BOOSTING A NEW WEST

BOOSTING A
NEW WEST

PACIFIC COAST EXPOSITIONS 1905–1916

BY JOHN C. PUTMAN

WSU PRESS
WSU PRESS
WASHINGTON STATE UNIVERSITY
PULLMAN, WASHINGTON

Washington State University Press
PO Box 645910
Pullman, Washington 99164-5910
Phone: 800-354-7360
Email: wsupress@wsu.edu
Website: wsupress.wsu.edu

First printing 2020
Printed and bound in the United States of America on pH neutral, acid-free paper.

LIBRARY OF CONGRESS CATALOGING-IN-PUBLICATION DATA
Names: Putman, John C., 1963– author.
Title: Boosting a new West : Pacific Coast expositions, 1905–1916 / John C. Putman.
Description: Pullman, Washington : WSU Press, Washington State University, [2020] | Includes bibliographical references and index.
Identifiers: LCCN 2020025622 | ISBN 9780874223811 (paperback)
Subjects: LCSH: Exhibitions—West (U.S.)—History—20th century. | West (U.S.)—Social life and customs—History—20th century.
Classification: LCC T395.5.U6 P88 2020 | DDC 607.4/79--dc23
LC record available at https://lccn.loc.gov/2020025622
ISBN: 978-0-87422-381-1

ON THE COVER Cover image is a detail from a poster promoting the Pacific-California Exposition movie. Poster credit is Ackerman-Quigley Litho. Co., Kansas City. Accessed as a digital object in the Archives and Special Collections at UC San Diego. *Design by TG Design.*
FRONTISPIECE View of Guild's Lake on fairgrounds of the Lewis and Clark Centennial Exposition. *Visual Instruction Department Lantern Slides (P 217), Oregon State University Special Collections and Archives Research Center, Corvallis, Oregon.*

CONTENTS

ILLUSTRATIONS

ACKNOWLEDGMENTS

As this odyssey finally comes to a conclusion, I want to take the opportunity to acknowledge the many debts I have incurred during this time. I would like to thank the staff at the numerous university and urban archives and libraries who found and copied letters, brochures, pictures, and other materials that made this study possible. I also must thank the editors at Washington State University Press who shepherded this project for the past couple of years. Along the way, other scholars, including referees and conference panelists, have taken the time to advise, and at times, cajole me to make this study better. Likewise, I want to thank my wonderful colleagues in the history department at San Diego State University who have always had my back and whose support never wavered. In the middle of this project, I assumed the role of director of the SDSU's International Business program and have benefited from the friendship and encouragement, whether they knew it or not, of several staff members, including Maribel, Marisela, Jessica, Roxana, Maria, and David. Finally, family means everything, and I would have never completed this journey without my precious wife Irene and my two wonderful children, Amanda and Joncarlo, who kept me going with their love, patience, and undying encouragement.

INTRODUCTION

In 1915 San Diego leaders invited the nation to visit their small but vibrant city to witness firsthand what the Far West had to offer. To highlight all the benefits of living in Southern California, the city erected an exposition on a plateau in the center of the city's sizable park. Fairgoers who wandered the newly christened Balboa Park, surrounded by lush gardens, could perhaps attend a concert at the Spreckels Organ Pavilion or stop in one of the large exhibit halls filled with the latest products from American industry. After a moment to catch their breath at the Plaza de Panama, they could head east on the fairground's promenade and discover the West they had hoped to experience—or so they thought. If they decided to turn left at the end of the promenade, fairgoers quickly encountered competing visions of the American West. Visitors could explore the rowdy and unruly world of the California gold rush at the Days of '49 Camp located in the fair's amusement zone, called "The Isthmus." Afterwards, sightseers could walk a few yards west and discover citrus orchards adjacent to a model farm with a well-furnished modern bungalow. This vision of a new rural life behind them, the guests could return to The Isthmus, where, if they looked north, they would spy a Pueblo Indian village, replete with adobe buildings, two kivas, and some three hundred Native Americans. Before heading back to El Prado, the exposition's main thoroughfare, fairgoers could stop at the Underground Chinatown exhibit to tour an opium den inhabited by Chinese slave girls. Upon leaving the amusement zone, these eastern visitors could perhaps rest for a few minutes and enjoy the lush flora at the Botanical Garden, where they might have pondered what exactly Far West fair officials wished to promote.

International expositions had become an integral part of American culture by the second decade of the twentieth century. From the 1876 Philadelphia Centennial Fair to the Panama-California Exposition held in San Diego on the eve of the Great War, millions roamed urban fairgrounds where they participated in the formation of a new American identity during a time of significant social and cultural change. Much more far-reaching than the typical county fair, expositions were expensive extravaganzas that took years to plan and drew visitors from across the globe. Often proposed as engines of economic growth, American expositions also offered businessmen, public officials, and intellectuals the unique opportunity to affirm their own political, racial, and cultural visions of American society. Impressive exhibits and educational displays provided visitors the opportunity to explore different aspects of both the past and present. Many Americans likely left the fairgrounds feeling proud of their nation's technological and cultural progress and confident about what the future held for their young country.[1]

Scholarly studies have demonstrated that these world's fairs represented more than simple booster efforts. The 1893 World Columbian Exposition held in Chicago, for example, has undergone significant scrutiny from a variety of disciplines and theoretical perspectives. These studies argue that the Chicago exposition's numerous technological, cultural, and educational exhibits can enlighten us about America's sense of itself, its power, and its place in the world.[2] The success of the 1893 fair soon inspired other American cities, from Buffalo, New York, to Omaha, Nebraska, to host similar events. Robert Rydell's seminal work, *All the World's a Fair: Visions of Empire at American International Expositions, 1876–1916*, laid the groundwork for studies about the cultural significance of American fairs. Examining nearly a dozen turn-of-the-century expositions, Rydell argued that they helped legitimate American imperial designs abroad as well as the racial/social order at home.[3]

These expositions, as Rydell made clear, reflected the desires and anxieties of a nation undergoing profound social, economic, and cultural change. In the wake of the Civil War, the United States experienced an industrial revolution that transformed the nation in myriad ways.[4] With the secession crisis behind them, the nation's leaders unleashed entrepreneurs who quickly altered the economic landscape, producing new products—and new problems. Railroads quickly crisscrossed the nation, unlocking new markets and resources as enormous factories attracted millions of immigrants to what some saw as the land of milk and honey. While Andrew Carnegie, John D. Rockefeller, and other capitalists built vast empires, workers and farmers railed against the "robber barons" who seemed to thrive at the expense of the common man. During the last three decades of the nineteenth century, substantial labor strife and political unrest threatened to tear the nation asunder. Meanwhile, economic pressure, cultural anxiety, and fortuitous circumstances permitted the country to fulfill what some believed was its imperial destiny. Convened during such dislocation, expositions could "alleviate the intense and widespread anxiety that pervaded the United States" and offer Americans "an opportunity to reaffirm their collective national identity."[5] Fairs thus reminded visitors that despite the problems, recent progress and the nation's untapped potential ensured a bright future.

Beginning with the 1893 Columbia Exposition, cities in the East, Midwest, and South took turns hosting international fairs. From Atlanta to Buffalo, local leaders relished the chance to showcase their respective communities and attract new businesses and settlers. Four of the final expositions hosted before World War I, however, took place along the nation's west coast. In 1905 Portland, Oregon, invited the American public to the region when it held the Lewis and Clark Exposition (LCE). Four years later, the rapidly growing metropolis to the north, Seattle, would stage the 1909 Alaska-Yukon-Pacific Exposition (AYPE).[6] Not to be outdone by its neighbors, California embraced exposition fever by hosting not one but two fairs in 1915. Celebrating the completion of the Panama Canal, San Francisco's Panama-Pacific International Exposition (PPIE) was christened the official national exposition, while its competitor to the south, San Diego, constructed the smaller, more regionally focused Panama-California Exposition.

While Rydell's 1984 study briefly detailed how the four Pacific Coast expositions contributed to visions of empire at the dawn of the twentieth century, several scholars have helped fill in his basic framework. Focusing particularly on statuary that dotted the grounds of the Lewis and Clark Exposition, Lisa Blee demonstrates how that fair's statues reflected the impulse for empire that began with the conquest of the American West.[7] In *Empire on Display: San Francisco's Panama-Pacific International Exposition of 1915*, Sarah J. Moore explores fair exhibits, images, and displays and argues that the Panama-Pacific International Exposition embodied the nation's imperialist fantasies and confirmed the manifest destiny of the United States.[8] Situating American desire for empire within the frontier anxiety sparked by Frederick Jackson Turner's address at the 1893 Columbian Exposition, the author suggests that the San Francisco fair celebrated the opportunity of new frontiers located beyond the continent that the newly completed Panama Canal promised.

Central to the story of how the turn-of-the-century expositions embodied notions of empire was the issue of race. The region's demographic diversity, combined with host cities located on the shores of the Pacific Ocean, meant that race figured prominently in these far western fairs. Matthew Bokovoy's *The San Diego World's Fairs and Southwestern Memory, 1880–1940*, for example, investigates San Diego's 1915 and 1935 fairs and illustrates how they reflected a contrived regional identity that simultaneously privileged the Spanish past and marginalized Mexicans and Native Americans.[9] Race, Bokovoy maintains, shaped both the conception and organization of San Diego's fairs, as well as Anglo-Americans' regional identity—like politics, sometimes race is all local. In her study of the Panama-Pacific International Exposition, Abigail M. Markwyn situates the San Francisco fair in the context of progressive-era California.[10] Leaders of San Francisco, home to the nation's largest Asian population, she argues, struggled to reconcile the goal of a Pacific empire with the city's deep-seated anti-Asian prejudice.

Race and empire, however, were not the only features of the 1915 Bay Area fair. Markwyn's *Empress San Francisco: The Pacific Rim, the Great West and California at the Panama-Pacific International Exposition* reminds us that cities were also sites of class, ethnic, and gender conflict, which often informed urban expositions. From Seattle to San Diego, fair directors had to mediate the social, political, and cultural upheavals of the progressive era with larger desires to promote their respective cities. Smaller Pacific Coast communities like Portland

and San Diego had the additional challenge of overcoming their cities' relative obscurity. As scholar Carl Abbott outlines in *The Great Extravaganza: Portland and the Lewis and Clark Exposition,* economic incentives were a powerful motivating factor behind the decision to host an exposition.[11] In the competitive economic environment of early twentieth-century America, Portland, Seattle, and San Diego vied with more established eastern and midwestern cities to lure new capital and settlers to the Far West. How westerners saw themselves and their homeland, then, figured prominently in the look, feel, and message of these four Far West expositions.

Although much of the extant historiography on the Pacific Coast expositions has focused on issues of race and empire, this study attempts to broaden our understanding of how these fairs sold the Far West to those living outside the region. Nearly a quarter-century ago, historian Clyde A. Milner II rhetorically asked: "Where is the West and who are westerners?" We might also ask: how did westerners understand their homeland, and how did they represent it to outsiders? Milner's question about the region preoccupied scholars of the American West for much of the latter part of the twentieth century, at least since the arrival of the so-called New Western History.[12] Numerous panels at academic conferences and special journal issues have energetically debated this question of *frontier versus region* or *place versus process.* In the end, let us say that we have agreed to disagree. Whether one favors region or frontier, most scholars believe that sometime at the turn of the twentieth century, western inhabitants began to see, if not define, themselves as distinctly western.[13] If these scholars are correct, we should look to this period to understand how westerners understood their homeland and how this informed their boosterism.

Locating the timing of regional boosterism might be the easier task; explaining what informs it is more daunting. The West, and even subregions like the Pacific Northwest or the Southwest, are more than physical territories imagined or defined by geographers. They are as much creations of the people who resided there as they were products of climate and natural landscapes. Few would disagree that cowpokes and ranchers of the Great Plains saw themselves as quite different from those living along the shores of Southern California. Although the American West may have shared some general characteristics that distinguish it from the South or East—such as aridity, racial diversity, or its troubled relationship with the federal government—these similarities in no way meant that residing in the desert Southwest was analogous to living in the Pacific Northwest. In other words, the collective memories and experiences of a region's inhabitants shaped how they saw themselves and their homeland. Yet this process reflected more than the impact of local events and personal encounters. As historian David Emmons has suggested, the national forces of "market capitalism and centralized nation state" that marked late-nineteenth-century America helped define the character of the West, and thus the timing of more aggressive booster activities.[14] Although regional differences informed the particular messages of each exposition's marketing campaigns, the four fairs also shared broader themes or concerns endemic to the Far West. San Diegans, for example, may have celebrated their sandy beaches as Portland residents did the majestic peak of Mount Hood, but collectively they promoted the bounty that nature bestowed on the region during a time when easterners lamented the ills of industrial urban life.

In contrast to the typical booster efforts by chambers of commerce, which often produced a few pamphlets touting local business opportunities, the Pacific Coast expositions represented far-reaching and comprehensive efforts to promote the region's short-term and long-term interests. Tourism, which has attracted the attention of numerous scholars, represented only a small slice of each exposition's marketing efforts.[15] Covering the considerable expense of hosting a fair, the costs demanded that publicity departments encourage people to attend the expositions. Tourists could ensure the success of the event by purchasing a fair ticket and spending money at local hotels and restaurants. However, tourism alone could not ensure the host city's long-term growth and prosperity. Despite declining travel costs, the trip from Chicago or New York was still a considerable outlay that was sensitive to economic fluctuations. Exposition publicity departments thus engaged in an overlapping two-prong marketing campaign, which attempted both to lure tourists to ensure the fair's profitability as well as promote the region to permanent settlers and investors.

Reams of marketing materials the Pacific Coast expositions produced reflected this bifurcated strategy. On one hand, the typical quarter- or half-page newspaper ad often focused on the fair's basic theme, or perhaps noted interesting sights like Yellowstone National Park or the Grand Canyon, which fairgoers could visit on their way to the host city. Exposition guidebooks similarly offered more detailed descriptions of the variety of events and exhibits visitors could expect. Often these guides spotlighted interesting places like Seattle's nearby Mount Rainier, San Francisco's Chinatown, or similar side trips that visitors could take during their holiday. Such booster materials reflected the fact that while exposition officials hoped to lure those looking to escape the East for a few weeks of leisure, they also recognized that a good deal of those who would likely attend the fairs lived west of the Rockies.

On the other hand, promotional brochures and fair-friendly magazine and newspaper articles often delineated the broader benefits of western living. Crafted by exposition publicity departments, these promotional pieces targeted potential settlers disenchanted with their current conditions. Readers learned how the unlimited economic opportunities in the Far West, together with its scenic landscapes and healthy climates, promised a better life. Equating progress with growth, leaders from Seattle to San Diego desired permanent settlers who would enhance the region's economy and ensure future prosperity for all. Yet "the majority of those who perused such sources," scholar David Wrobel has suggested, "did not relocate to the West."[16] Westerners no doubt understood that few would immediately pull up stakes and move across the country. But like any product-marketing campaign, exposition publicity officials hoped to create a favorable impression so that when customers were ready to purchase, then or in the future, they would consider the Far West.

Whether targeting tourists or settlers, the four expositions were at their heart acts of boosterism. By the nineteenth century, urbanist Carl Abbott has argued, boosterism was "a response to concrete problems of urban growth and a literature of prophecy, an affirmation of the great destiny and mission of the American people."[17] Little had changed by the time railroads had extended their tracks to the Pacific Ocean. Like Abbott's Midwest businessmen, boosters along the Pacific Slope promised that tourists and settlers alike would discover Gardens of Eden, Fairylands, or even a New Italy if they ventured to the West.[18] Boosters' success, historian Hal Rothman has suggested, relied on the "combination of such entrepreneurship and the relationship of places to the dominant cultural themes of the different eras."[19] Recognizing the powerful impact of urbanization and industrialization, Pacific Coast exposition publicity departments aptly tapped into the cultural values and anxieties of turn-of-the-century America.

Mirroring corporate advertising campaigns designed for sewing machines, soaps, and baking powder, the four Far West expositions crafted marketing strategies that furnished solutions to the ills that plagued the nation. Appealing to anxious single women, a facial soap ad, for example, might promise not only to clean one's face, but also help lonely women attract a desirable mate. Such advertisements vowed to do more than just remove dirt from the buyer's face. Fair brochures similarly assured potential settlers that they could overcome woes and disappointments and achieve some personal or financial success by relocating to the Pacific Northwest or California. In contrast to earlier booster undertakings, the expositions drew upon the emerging science of consumer marketing to construct more effective advertising campaigns and target those open to such appeals. Seasoned newspaper executives familiar with the art of advertising often managed fairs' publicity departments. Yet, as scholars of urban marketing have argued, "[P]laces are obviously different from many other products offered on the market both in the composite nature of the product and the way it is used by the customer."[20] When selling a city or region, unlike a bar of soap, it is not exactly clear what is being sold and how or when it is consumed. Advertisers or marketing agents may have tried to treat places like any other product, but as scholars John R. Gold and Stephen V. Ward have suggested, "they are in reality complex packages of goods, services, and experiences that are consumed in many different ways."[21] Selling the Far West, then, would depend greatly on how fair publicity departments successfully packaged both the region's tangible and imagined qualities.

By the early twentieth century, advertising had become a profession that counseled practitioners to embrace new techniques and approaches informed by the social sciences, psychology, and the demands of modern industrial capitalism.[22] Modern advertising professionals studied consumer psychology and designed new styles that helped connect the customer to the product. Aided by the rise of mass-produced magazines that reached a national audience, marketing campaigns did more than just sell the benefits of the product; they also helped cultivate a desire or need for it. Whether it was the use of testimonials, emotion-evoking images, or "reason-why" advertising, Pacific Coast exposition publicity departments possessed a wide range of new strategies to mine in selling the Far West. However, while these new techniques may have helped more effectively present the region to the target audience, fair officials still had to craft a persuasive and meaningful message. In other words, to sell the product, they had to define first its qualities and benefits and then determine how to persuade the potential "customer" to purchase it.

Whether exposition leaders touted the region's climate, landscape, or economic opportunities, the selling of the West "still hinged on comparison and contrast with the eastern part of the United States."[23] As this study will show, westerners were mindful of the area east of the Mississippi when framing their marketing campaigns. Fair officials and local leaders, out of a sense of inferiority or just simple pride, rarely missed an opportunity to point out the superiority of western living. By hyping the region's advantages, boosters attempted to woo capitalists and new settlers, and in doing so, also reminded their fellow residents about what made the Far West different. Pioneers' stubborn hold on the past, for example, helped local inhabitants remember their territory's unique qualities, while new leaders advertised the virtues that made the West central to the nation's future. The Pacific Coast expositions offered an opportunity to lash together the strands of these developing perspectives into a marketing strategy that confirmed the benefits of western life to all.

The Far West may have had a good deal to offer potential settlers, yet fair officials also had to confront the ideological and cultural consequences of the conquest of the West. Influenced by widely read dime novels and popular Wild West shows, the West often evoked images of savage Indians, violent gunslingers, and unbearable desert climates.

However accurate or true this perception of the region, what mattered was how those living outside understood the West. Unless easterners had a relative who lived in the Far West, they had little else but those novels and Wild West shows to help them fully comprehend the region. Held little more than a decade after Frederick Jackson Turner sparked a frontier crisis, Pacific Coast exposition organizers crafted a different and competing vision of the post-frontier West. Beginning with the Portland fair in 1905 and ending with San Diego's 1915–16 exposition, westerners attempted to help the public move past the popular stereotypes of the American West, and in doing so, helped draw the nation away from its Atlantic Coast inclinations toward a future where the West captured more than just the imagination of the American public.

Boosting a New West: Pacific Coast Expositions, 1905–1916, explores exposition officials' efforts to fashion an advertising campaign that confronted contested understandings of the American West and appealed to the dreams and aspirations of city dwellers and rural folk who lived east of the Rockies. Between the opening of the Lewis and Clark Exposition's gates in 1905 to turning off the lights in San Diego a decade later, millions of Americans visited the exhibits, watched live performances, and wandered the amusement zones of the four Pacific Coast fairs. Millions more thumbed through exposition brochures or read firsthand accounts of each fair in newspapers and national magazines. Selling the Far West required fair officials and local leaders to define the region, first to themselves and then to those living outside the territory. National economic, cultural, and social anxieties, as well as popular misconceptions of the West, no doubt informed this process. As David Wrobel has argued, fair promoters and other western boosters "influenced both the sense of place of western residents and the sense that prospective residents and other Americans had of western places."[24] In the end, westerners perhaps learned as much about themselves and their homeland as did those who perused the pages of national magazines or who trekked west to attend a fair.

1 ⟻ TO HOST A FAIR
THE PACIFIC NORTHWEST

During the late-nineteenth and early-twentieth centuries, international expositions became an integral part of American culture by introducing visitors from around the world to the wonders of American society. From the 1876 Philadelphia Centennial International Exposition to the Panama-Pacific International Exposition (PPIE) held in San Francisco on the eve of the Great War, millions roamed urban fairgrounds, where they participated in the formation of a new American identity during a time of significant social and cultural change. At the dawn of the new century, with the nagging depression of the 1890s behind them, western residents entered a new and more aggressive "second boosterist phase" in which they sought to reshape the discourse about their home region.[1] Co-opting the vehicle of the international fair, Oregon, Washington, and California leaders sought to direct the nation's attention to the Far West by hosting four expositions in less than ten years.[2] Leading politicians and businessmen believed that if done right, a fair could not only bring more attention to their respective communities and regions, but also could serve as launching pad to a better and more lucrative future. In the first two decades of the twentieth century, Pacific Coast cities energetically constructed expositions that highlighted the Far West's economic and trade opportunities, as well as the region's purported superior living conditions. By showcasing the advantages of western living, these expositions sought to encourage the American public to reimagine the twentieth-century West as the nation's future site of opportunity, progress, and modern life.

Portland: The Lewis and Clark Exposition

Portland's step into the exposition field began during the punishing 1890s depression. The brainchild of dry goods merchant Dan McAllen, the proposed fair initially produced little enthusiasm. Undeterred, McAllen, who believed that his city seemed to be "dying of the dry rot," refused to admit defeat.[3] By 1900 business leaders finally came around when, at the urging of newspaper publisher H. W. Scott, the Oregon Historical Society endorsed the concept of an exposition to be held in concert with the commemoration of the one hundredth anniversary of Meriwether Lewis and William Clark's exploration of the Pacific Northwest. From its inception, Portland leaders linked

Bird's-eye view of Lewis and Clark Centennial Exposition with mountains in background. *Library of Congress, Prints and Photographs Division, LC-DIG-ppmsca-44796.*

the celebration of this historical milestone to the city's proximity to the increasingly lucrative trade with the Orient. Fair officials quickly obtained federal and state government subsidies, in addition to firm commitments from surrounding western states to both participate in and promote the exposition. By 1903 they had chosen Guild's Lake, located in northwest Portland, as the site of the fair. All that remained was construction of the fairgrounds, securing exhibits, and advertising the nation's first exposition held in "a relatively new and practically undeveloped country."[4]

Founded in 1843, Portland quickly became the dominant city in the Pacific Northwest for much of the late nineteenth century. Located inland along the Columbia River, the city slowly grew as the Donation Land Claim Act offered 320 acres of free land to those who wished to settle in Oregon territory in the early 1850s. Without the lure of gold or silver, Portland attracted more conservative New England transplants, many of whom engaged in trade up and down the Willamette and Columbia Rivers.[5] By 1880 Portland's population had topped 17,000, but with the completion of the Northern Pacific Railway (NP) in the mid-1880s, the city soon surpassed 90,000. Growth accelerated when Portland merged with East Portland and Albina into a single city in 1891. European immigrants, joined by a growing Asian population, helped diversify the city. Portland's Chinatown, for example, had nearly 8,000 residents by the turn of the century, making it second to San Francisco's in size.[6] Germans, Britons, and Canadians comprised the next-largest foreign-born populations, with the newer southern and eastern European immigrants lagging further behind.

By 1900 Portland had recovered from the depression that struck the nation in 1893. The city continued to add population and constructed more than five thousand buildings in the first few years of the new century. The Columbia River's greatest port was the nation's fifth-largest shipper of wheat, and the city saw manufacturing double and bank deposits increase by one and a half times in the run up to the Lewis and Clark Exposition.[7] Visitors to Oregon's largest city may have been surprised to discover electrified trolleys, excellent middle-class suburban homes, and a vibrant civic and social scene. While still less industrial compared to established cities in the Northeast and Midwest, the city's lumber mills typically employed a hundred workers or more. Recognizing both the city's economic growth and desires to expand business opportunities, the Portland Chamber of Commerce was founded in 1890. Portland's elite also enjoyed an array of social and civic clubs, including the exclusive Arlington Club, several newly built places of worship, and an active women's movement led by suffragist and newspaper publisher Abigail Scott Duniway.[8] By 1900 a well-established business community and favorable location seemingly positioned Portland to become the metropolis of the Pacific Northwest.

Despite its strong standing in the region, Portland business leaders may have felt a little uneasy about its future, with Seattle to the north enjoying the benefits of a gold rush in Alaska and the Yukon territory. Hosting a world's fair would help the city maintain its power and status by drawing the nation's attention to the Pacific Northwest. Facing criticism that expositions had run their course, proponents of Portland's fair suggested that it would do more than simply showcase the city's business opportunities. The director general of the Lewis and Clark Exposition, H. W. Goode, claimed that expositions provided a "common meeting ground of the identical men who are looking for one another for the promotion of mutual interests."[9] A local newspaper likewise declared fairs as "one of the best mediums of education of the day."[10] Fair officials argued that they envisioned the Portland exposition as a regional event that would attract those intrigued by the mysterious and unknown Far West. According to one state commissioner, the Lewis and Clark Exposition was a two-way street—exposing the East to the West while simultaneously "exhibiting to the masses in Oregon what the outside world is doing."[11]

Rejecting the premise that Portland was unworthy of hosting a world's fair, city leaders still had to show that the city could handle such a gathering. Tom Richardson, manager of the Portland Commercial Club, touted the city's urban amenities and its fantastic views. Not only did Portland possess an extensive trolley line and modern buildings, it stood under the gaze of mountains and alongside impressive rivers. Moreover, official publications produced for the exposition offered concrete statistics supporting Portland's qualifications. Books and pamphlets reminded readers that Portland's population of 90,426 surpassed that of nearby Seattle, Tacoma, and Spokane and that the city had more than 2.8 million square feet of paved roads. Visitors, in short, would discover an up-to-date city that also offered pure mountain drinking water and an appealing summer climate.[12]

Despite the apparent health of the city, Portland officials decried the community's rather stagnant population and commercial growth. In 1901 the Portland Chamber of Commerce, for example, proclaimed its new motto: "For 200,000 population in 1905."[13] The president of the Lewis and Clark Fair, H. W. Corbett, admitted that the city was holding the exposition "for the primary purpose of peopling unoccupied areas."[14] While buildings quickly filled the Guild's Lake site, fair officials continued to promote the event as central to Portland's future growth. Months before the fair's opening day, the *Evening Telegram* urged residents to pay special attention to home seekers who might visit the city because "Portland needs a population."[15] A year later, when residents celebrated "Portland Day" just weeks before the closing of the exposition, city leaders again expressed their faith that the fair would positively transform their community by handing out round pins imprinted with "Portland great! Portland fine! Five hundred thousand in nineteen-nine."[16]

Oregonians' anxiety about growth reflected not only larger cultural beliefs that equated growth with progress, but also a nagging fear that the state was slipping behind other Pacific Coast states. Newspapers grumbled about neighboring states that witnessed fantastic rates of growth. In a 1901 speech on the impending fair, Edward Everett Young, editor of the *Baker City Republican*, alleged that there "is one thing Oregon cannot afford to overlook. California, on the south, and Washington, on the north, are rapidly outstripping us on the question of population . . . let us not forget that Oregon's greatest need is population."[17] Oregon's future, then, hinged upon the ability of the Lewis and Clark Fair to accentuate the region's promise. "Good hard work," the *Eugene Register* concluded, will make "the exposition the crowning glory of the Oregon of the past [and] will forge us to the front as the mighty Oregon of the future."[18] Perhaps masking their city and region's economic weaknesses, business leaders and fair promoters hitched Portland's future, and in some cases their own profits, to hosting the fair.

Oregon boosters offered more than simple platitudes in defense of the state's potential. Fertile soils and open space were just two of the purported benefits they highlighted when comparing Oregon to eastern states. Excellent farmland might attract new settlers, but Lewis and Clark Fair officials also craved new businesses and capital investment. Fair president Corbett admitted that Portland leaders had "extended every means within our power to attract immigration and capital, but our progress has been but slow."[19] More discouraging in his eyes was that other regions of the nation continued to surge ahead of Portland. The compulsive search for outside capital, as Richard White has argued, dominated western politics during the late nineteenth century, especially at the local level.[20] The Lewis and Clark Exposition would obviate this growing disadvantage by promoting the city's potential to capture trade with the Orient. "We would advertise our commercial importance to the world," wrote chamber of commerce chairman J. M. Long, "and our importance as an Oriental trade port, thereby direct capital from all parts of the Union to our city."[21] The Portland fair, then, would reward the city with settlers, capital, and national prominence.

By the time the entrance gate closed for the final time, exposition officials, city leaders and other observers could only crow about the success of Portland's fair. Despite dire predictions that the Lewis and Clark Exposition would fail and that the expected economic boom would not materialize, all evidence indicated that the event was an undisputed success. Numerous publications noted that the fair turned a small profit and that Portland's economy prospered. Not only did the event attract capital investment to the city, but the *Lewis and Clark Journal* boasted that many visitors "sent back for their belongings and stayed" in Oregon.[22] Fondly reminiscing about the exposition a year later, local newspapers and official reports proffered a cornucopia of economic statistics, including bank deposits and real estate transactions, to support the fair's impact.[23]

The 2.5 million customers who pushed through the turnstiles aside, few could challenge the notion that Portland was much healthier after the exposition than before. The Portland *Oregonian* illustrated this in a 1906 cartoon that showed a sickly, old man labeled "Portland Then" next to a rotund man with the word "prosperity" on his large gut and the words "and Now" next to him. Off to the side was a note to a doctor from "Portland," which thanked the physician for prescribing the "Exposition Specific," which so improved his health that he urged his neighbors to take the remedy.[24] For some observers, however, the financial bliss that the fair produced was equaled by the confidence the community gained. The *Evening Telegram* declared the exposition's success meant the "defeat of timid conservatism" that questioned hosting the event. Richardson of the Portland Commercial

Club perhaps summed it best: "It has given Portland people confidence in themselves."[25]

While Portland citizens basked in their fair's success, the idea of another Pacific Northwest exposition began to take root. During a 1905 trip to gather Alaska products and resources to showcase at the Lewis and Clark Exposition, Godfrey Chealander, an Alaskan businessman, grew frustrated with the underwhelming size of the region's display. Confident that Alaska had much more to offer, he contacted John E. Chilberg, a Seattle businessman and president of the local Alaska Club, about organizing an exposition in Seattle that would do Alaska justice. Over the next year, city leaders worked with Chealander to gather support from Seattle newspapers and the chamber of commerce for a proposed 1907 fair. In May 1906 proponents formed the Exposition Company and announced plans for an exposition, which would showcase the resources of Alaska, the lucrative Yukon territory of western Canada, and the Pacific Northwest.[26]

Seattle: The Alaska-Yukon-Pacific Exposition

Settled by a small band of midwestern migrants who ventured to Puget Sound in 1852 in search of a good harbor and abundant land, Seattle quickly became home to a timber industry that would shape the city's economy for decades to come. The sound emerged as an early source of lumber for San Francisco merchants—despite the great distance—because it offered safe, deep harbors. The region's promise attracted many entrepreneurs to the area, including the father of Seattle's lumber industry, Henry Yesler.[27] In the 1870s the Northern Pacific Railway, under the leadership of eastern financier Jay Cooke, began to construct a transcontinental railroad that would link Lake Superior to the Pacific Northwest. Over-speculation, shady dealings, and Cooke's ego combined to bring down the shaky foundation upon which he had built the NP. A depression stalled further construction of the railroad until a German immigrant, Henry Villard, reorganized and finally completed the NP, tying the Great Lakes to the Puget Sound by the mid-1880s.[28]

Despite the economic growth that the railroad brought to the Puget Sound, racial discord and class conflict hounded Seattle during the late

1880s. Led by the Knights of Labor, workers not only drove hundreds of Chinese workers from the city, but they also temporarily seized control of city government. However, by the early 1890s labor was in disarray, and the region became home to the several utopian colonies as Seattle residents suffered under the depression that struck the nation.

Pessimism and economic woes quickly evaporated in July 1897 when the steamship *Portland* docked at the wharf at the foot of downtown Seattle with more than a ton of gold in its hull: a precious cargo that forever changed the city. The discovery of gold in the Yukon territory and Alaska generated a decade of unprecedented growth, catapulting Seattle into the elite of western cities. While San Franciscans probably had expected to dominate the gold trade as they had all other coastal trade, Seattle held certain advantages over the California city. Not only was Seattle closer to Alaska than other West Coast cities, but it was large enough to provide a wide array of supplies needed by gold seekers. The city's proximity to Alaska, its two rail lines, and commercial contacts forged prior to the gold strike positioned Seattle well to capture and dominate most of the Alaskan trade for years to come.[29]

In nearly every conceivable way—banking, real estate, and retail sales—Seattle witnessed tremendous growth. In 1900 the value of trade from the city to Alaska topped $20 million annually, and within three years, that had more than doubled. Banks represented one of the greatest indicators of this windfall. In 1898 total deposits in Seattle banks stood at only $7 million, but by 1906 they had reached $60 million.[30] Retail sales likewise reflected this surging business activity as grocery and hardware sales more than doubled in the first year following the strike. Seattle's economic growth during the first decade of the twentieth century also produced an exceptionally healthy real estate climate. In 1900 twenty-four new business blocks were developed, and the assessed land value in the city nearly quadrupled from 1900 to 1907. In short, as one contemporary observer summed up the Klondike gold strike, "[t]hey [gold seekers] all had that for want of which Seattle suffered long and painfully: money. . . . In one day the destiny of Seattle was changed."[31]

Seattle's economic growth at the turn of the century was quite impressive, yet it did not necessarily translate into significant economic development and diversification. The number of businesses did indeed grow, but by the end of the gold rush in 1910, Seattle still possessed a primarily local-oriented economy dominated by rather small firms. In particular, the city still suffered from a rather anemic manufacturing sector—in 1910 the city still lacked a single mass-producing iron or steel firm. After a decade of tremendous growth, the Puget Sound's major city was second to last in manufacturing in the nation for cities of comparable size. The difficulty competing in a national market economy dominated by eastern and midwestern firms, as well as the limited markets in the rather sparsely populated Pacific Northwest, largely explains Seattle's weaker manufacturing base. While the city possessed a rather vibrant economy in the early years of the twentieth century, it remained a commercial center dependent on a larger regional economy more "devoted to the extractive industries, to extensive agriculture, to mining, and to logging than manufacturing."[32]

As the first decade of new century came to a close, Seattle leaders still yearned for a stronger manufacturing base, but they were hardly disappointed with the city's economic and demographic growth in the previous decade. Its economy appeared strong, and Seattle had become a true metropolis. During the first ten years of the twentieth century, the city's population nearly tripled to just over 237,000, surpassing Portland as the largest city in the Pacific Northwest. Yet at the same time, this was a rather restless and unsettled population. As the stepping off point to Alaska, Seattle attracted tens of thousands of rootless men who resided in the city for only a brief period while awaiting transportation to the gold fields, or perhaps working odd jobs to raise additional funds needed to make the trek.[33] Striking while the iron was still hot, Seattle leaders believed that the city's future rested on the planned exposition. Building upon Portland's Lewis and Clark Exposition, a successful fair could attract more permanent settlers and business to Puget Sound. If done right, the Alaska-Yukon-Pacific Exposition could launch the city forward just as the gold rush had a decade earlier.

Recognizing that Seattle had already benefitted greatly from the gold strikes in Alaska and the Yukon due to the city's proximity to the region, exposition leaders decided to expand the scope of the event to include nations that lined the Pacific Ocean. "Because of the importance of Oriental business to Seattle," Chilberg noted, "we added the name Pacific to our corporate title."[34] By expanding the scope, the *Seattle Daily Times* suggested that not only could Seattle tap into the rapidly growing interest in Asian trade networks, but it also would encourage the United States government "to spend a goodly sum of money in exploiting the resources of the Hawaiian and Philippine Islands."[35] Fair officials did not hide from the clear commercial nature of the proposed exposition. Unlike earlier expositions in Chicago, St. Louis, and Portland, which celebrated notable historical events like Columbus's discovery of the New World or the Lewis and Clark Expedition, Seattle leaders stated that their event was "simply and frankly a broad, commercial proposition."[36] The rather short time frame and the scheduled 1907 Jamestown Exposition persuaded fair officials to move the opening of the exposition to June 1909.[37]

Like Portland, Seattle leaders first and foremost saw the fair as a tool to further the growth and development of their city and region. By 1906 the trade and foot traffic brought to Seattle by the gold strikes in Alaska and the Yukon had begun to diminish. A primary purpose of the exposition was to reveal Alaska and the Yukon's vast opportunities and resources, which Seattle could continue to exploit with its shipping and national railroad connections. Yet fair officials did not forget their own city. A report to the United States House of Representatives added that the AYPE's "object is to demonstrate the progress and the resources of the entire region of the Pacific and to forecast the future possibilities of the oriental trade."[38] In particular, stated one exposition information guide, "the A.-Y.-P. points the field of his future exploitations, the source of future millions."[39] As the closest mainland American port to the Far East, Seattle leaders recognized the economic benefits the AYPE could provide their fine city.

Key to developing Seattle was promoting a better understanding of the American West. According to the AYPE's official declaration, the third stated purpose of the exposition was "to demonstrate the marvelous progress of Western America."[40] Fair officials noted that unlike earlier large expositions in Chicago and St. Louis, their event "gives especial attention to a part of the country which was necessarily neglected in those exhibitions which covered the world."[41] In many ways, local officials envisioned the AYPE as a coming-out party for Seattle and the American West. Newspaper reports announced that the fair "will do much towards giving the East a proper appreciation of the West." At groundbreaking ceremonies in 1907, Henry Alberts McLean, president of the Washington state commission for the exposition, declared that the AYPE would bring to an end "one epoch of this Commonwealth's history and open another. The pioneer days, the days of adventure, the days of uncertainty, the days during which we have been practically unknown to the great body of the people of the nation, will, when the exposition is over, be ended forever."[42]

A central byproduct of selling the Far West to the nation was the subsequent economic boon fair officials predicted for Seattle. Lessons from earlier fairs seemed to support these expectations. The *Seattle Daily Times*, for example, highlighted St. Louis's economic growth and the development of its downtown area following the 1904 Louisiana Purchase Exposition. City leaders had only to look at the "phoenix-like" rise of Portland, "where thousands of visitors from the overcrowded cities and states of the Atlantic seaboard found a new field for the investment of capital, for the use of brain and brawn in its workshops, mills, fields, farms, forests and orchards."[43] Local Seattle real estate developers like Ferninand Whitaker learned that property values increased in Portland after its exposition.[44] As AYPE chief of publicity Frank Merrick argued, the fair would bring the East closer to the Pacific West and thus bring "more capital to this section" and "stimulate every line of business" in the region.[45]

Located on the University of Washington campus north of downtown Seattle, the AYPE opened on June 1, 1909, with the press of a telegraph key from the East Room of the White House. When the gates closed on October 16 after a 138-day run, total attendance topped 3.7 million.[46] Exposition officials proudly declared the fair a great success. The *Seattle Daily Times* reported that "tourist travel has exceeded all predictions and the direct and immediate benefits from the exposition have been felt throughout the Northwest." The AYPE provided an additional benefit to the city when it transferred seven fair buildings to the university to house laboratories and lecture halls.[47] As the city looked forward to the next decade, residents could celebrate the notoriety their community had gained from the exposition and its continued growth as it quickly surpassed Portland as the most populous city in the Pacific Northwest in 1910.

The AYPE's success did not escape the eyes of businessmen down the coast in Southern California. Even before the gates closed in Seattle, San Diego banker G. Aubrey Davidson urged members of the chamber of commerce to consider hosting their own exposition in 1915. Reeling from the effects of the 1907 Wall Street panic, Davidson argued that the completion of the Panama Canal in 1915 offered a unique opportunity because San Diego was the first American Pacific Ocean port located north of the canal. By September the chamber formed the Panama-California Exposition Company and settled on the City Park site as the location of the fair. Excited about the prospects of hosting an international exposition, city leaders also recognized that significant obstacles stood in their way. With a population of less than forty thousand, San Diego would be by far the smallest city to attempt this feat. More importantly, by the end of 1909, San Francisco announced its intention to hold its own Panama Canal exposition in 1915.[48]

San Diego: The Panama-California Exposition

Although it was the birthplace of California following the founding of Mission San Diego de Alcala in 1769 by Father Junípero Serra, San Diego grew rather slowly for the next century. The gold rush may have attracted hundreds of thousands to California; however, few made their way to state's southernmost city. In the late 1860s, booster Alonzo Horton purchased land south of the original settlement, and by the next decade others followed his advice to relocate to his New Town, making it the heart of San Diego. Nevertheless by 1880, less than three thousand people called San Diego home. The completion of the Atchison, Topeka, and Santa Fe transcontinental line by way of the southern tier of the country terminated in San Diego in 1885, ushering in a short population boom. Despite its natural harbor and railroad line, San Diego's population stood at less than twenty thousand at the turn of century.[49]

View of Panama-California Exposition, located in San Diego's Balboa Park. *San Diego State University Special Collections, John and Jane Adams Postcard Collection.*

Looming under the shadow of San Francisco and the rapidly growing city of Los Angeles, San Diego leaders searched for something to put their community on the map. City leaders discussed a number of ideas, yet seemingly failed to provide the necessary incentives to attract new settlers and businesses. Meanwhile, Los Angeles continued to grow, prosper, and extend its influence throughout Southern California.[50] For example, in 1910 Harrison Gray Otis, publisher of the *Los Angeles Times*, visited San Diego to encourage local merchants to enact a free-speech ordinance to undermine the growing influence of the Industrial

Workers of the World (IWW). Having already announced plans to host the exposition, San Diego leaders eagerly followed his advice to confront the radical labor organization. With the fair's opening less than three years away, businessmen and local officials wanted to drive the IWW out so as to make their city attractive to outside capital investment. By the end of 1912, IWW leaders and many of the rank and file were either in jail or had been driven from San Diego County. With this apparent threat behind them, San Diego leaders looked forward to the windfall that the Panama-California Exposition promised to deliver.[51]

Competition from San Francisco posed an even greater challenge to San Diego. To tip the scales toward their city, San Diego leaders attempted to woo Los Angeles officials to support the Southern California event. When San Francisco suggested that San Diego withdraw its proposal, Panama-California Exposition (PCE) proponents refused to budge. Complicating matters was a late bid by New Orleans to host the official Panama Canal celebration, which meant that the two California cites might potentially divide congressional support, allowing the Louisiana port city to win federal recognition. Concerned state leaders, including prominent Los Angeles businessmen, rallied support behind the larger, more established San Francisco, leaving San Diego to accept a lesser status as a smaller, regional exposition. Los Angeles booster Charles Lummis aptly described San Diego's position: "'Good enough! You have your Fair, and we'll have ours. There's room for two. We'll make ours Different.'"[52] Outmuscled by the northern metropolis, San Diego officials pushed forward to develop a different and unique exposition that would distinguish it from the Bay Area event.

San Francisco's decision to offer a competing exposition forced San Diego leaders to envision a different kind of fair in terms of architectural style and themes. Rather than follow the typical neo-classical and Beaux Arts style of earlier expositions, the PCE instead drew inspiration from the Spanish Colonial style.[53] Likewise, previous fairs emphasized the achievements of the past and present but said little about the future.[54] San Francisco's Panama-Pacific International Exposition intended to do much the same, so San Diego leaders felt they had found their focus. *Sunset Magazine*, for example, claimed: "San Francisco's Exposition was universal, all-inclusive. It proposed to record, in visible, tangible form, the progress of civilization in all its phases; it was to be the final summary of man's past achievements. San Diego could not do the same thing on a smaller scale."[55] The choice to include California in the title of the fair indicated the particular regional focus of San Diego's event compared to San Francisco's international flavor. "[I]t was not placed there by chance or mistake," the *San Francisco Chronicle* claimed; "[t]he main object of the Panama-California Exposition is to display the glories of California."[56]

San Diego's confidence reflected the earlier success of Portland and

Seattle. PCE director David C. Collier noted that "[t]wice during the past five years has the northwest called to the nations of the world through the medium of a great exposition, and twice has the tide of travel toward the land of the totem pole been double and tripled and many times expanded."[57] Initially, some leaders hoped that just as Seattle tapped into growing interest in trade with Alaska and the Orient, the San Diego fair would do the same with Latin America.[58] When Congress proclaimed the PPIE as the nation's international exposition and the president announced that he would officially invite nations of the world to San Francisco, San Diego leaders had to quickly pivot. Even before the first shovel of dirt was turned, fair officials had declared that the "scope of the San Diego project was limited to the resources and products of the Southwest and the countries contiguous or tributary to that region."[59] Rather than competing with San Francisco, San Diego would carve out of the American Southwest its own regional empire.

Central to the San Diego's bold plans was the completion of both the Panama Canal and local magnate John D. Spreckels's railroad project, which sought to link the city with the greater Southwest. The canal promised shipping costs to and from the region that were cheaper than using current transcontinental railroad lines.[60] When Spreckels's San Diego and Arizona Railway was completed, local officials firmly believed that San Diego would emerge as the trade center of the American Southwest. The Panama-California Exposition, then, would showcase this region and San Diego's place in "the limitless future opportunities of this great American Southwest."[61] To help visitors visualize this, one fair brochure printed a map that showed "New Routes of World Commerce After Completion of Panama Canal," with San Diego central to what the map titled the "Great Circle of Commerce."[62]

Choosing to focus on the opportunities the Southwest offered meant that exposition directors had to overcome the common perception that the region was unfavorable to farming. Simply rejecting or dismissing this view was insufficient. San Diego leaders declared that the PCE would provide real demonstrations of how agricultural products could be successfully grown in the region. "Processes, not products" was one of the fair's slogans. Rather than just displaying products on shelves or in exhibit halls as other fairs typical did, San Diego would show visitors real farms or actual demonstrations of industrial products and machines.[63] *Sunset Magazine*, for example, described how a fair director rejected a proposal to exhibit a European country's famous line of art bronzes, because San Diego "made it a rule to accept exhibits only if the goods shown have a market or can create a market in our territory, and for art bronzes there is no demand."[64] Not only did exposition officials believe that this approach promoted the region's commercial potential, it also helped insure the event's success by further distinguishing it from the San Francisco fair.

San Diego's success, however, rested on the agricultural potential of its far-reaching hinterland. Exposition officials shamelessly claimed that the region possessed forty-four million acres, which could provide upwards of seven hundred thousand farms.[65] The city's natural harbor, they added, was the "most convenient inlet and outlet for commerce for all of that rapidly-developing portion of the United States as the Great Southwest."[66] With access to a good deal of Southern California's citrus production, the new railroad promised to extend that reach to the growing fertile Imperial Valley, with its hundreds of thousands of cultivated acreage.[67] Exploiting the agricultural potential of the Southwest was important not just for San Diego but for the future of the American West. PCE president Davidson added that the city's future hinged on convincing visitors of the region's agricultural possibilities and providing "a promise of sure fulfillment" to capital and labor.[68] As *Sunset Magazine* succinctly put it, San Diego was "holding its exposition not to take business away from other cities, but to create new business."[69]

On January 1, 1915, San Diego swung open the gates to the first year-round exposition. Touting the city's mild climate, fair leaders hoped that a year-long event would not only ensure its financial success but further distinguish it from San Francisco's larger exposition. After a strong opening week, attendance was somewhat disappointing until the late spring—when the impact of PPIE opening helped increase railroad traffic to the Pacific Coast. By October, Los Angeles businessmen had pledged $150,000 to encourage San Diego officials to continue the fair for a second year.[70] Aided by exhibits borrowed from the San Francisco fair after it closed in late 1915, San Diego could now call the 1916 fair an "international" exposition. Fair officials added foreign exhibits, including those representing France, Canada, Brazil, and several other nations, as well as a few popular attractions from the PPIE's entertainment zone. In 1915 more than two million had passed through the gates, and when the fair closed a year later, total attendance topped 3.7 million.[71] President Davidson declared upon its closing that the "West has been seen at its best. The wonderful and vast possibilities of this great empire have been successfully exploited to the amazement and enlightenment of our visitors."[72]

San Francisco: The Panama-Pacific International Exposition

Rightly proud of the Panama-California Exposition, few San Diego leaders could deny that the fair's success hinged on the competing northern California exposition. Just six weeks after San Diego's fair opened, San Francisco had launched the Panama-Pacific International Exposition. Plans for the exposition began more than a decade before, when local merchant Reuben B. Hale proposed the enterprise to celebrate the future completion of the Panama Canal. In a 1904 letter to the San Francisco Merchants Association, Hale asked, "Is not the time right . . . for us to consider a world's exposition in 1915?"[73] As the nation's eyes focused on the Louisiana Purchase Exposition, Hale and other business leaders believed that their city's economic might compared favorably to St. Louis. The early momentum was stopped in its tracks when an earthquake in April 1906 devastated the Bay Area. Remarkably, San Francisco quickly rebounded, and by 1910 had revived plans for hosting the nation's celebration of the Panama Canal. City leaders incorporated the Panama-Pacific International Exposition Company, and within a few weeks they had raised several million dollars to fund the event.[74]

Born out of the California gold rush, San Francisco had been the premiere city in the American West for more than a half century. Formerly known as Yerba Buena, American officials changed the name of the community soon after seizing control of California from Mexico in the late 1840s. Its population exploded following the discovery of gold in early 1848. By the end of the first year of gold rush migration, more than twenty-five thousand called it home. Over the next decade,

View of Panama-Pacific International Exposition fairgrounds with San Francisco in the background. *Wikimedia Commons.*

the city's population grew in both size and diversity as the gold rush attracted people from around the world. Even as the gold rush subsided, the Comstock Lode strike in nearby Nevada and the construction of the transcontinental railroad in the 1860s continued to draw settlers to the growing Bay Area metropolis.

The completion of the Central Pacific–Union Pacific railroad line in 1869 not only encouraged more migration westward, but it also tied California to a growing national market. With nearly 150,000 calling San Francisco home, the city quickly emerged as the manufacturing capital of the Far West. Growth did not come without some pain, however. Tension between San Francisco capitalists and white workers contributed to a wave of anti-Chinese sentiment throughout the 1870s,

culminating in a political upheaval that saw labor acquire significant power in the state. Through the newly formed Workingman's Party of California (WPC), labor pressured state officials to address complaints about the Chinese and the growing power of the railroads. The WPC not only helped insert anti-Chinese and anti-railroad amendments in the state constitution, but the threat of further labor dominance compelled California officials to call for the 1882 Anti-Chinese Act ending immigration from the Far East country.[75]

By the turn of the twentieth century, San Francisco suffered from political corruption and machine politics. Political reformers' efforts to try to right the ship largely proved ineffective. Growing class conflict encouraged workers to form the Union Labor Party (ULP) in 1901 under the leadership of Abraham Ruef. That year San Franciscans elected a musician union president as mayor, ushering in several years of labor rule. However, widespread corruption by Ruef, who largely ran the city, led to a celebrated graft trial that ended in convictions for both Ruef and the mayor. Outrage at the level of corruption in government helped usher in California's progressive movement.[76] Bribery scandals were not the only issues the city had to face. Just before the trials began, the devastating earthquake of 1906 destroyed much of the city. Home to more than three hundred thousand, the state's largest city quickly recovered from the shock and rebuilt the city anew. By 1910 San Franciscans brimming with confidence announced plans to host an international exposition celebrating the completion of the Panama Canal.

Before the ink dried on the incorporation papers, San Francisco exposition officials faced two rather different challenges to their claim. Several months earlier, San Diego businessmen G. Aubrey Davidson had proposed that the Southern California city should draw up plans to host an exposition in 1915. When San Francisco leaders announced their fair, they quickly dismissed the proposed venture from the small city to the south. The *San Francisco Chronicle*, for example, ridiculed San Diego's challenge, declaring: "As OUR readers know, San Diego's latest flower of an imperial fancy is her idea of holding a Pacific-Panama exposition." The paper argued that San Diego's population of no more than fifty thousand could not attract interest of nations like Japan or China, nor would the federal government choose it over a "hotel city" like San Francisco. It concluded that San Diegans "are energetic, but so is a dummy engine; and, however a dummy engine may fret and stew and toot its whistle, it can't pull an overland train." While San Francisco officials saw little competition from the Southern California city to the south, others in the state expressed concerned that if the state did not unite behind one city that Congress might reject both proposals.[77]

Hoping to avoid what many viewed as a potential catastrophe for the state, several Los Angeles bankers organized a statewide meeting to resolve this dispute. At a meeting held in Santa Barbara in the spring of 1910, over one hundred delegates from some fifty cities tossed their support behind San Francisco. One Los Angeles businessmen, William Garland, declared that "[i]f the fair is to be held at all . . . it must be held in San Francisco." PPIE official Charles C. Moore added that "San Francisco is the metropolis of the Pacific Coast. You did not make it so, and we did not make it so. Nature and time have done that and now San Francisco must discharge her obligation to the whole Pacific Coast." Despite the widespread support for San Francisco, San Diego leaders refused to recognize the Santa Barbara decision. Months later, after numerous negotiations involving local congressmen and commercial organizations, PCE officials forged a compromise that endorsed the San Francisco fair in return for its support for a narrower regional exposition in San Diego.[78]

While the San Diego conflict turned out to be a small irritant for PPIE officials, a competing proposal from New Orleans to host the 1915 exposition proved more challenging. As Californians debated which city in their state should host the fair, New Orleans exploited this dispute to tender its own bid in early 1910. The Louisiana city claimed that a national exposition should not be held in a frontier post distant from the bulk of the American population. Soon after the San Diego skirmish ended in March, San Francisco leaders went on the offensive, rallying support from California politicians and raising millions to fund their fair. The lobbying effort included sending some two million postcards a week to Congress and an aggressive crusade to "Flood Whole Country With Pamphlets and Literature."[79] The campaign also attacked New Orleans, claiming that few "would choose to spend a summer there" and that "[f]ully 1,000,000 active, prosperous, pleasure-loving white people live in San Francisco. New Orleans has not half this number in fifty miles." Furthermore, California leaders noted that New Orleans had hosted a fair before in the 1880s, and the federal government had to pay off that event's debt.[80]

Undermining New Orleans's bid was only one strategy employed by California officials. Politicians, newspaper editors, and PPIE leaders also promoted San Francisco's strengths and advantages. A "peculiarly salubrious climate for a summer exposition" distinguished San Francisco from the hot, humid Gulf Coast city.[81] Boosters also leveraged the growing belief that California had captured the imagination of the American people. It is, one prominent supporter claimed, "a part of the earth which every traveler, the world over, holds the wish to see and which disappoints no one who has come under the spell of its scenic beauty."[82] Holding the exposition on the Pacific Coast also made logical sense, since the Panama Canal promised to open the Pacific Ocean and Orient to American commerce. Visitors could easily travel to San Francisco through the canal and return home "overland through the West that the canal is to develop and bring into prominence and power."[83] The significant railroad construction in the West, the *San Francisco Chronicle* explained, symbolized the future of the nation evidenced by the growing travel and trade to the region. In short, the paper concluded, there "is 'nothing doing' in the South."[84]

San Francisco's effort paid off on January 31, 1911, when Congress granted the official right to host the 1915 American exposition to the Pacific Coast metropolis. Central to San Francisco's success was its location on the Pacific Ocean. As early as 1904, the PPIE's founding father, Reuben Hale, had maintained that the fair would do more than just commemorate the completion of the Panama Canal. He wrote: "Horace Greeley said 'Go West, young man'; but when he goes west from San Francisco he goes east. It is the beginning of the east, and the end of the west. We are the center around which trade revolves between the United States and all European countries that are looking for trade with the Orient and other Pacific Ocean points."[85] Not only would the city milk the commerce between Europe and Asia, but it also would serve as the staging point for American businesses that sought to reach the markets of China, Japan, and other Pacific nations. One local merchant, J. R. Howell, believed that the "advertising value of the world's fair alone will be $40,000,000 to $50,000,000, for it will bring hundreds of thousands of people out here." Even the *Washington Post* recognized that the 1915 exposition would mark an important moment in the commercial future for San Francisco, as well as the entire nation.[86]

Plans for the Panama-Pacific International Exposition moved along well until August 1914, when a brewing conflict in Europe erupted into a world war. Fair officials quickly realized that any equivocation about the potential impact of the war might undermine faith that the exposition would go forward. Observers claimed that the war would impede European participation and might force a postponement of the fair's opening. PPIE officials responded that the opening would not be delayed and that the war's key players—Great Britain, Germany, and Russia—were not officially participating in the event. Moreover, exposition president

Moore argued that the fair took on more importance because it could help maintain international friendliness in the midst of war.[87] Likewise, a noted journal proclaimed that in "the shadow of the calamity of war the struggling nations saw the exposition as a beacon lighting the road to future restoration and rehabilitation."[88] Inspired by the exhibits fairgoers witnessed at the PPIE, the national magazine *Current Opinion* stated that the "whole effect of the Exposition becomes, thus, in a way, that of a counter demonstration against the war."[89] Rather than subverting the exposition, World War I added a new dimension to its importance beyond the economic benefits it promised to San Francisco.

Beyond raising the geo-political significance of the fair, San Francisco leaders saw another silver lining in the clouds of war. Reuben B. Hale, now vice president of the PPIE, stated that the "European war will turn to the West and to the expositions next summer the tide of tourists from the United States and from South America." Hale maintained that Americans who traditionally vacationed and spent some $200 million in Europe each year would now look to California to spend their idle time.[90] To encourage tourist travel westward, fair officials quickly exploited the growing "See America First" campaign that the Great Northern Railway had adopted as its company motto. Western boosters recognized that "defining tourism as a patriotic ritual of citizenship" could aid efforts to attract settlers and capital.[91] California senator James D. Phelan, for example, acknowledged the benefits of the "See America First" idea and argued that the exposition's art and educational exhibits were enough to induce travel to the Pacific Coast. "[T]he American people, moved by a patriotic impulse," he suggested, "should turn their faces towards the West, and so, at the same time, acquire a knowledge of their country and the latest achievements of the world's civilization."[92] While the world war posed a challenge to exposition officials, it also offered a greater opportunity to help redefine the West in the American mind.

On February 20, 1915, the gates to the Panama-Pacific International Exposition opened to a flood of visitors, which by day three totaled 442,957. Fair officials crowed that this early success surpassed the initial attendance of both the 1893 Chicago and the 1904 St. Louis celebrations. Newspaper editors from numerous western communities likewise heralded the San Francisco fair. The *San Bernardino Sun* declared that a tremendous influx of people to the Pacific Coast would continue beyond 1915 and that "California will be a commonwealth as populous as it is rich and productive and pleasing." The *Humboldt Times* added that the opening of the gates marked the arrival of the West and its residents. Even Portland's paper acknowledged that San Francisco was the best-qualified city to host the exposition because it "is the premier city of the Pacific Coast, it is the center from which radiated the greatest development of this Coast." Over the next ten months, some 18,875,294 people passed through the PPIE turnstiles, including nearly a half-million fairgoers on closing day in early December.[93]

THE END OF THE PPIE WAS NOTHING BUT A TRIUMPH for San Franciscans. No other fair, the *San Francisco Chronicle* claimed, "has so stirred the imagination. The world never had before so great a lesson in simple beauty. It has never before been shown such high standards in so many lines of human endeavor."[94] John F. Shafroth of Denver, Colorado, noted that World War I made the exposition more significant, because in a world of hatred and conflict, the PPIE offered mankind "participation in a communion of brotherhood." Others did not forget the economic benefits the fair bestowed. An Ohio resident remarked that the San Francisco event exposed the nation and the world to the commercial opportunities of the West, a "great region [that] has been more foreign than Europe."[95] Perhaps a *San Francisco Chronicle* editorial summed it up best: "From every point of view the exposition has been a glorious success. In its beautiful appeal, its influence on the public mind, its satisfactory attendance, its financial achievement, the pleasure it has given, and the extraordinary advertisement it has given the State, the exposition is a triumph for San Francisco and for California."[96] As the lights were turned off and workers began to dismantle exhibits, residents up and down the Pacific Coast no doubt saw a bright future for their young region.

2 ⊱ PROMOTING THE FAIRS

WITH THE CALIFORNIA GOLD RUSH AND THE RAILROAD boom period of the 1880s a distant memory, West Coast communities from Seattle to San Diego hitched their futures to their respective expositions. Recognizing the utility of an urban fair was just the beginning. Ensuring success hinged on promoting and advertising their expositions to faraway audiences. Separated from the Far West by steep mountain ranges, bone-dry deserts, and grassy plains meant that only a relatively small number of Americans had ventured across the continent to the Pacific Ocean. Local leaders would spend several years carefully defining their fairs and crafting marketing plans to convince Americans that they would not regret the cost and time traveling to these West Coast extravaganzas. Drawing on new tactics and approaches developed by the modern advertising industry, exposition publicity departments determined the desires of their target audience and devised national promotional campaigns that would have impressed executives at any American manufacturing firm. With the aid of the transcontinental railway companies, national magazines, and thousands of local newspapers, fair officials both highlighted the benefits of western living and challenged popular misconceptions of the American West in their quest to sell their homeland to the rest of the nation.

⊱ The Transformation of Advertising

Soon after Pacific Coast cities decided to host an exposition, one of their first tasks was to appoint a director of publicity or—what some called—exploitation. Fair officials correctly understood that advertising was crucial to staging a successful event, and they wasted no time devising a marketing strategy. Writing about Portland's exposition, historian Carl Abbott argued that "[e]ffective advertisement meant large attendance, and large attendance, combined with a successful image for the fair and the city, would mean success as a booster enterprise."[1] Five years before the gates opened in San Diego, for example, the Panama-California Exposition Executive Committee debated the importance of establishing the publicity committee as the fair's first official department.[2] Likewise, within days of incorporating the Panama-Pacific International Exposition in March 1910, the newly minted board of directors formed a Committee on Exploitation and Publicity chaired by future fair president Charles. C. Moore.[3] "Advertising an exposition," a Seattle publicity piece declared, "is a mighty task." It added that "the most important work in connection with building an exposition is advertising it."[4] Plans included determining not only how best to disseminate information to potential visitors, but also the specific themes and content of promotional material. Exposition officers, in concert with local politicians and businessmen, quickly gathered data about their cities and the surrounding region in order to explain the economic, social, and cultural advantages their community had to offer visitors. Meanwhile, publicity committees reached out to the nation's newspapers, magazines, and transcontinental railroads to advertise their expositions.

Advertising as both an activity and industry grew significantly in the latter decades of the nineteenth century. The impact of industrialization, urbanization, and new transportation innovations spawned not just new businesses and products, but also rapidly expanding national and—in some cases—international markets. The days when a local shopkeeper's customers could be reached through a simple notice in the town's paper were quickly disappearing. Transcontinental railroads and telegraphs reduced the distance between producer and consumer, allowing companies to expand both their markets and their operations. By the 1880s, mail-order firms like Sears and Montgomery Wards connected once regionally restricted companies to vast numbers of consumers in small towns and rural communities. In the competitive marketplace of late-nineteenth-century America, more and more companies turned to advertising to promote their products and persuade Americans to purchase their wares.[5]

By the dawn of the twentieth century, businessmen increasingly sought out more skilled and professional advertising agents. While small-town shopkeepers might still write the copy for advertisements listed in the community's newspaper, larger firms recognized the need for more persuasive ads and a clear marketing strategy. A national trade journal, *Printers' Ink*, claimed that the "success of all advertising hinges on its plan—the theory on which it is based."[6] To this end, growing specialization and a new corporate culture led many large manufacturers to set up their own advertising divisions to reduce the role of the middleman. Success in the competitive marketplace demanded marketing strategies that differentiated their products and persuaded customers to buy them. The advent of new mass-market magazines with large, national readership likewise contributed to the need for more professional advertising agents. By the 1920s, the appearance of national advertising firms marked the final step in the evolution of modern advertising.[7]

The transformation of advertising by the early twentieth century influenced expositions' promotional campaigns. Fair directors' choice of journalists and experienced newspaper executives to head publicity departments was based on more than their professional skills at crafting good stories. While an AYPE state commission report wrote that an exposition "is primarily a gigantic plan of advertising," exploitation directors from Seattle to San Diego correctly understood that a successful event depended on more than just advertisements in the nation's newspapers.[8] San Francisco's PPIE director of publicity, George Hough Perry, declared that "[a]dvertising is an exact science" that must be practiced like other sciences; he suggested that it was not the same as publicity and should be measured in real results—not just attention paid to one's products or store.[9] As a leader in his industry, Perry brought a good deal of expertise to the San Francisco fair. Before taking on the role of publicity director, Perry had worked in advertising in New York and delivered papers and lectures at several professional conventions, including a talk on the fundamentals of advertising to the Annual Convention of the Associated Advertising Clubs in 1911.[10]

Perry had a well-established place in the advertising world prior to taking on his duties for the San Francisco fair, but national experts also recognized the success of other western cities in municipal advertising. At the same convention where Perry spoke, the Municipal and State Publicity Department held a two-day session where several speakers noted that "scientifically applied advertising . . . has spread like wildfire all over the South and West." The department's chairman especially singled out "Pacific towns and cities" like Seattle and Los Angeles, where "this method of setting forth the attractions and possibilities of its communities is in full swing." At the close of the two-day session, chairman Thomas F. Anderson declared that municipal advertising was "destined to be one of the most important phases of advertising in this country." Moreover, he believed that a city's success hinged less on its publicity bureau's budget than on the quality and expertise of its manager.[11] The Pacific Coast fairs' exploitation departments would no doubt agree.

The Associated Advertising Clubs' annual convention program confirmed that all advertising was not the same. Along with the Municipal and State Publicity Department, the program listed ten other department sessions ranging from periodicals to outdoor advertising.[12] While all advertising may have involved selling something to someone, industry professionals understood that selling a product was inherently different from selling a place or lifestyle. Place promotion, as scholars call it, is "defined as the conscious use of publicity and marketing to communicate selective images of specific geographical localities or areas to a target audience."[13] Whereas companies might market a tangible product to a specific type of customer, scholars Steven V. Ward and John R. Gold argue that marketing a locale is less clear because advertisers are selling "complex packages of goods, services, and experiences that are consumed in many different ways."[14] Determining success, then, is difficult because measuring "sales" is imprecise, and connecting the promotional campaign to the customer's decision-making process is nearly impossible, since it might be years before results would show. Whether Pacific Coast business leaders and city officials realized these concerns is not clear. However, in the competitive environment of the early-twentieth-century Far West, most likely felt that doing nothing was unacceptable.

Advertising Techniques

Despite the challenges of place promotion, exposition officials embraced the opportunity that the fairs offered to boost their cities. Municipal advertising was not limited to less developed areas like the Far West. A 1910 *Putnam's Magazine* article on the role of civic advertising declared that "any city which does not make some active effort at direct advertisement is dead, and sure to fall behind the times." If publicity bureaus and advertising agents helped elect presidents and marketed the "latest brand of soap," the magazine added, why should cities not do the same to ensure their futures? Urging local officials to join forces with commercial organizations like the chamber of commerce to engage in civic advertising, the article concluded that "[t]he day has come when the American city, to be progressive, must advertise itself."[15] By hosting expensive expositions, local leaders along the Pacific Coast demonstrated that they eagerly shared this conclusion.

Agreement on the need to advertise was only the first step. Cities and regions had been engaged in such boosterism for decades, and even the use of expositions was three decades old when Portland hosted the Lewis and Clark Exposition in 1905. Moreover, fair publicity directors operated in a time where the advertising industry was changing. Not only were professional advertising agents increasingly dominating the production side of the industry, but also the style or approach to advertising was evolving. The days of the carnival barker or patent medicine ads—in which the product's benefits bore little resemblance to its wild claims—was coming to an end. By the early twentieth century, "reason-why" advertising had become the accepted practice. Simply put, this new approach aimed to convince the consumer to purchase a particular brand or product by highlighting its distinctiveness. Signifying a shift from emphasizing the features of the business or product to how it could benefit the consumer, advertisers were encouraged to design ads to persuade the consumer to identify with the product.[16] During the progressive era, some psychologists and social scientists went one step further suggesting that consumers were non-rational beings whose desires and hopes could be manipulated. To enhance the effectiveness of advertising, experts argued that promoters should utilize techniques "to connect the product with the instinctual wants and needs in the consumer's mind."[17] By the time the Pacific Coast cities opened the gates to their respective expositions, fair directors had some new weapons to employ in their quest to sell the Far West.

Publicity material churned out by the four expositions' presses demonstrated that fair officials had readily embraced these new techniques and approaches. Exploitation departments understood that simple informational ads notifying potential visitors of their plans to host a fair, regardless of how many column inches of space they occupied, would not convince people to trek thousands of miles across the country. Just like manufacturers and large corporations, exposition officials had to persuade "consumers" to make that purchase. Fair marketing materials, for example, often drew upon the reason-why techniques advocated by leading advertisers to convince readers why they should consider visiting or moving to the Pacific Coast. Testimonials by people who had recently settled in Seattle, San Diego, or wherever the fair was held likewise borrowed from new techniques employed by the advertising industry. In some cases, publicity directors used emotional response advertising techniques, attempting to touch or move the reader: a picture of Mount Hood or a Southern California beach or a story about someone who overcame a health condition due to the region's salubrious climate might compel an Ohio farmer or Pittsburgh merchant to pull up stakes. Whatever new technique exploitation departments borrowed, in the end, they agreed with one advertising leader who proclaimed that advertisements must "educate the people to a knowledge of the comforts, conveniences, and luxuries of life and create the desire to share in their enjoyment."[18] This desire could not be produced by a quarter-page advertisement buried in the in a newspaper's classified ads section.

Understanding the consumer emerged as one of the central principles of modern advertising in the early twentieth century. Psychologists urged advertisers to comprehend "the workings of the minds of his customer" in order to design effective ads.[19] Crafting a persuasive message required fair publicity directors to use language and values shared by those whom they attempted to reach. An effective campaign, one scholar has argued, relied on "images and symbols [that] are selected from reality by the advertisers but fashioned to meet the audience's needs. The frequency with which they occur and recur strongly implies that language is shared by both parties."[20] When exposition publicity directors crowed about the specific benefits of western living, they were in many ways speaking about what drew them to the region. They shared with those living east of the Mississippi a set of concerns, anxieties, and desires, which informed the advertisements and brochures they produced. In short, they truly understood their "consumers," because they once stood in their shoes. Their task was to help the merchant and farmer envision themselves spying Mount Rainier from a Seattle street or eying the bushels of oranges harvested from their orchard in San Diego's backcountry.[21]

Fortunately, the four Pacific Coast cities had the experiences of earlier expositions to draw upon when formulating their promotion plans. Since the 1893 Columbian Exposition, several smaller fairs were held in Buffalo, Omaha, and St. Louis, which provided models for Portland in 1905. However, the considerable distance between the Pacific Coast and the intended faraway audience, as well as the East's relative lack of knowledge of the Far West, posed additional barriers.[22] Publicity directors from smaller, less well-known cities first had to acquaint Americans east of the Mississippi with their communities. James A. Wood and Welford Beaton, the Alaska-Yukon-Pacific Exposition exploitation directors, believed that to host a successful event, "a desire to visit the country must first be created." Once potential visitors understood what the Pacific Northwest had to offer, publicity efforts could then turn to advertising the AYPE. Similarly, Lewis and Clark Exposition directors may have featured the Pacific Northwest prominently in publicity materials, but they never failed to highlight Portland, in order to "place the city before the eyes of the world."[23] Unlike the other smaller cities, San Francisco may have had less need to raise its profile because not only had the U.S. government picked it as the national exposition after a bruising public fight with New Orleans, but it was also the largest and most well-known city in the West.

While exploitation departments quickly developed promotion plans to generate interest in their expositions, they also simultaneously sought participation from other cities, states, and, if possible, foreign countries. PPIE's by-laws, for example, required the publicity committee to include procuring state and international participation.[24] Besides soliciting exhibits, city leaders marshaled the support of numerous Pacific Coast commercial organizations and newspapers to raise "a mighty sum with which to further to advertise the Pacific Slope."[25] After alerting the nation to its plans to host an exposition, San Diego similarly turned its attention to persuading other states and counties to join its celebration.[26] Pacific Coast boosters understood that an exposition's success hinged on encouraging many western states and cities to provide exhibits or displays that advertised their resources and economic opportunities. Henry Reed, who served as the director of exploitation for the AYPE before resigning in 1908, organized a letter-writing campaign to drum up support for the 1909 fair.[27] Expressing his concern to one AYPE official, Reed wrote that "if there is no considerable western participation, the eastern states and manufacturers will not have the inducement for exhibiting."[28] In short, publicity committees from Seattle to San Diego had their hands quite full well before their respective expositions opened their gates.

From the beginning, fair directors focused on newspapers as the primary vehicle for advertising the fair. Reed, who also served as the Lewis and Clark Exposition (LCE) secretary, wrote that "we are doing straight out newspaper publicity."[29] Defined largely by geography, newspapers allowed fair officials to target specific audiences—in both the small towns and large metropolitan centers—whom they believed might be open to visiting or moving to the Far West.[30] To that end, fair officials often chose newspaper editors or journalists to serve as publicity directors. Before taking on his role with the LCE, Reed had worked for the *Portland Oregonian*. Similarly, the AYPE's James A. Wood and Welford Beaton both had newspaper training. Exposition officials did not ignore their local press either. Lewis and Clark fair executives, for example, created a separate department just for Portland's papers to stimulate local attendance. San Diego and Seattle exploitation directors also sent special issues of their papers to other cities because, they believed, it "is the local newspapers that publish all the details of what is transpiring in that locality."[31]

Regardless of how well crafted an advertisement might be, none of the Pacific Coast expositions could afford to just place ads in the nation's newspapers. Moreover, few newspapers were willing to offer ad space for free. As one PPIE official put it, "the day of free publicity had passed."[32] Newspapers were businesses, and the space on their pages was quite valuable. Nevertheless, exposition officials prided themselves on spending little or no money on direct advertising. San Francisco's fair president, Charles Moore, for example, resisted pressure to spend one million dollars on advertising space. Likewise, the Panama-California Exposition's publicity bureau noted in 1911 that, after more than a year, it had not spent a single dollar advertising the fair.[33]

In the end, exposition publicity departments rarely paid for advertisement space, but instead submitted articles to national newspapers that accomplished much the same goal. As one AYPE official explained, to "get into the newspapers is essential to the success of a comprehensive advertising campaign. It therefore becomes necessary to make news, and to give it to the newspapers in a manner that will make it acceptable to editors who view with suspicion all matter sent them by press agents."[34] He added that in Seattle's case, publicity director James A. Wood devised the news, and his assistant Welford Beaton placed it in the most appropriate papers. Winfield Hogaboom, director of publicity for the San Diego fair, likewise declared that if newspaper promotional material "appears to the reader as publicity, and not as news, it is of no more effect than straight advertising because it is accepted in the reader's mind as advertising."[35] Illustrating the effectiveness of this approach, San Francisco officials claimed they did not even have to seek out venues to advertise their fair since many distant newspapers requested "news 'stories'" and pictures about the PPIE.[36] Exploitation departments thus spent much energy constructing articles that would capture readers' attention and generate excitement for their respective fairs.

Devising the most appropriate message was only the first step of successful publicity. Exploitation directors also tried to target their marketing outreach to produce better results. Portland's General Press Bureau, for example, did not disseminate information indiscriminately, but instead sent a specific article to only one paper in a particular city because it believed that the paper's editor would be more likely to publish it if he or she thought it was an exclusive.[37] LCE directors were likewise careful not to focus too much advertising on Portland at the expense of the rest of Oregon. If Portland garnered too much attention, they feared it might alienate other nearby communities and imperil fair attendance.[38] Protecting an exposition's image was also an important responsibility of some exploitation departments. PPIE officials even applied to the secretary of state of California to protect the fair's name from improper use by outside groups and businesses who might misrepresent the event and seriously undermine the exploitation department's carefully crafted message.[39]

While newspapers provided exposition officials an inexpensive way to reach a large swath of the nation's population, publicity directors also looked to popular national magazines and trade publications to promote their fairs. As place-promotion scholars have argued, both the message as well as how, or through what venue, information is transmitted influences the level of receptivity by the targeted audience.[40] During the late nineteenth century, changes in postal rates and technology advances helped produce a wave of new, inexpensive magazines that were within the reach of millions of Americans. National magazines offered several additional benefits that a typical newspaper article did not. Publishers, for example, not only pursued more advertisements, but they also needed more content to attract readers.[41] *Collier's Weekly*, the *Saturday Evening Post*, and similar magazines allowed fair publicity departments to publish longer and more comprehensive articles that could attract the eyes of hundreds of thousands of readers in a single issue. The Panama-California Exposition's publicity department reportedly targeted more than a dozen magazines and another nine farm journals that together could reach upwards of ten million readers.[42] Frank Merrick similarly noted that the Portland's General Press Bureau often wrote special articles for magazines and the trade press.[43]

More importantly, many of these national periodicals supplemented written descriptions with numerous pictures and illustrations that many newspapers could not or would not print. In his final report, Merrick affirmed that the Press Bureau recognized the significance of pictures in accentuating the written words.[44] Like many large companies or manufacturing firms, fair officials understood that national magazines not only offered a larger audience, but also reached subscribers who were more likely more affluent and possessed the means to travel to a Pacific Coast exposition. Newspapers allowed publicity departments to target certain geographic populations—midwestern farmers, for example—but national magazines were defined by class and interest and thus offered access to potential targets like merchants and investors.[45]

Fair publicity directors particularly found special issues of magazines focused solely on the expositions most beneficial. In 1909 *Harper's Weekly*, for example, published a special Pacific Northwest issue in which the AYPE figured prominently. The exploitation office and the Seattle Chamber of Commerce provided numerous articles and pictures highlighting the fair and the opportunities the region offered visitors and settlers. The *Seattle Daily Times* declared that this issue "contains more valuable publicity regarding the A.-Y.-P.E. and Seattle than any of the larger and more widely circulated Eastern periodicals have given this part of the country."[46] In 1915 the monthly *Timken* magazine, a trade periodical aimed at the automobile industry and motorcar enthusiasts, published a special California volume. The front cover conspicuously displayed pictures of the San Francisco and San Diego fairs, and between the covers included several articles on the expositions and the surrounding territory.[47]

While exploitation departments utilized scores of national magazines and trade journals to promote their fairs, certain periodicals were willing to offer more significant and continuous coverage of them. *Sunset Magazine* was one periodical that provided the Pacific Coast expositions much space. Created by the Southern Pacific Railroad in 1898, *Sunset* was devoted to tourism and the promotion of the American West. With backing of a large railway company, the magazine had both the resources and the reach that exceeded anything an exposition or a chamber of commerce could achieve. The Southern Pacific Railroad believed that the magazine's positive coverage of the region could encourage more tourists to travel to the West and, in doing so, increase its ridership, so support for the Pacific Coast fairs fit well with this goal. G. W. Del Carlo, circulation manager for *Sunset*, pledged his magazine's support for the 1915 California fairs: "Sunset will do all it can to move people out here and will see that every month both the San Diego and San Francisco Expositions are well reported in pictures and articles to inform the eastern people of the Expositions." Del Carlo noted, for example, that the magazine distributed posters to the eastern communities that featured "a huge magnet lying in the Pacific ocean with the two poles at San Francisco and San Diego, labeled Expositions. The drawing showed railroad trains all over the United States being drawn to the poles of the magnet during 1915 by the magic attraction of the Expositions."[48] *Sunset Magazine*'s commitment to the PCE and PPIE, in short, helped provide free and comprehensive descriptions of the Far West to a larger national audience.

Sunset was not the only periodical that furnished San Diego's fair considerable attention. In 1909 the PCE's board of directors had a spirited debate about whether to declare a magazine called *Scenic America* the official organ of the San Diego fair. Director D. C. Collier believed that doing so was a great opportunity since material would be published for free, and thus the fair "had everything to gain and nothing to lose." However, a few board members, perhaps concerned that this decision might lead other magazines to ignore the exposition, argued that no periodical should have such standing.[49] *Sunset Magazine* may have favored California, but Oregon and Washington were not completely ignored. *Pacific Monthly*, which launched in Portland, offered more highbrow literature that served to promote Far West, especially the Pacific Northwest.[50] Similarly, the Northern Pacific Railway magazine *Wonderland* provided the Lewis and Clark Exposition significant exposure. In the buildup to fair, the magazine expanded its coverage of the LCE, culminating in a special 1905 issue showcasing the event.[51] However the expositions attracted such attention and support, the free national publicity was a welcomed addition to exploitation efforts.

Promoting expositions depended on more than just the willingness of newspapers and magazines to provide free space. Publicity departments produced their own guidebooks, brochures, picture books, and sometimes their own journals and newspapers to advertise their respective fairs. Much of the content often resembled articles found in newspapers and magazines, since most publicity directors recognized the savings in time and money of recycling previously written material. In 1904 the *Lewis and Clark Review and Gazetteer*, the *Exposition*, and the *Lewis and Clark Journal* hit the newsstands replete with articles about the

Santa Fe Railroad advertisement, announcing that both California expositions will open on time, despite outbreak of war in Europe. Rotarian Magazine, *January 1915*.

region's resources, the advantages of the Pacific Northwest living, and updates on what visitors could expect at the Portland fair.[52] San Francisco officials produced and distributed their own biweekly twenty-page promotional portfolio that included photographs, descriptions of the fairgrounds, and articles detailing the exhibits and key buildings. More often than not, these periodicals, including the Panama-California's *Exposition News*, began publishing six months to a year before a fair's opening.[53] Exposition officials did not always have to craft their own materials, but instead they could disseminate favorable federal or state reports that supported the fair's messaging. Washington's AYPE Commission report, for instance, claimed that "chief means of exploitation was distribution of 32,000 copies of the Biennial Report of the Bureau of Statistics and Immigration for the year 1909."[54]

Picture books were also very popular among both exploitation departments and potential visitors. Seattle officials, for example, published a volume called *The Alaska-Yukon-Pacific Exposition and Seattle: The Beautiful Exposition City* replete with pictures of the fairgrounds and city landscapes. Likewise, the PPIE produced *The Red Book of Views of the Panama-Pacific International Exposition* with numerous photographs of the fair, including a few nighttime scenes demonstrating the impact of electric lighting. Perhaps less expensive but no less impressive was a San Diego booklet that offered a number of pencil drawings of the PCE.[55]

The use of images, especially photographs, emerged as a powerful force in the advertising world by the early twentieth century. Magazine articles accompanied by images and picture books presented an exposition's exploitation division the opportunity to provide concrete visual support for their written claims.[56] Together these picture books, guidebooks, and specialized periodicals helped publicity departments advertise their respective fairs and highlight the benefits surrounding communities offered potential settlers.[57]

The Railroads

Next to newspapers and magazines, the region's railroads proved to be the most important avenue for marketing the Pacific Coast expositions. Following the great railroad rate war in 1886–87, historian Earl Pomeroy argues, railway companies recognized the potential windfall of western travel. Journalist Ray Stannard Baker, in a discussion about the railroad's impact on the region, suggested that "the West was inevitable but the railroad was the instrument of its fate."[58] Well before the Pacific Coast fairs opened their gates, railroad companies boosted the West to sell large swaths of land the federal government had granted to them. By the early twentieth century, railroads recognized that tourism could help ensure profits. Companies expanded their promotional efforts and affiliated with western communities and governments to boost the region.[59] A Santa Fe railroad executive, for example, stated that "We are great believers in the unconscious or subconscious influence of advertising. We try to keep the Santa Fe route in the mind of all the people."[60] Railway companies no doubt recognized the natural synergy that the Far West fairs provided.

Exposition directors clearly understood the critical role railroads played in advertising both the fairs and the larger region. Seattle's James A. Wood, for example, claimed that next to city's residents, the "most efficient aid comes from the railroad companies."[61] Likewise, a LCE official stated that without the "friendly interest of the railroads," Portland could not have successfully promoted the Pacific Northwest.[62] Soon after the Panama-California Exposition opened its gates, the *San Diego Union* proclaimed that the "Union Pacific [Railroad] is proving a loyal supporter of the San Diego Exposition" by attempting to reach through its advertising division every potential visitor to Southern California in 1915.[63] Railroad officials often confirmed the significance of their aid. During a tour of Seattle in 1908, Northern Pacific Railway president Howard Elliott claimed that his company had done everything it could to make the AYPE a success, including placing references to the event in all railroad advertising material.[64]

Railroads serving the Far West did more than just note the date and place of the fairs. As some scholars have noted, "Railway companies and their passenger agents became more sophisticated in the use of persuasion, becoming true masters in their mission to lure Easterners to the West."[65] Firms hired writers, photographers, and artists to produce lavishly illustrated brochures describing the region's natural wonders and the opportunities available to potential settlers. According to the advertising agent for the Oregon Railway and Navigation Company, railroad companies distributed a variety of literature "exploiting the wonderful resources of the section, advertising the Lewis and Clark Exposition and introducing the West to the East."[66] Railroad guidebooks, for example, highlighted the climate, resources, and economic potential of the Pacific Northwest, as well as natural wonders one could see on the trip to Portland.[67] Similarly, a 1915 Union Pacific advertisement in the *New York Times* described a circular excursion route that travelers could take while visiting the California fairs. The ad included small sketches surrounding the text depicting key cities like Seattle, Portland, and Denver, as well as points of interest that sightseers could tour, such as Yellowstone National Park and the Columbia River.[68]

Railway companies understood that spotlighting popular destinations like Yellowstone or nearby western cities in addition to the expositions made it easier to fill seats on their western transcontinental lines. In the end, this mutual relationship benefited both parties well.[69]

While the railroad's advertising generally appeared about a year prior to the exposition's opening, the relationship between railway companies and fair directors often originated much earlier. Before San Francisco even secured federal support of the PPIE, the Southern Pacific Railroad, for example, declared its "interest in the project and expect to assist it in every manner possible." By 1912 the fair's exploitation department sent letters to passenger agents of fifty-three railroads, urging them to promote the San Francisco exposition in all their advertising materials.[70] That same year, the *San Diego Union* noted that initial efforts to promote the PCE included getting the railroads on board, especially "the Santa Fe system, the Salt Lake Route and the Southern Pacific Company, all three seeing the advantage to themselves in advertising the Panama-California exposition."[71] The Northern Pacific Railway, a Seattle paper explained, similarly commenced its "extensive campaign of publicity" two years before the AYPE gates swung open.[72] Excitement about these expositions was not the only reason railroads engaged in such early promotion. The great distance and cost fairgoers had to incur traveling to the Far West required railroad officials to undertake advertising efforts years in advance of the expositions.

Exposition officials also recognized that railroad companies could do more than just advertise their fairs. San Francisco leaders, for example, enlisted the aid of several transcontinental lines in their early struggle with New Orleans to win federal support for the Pacific Coast proposal. A Chicago business journal claimed that "[i]f all of the East and West roads bring pressure to bear upon their Congressmen it is probable that San Francisco will win with ease."[73] Fair officials sometimes asked rail companies to subscribe to capital stock to help fund their events. LCE directors also asked the Great Northern Railway Company to provide free rides for their representatives to travel across the West to drum up interest for the Portland fair.[74] Perhaps more important than securing the support of railroad officers was cultivating strong and effective relationships with railroad passenger agents. These frontline railroad employees interacted directly with potential exposition visitors, and fair officials understood that they could ensure better attendance if these agents were sold on their fair. Portland's Henry Reed, for example, convinced the Oregon state government to appoint Union Pacific Railroad agents as honorary commissioners of immigration for Oregon. Several months before the PCE opened its gates, San Diego hosted four hundred passenger agents to showcase its fair so that these railroad representatives could "tell of it intelligently to those intending to visit San Diego" in 1915.[75]

Passenger agents' ability to persuade potential visitors to attend Pacific Coast fairs was influenced significantly by the cost of travel. Exposition officials concluded that railroad fares were the single most important factor in drawing visitors from east of the Mississippi. Without the "favorable rates to the Portland centennial," wrote one fair director, the exposition may not have succeeded.[76] Commenting on the increased traffic to the West in 1909 at the height of the AYPE, the *New York Times* noted that "[t]housands of persons are going West this year who could not be tempted by a mere fair, however great. The low rates are filling the trains."[77] The Great Northern Railway, for example, announced that it would offer "cheap round-trip excursion tickets" to nearly all important eastern cities, whereas before it had provided such low-price tickets only to larger, important cities.[78] Finally, in addition to low rates, some railroads offered stopover privileges that allowed visitors to enjoy a short stay at popular destinations, such as Yellowstone National Park, on their way to Pacific Coast fairs.[79]

Low rates, energetic passenger agents, and an impressive advertising campaign by the nation's railroad helped encourage travel to the Far West expositions. Soon after the gates opened at the PPIE in February 1915, a Union Pacific Railroad executive, for example, announced that his company had received more than a hundred thousand inquiries in just ten days, requesting rates to California.[80] Later that year, the *Railway Age Gazette* claimed that railroad traffic was considerable, and available statistics indicated that passenger business increased more than threefold on some transcontinental lines—and even more on regional railways.[81] No doubt the amount of material railroad companies dispersed was quite impressive: one railroad advertising agent claimed that his railroad distributed more than 2.5 million pieces of literature on behalf of the Lewis and Clark Exposition.[82] Outlining the Northern Pacific Railway promotional efforts, the *Seattle Daily Times* stated that on average, each month the railroad alone distributed 164,000 pieces of printed matter with AYPE advertising, including 80,000 folders, 60,000 schedules, and 1,000 buffet and café cards. Moreover, the railway company placed so many articles, illustrations, and other descriptive matter in numerous eastern newspapers that the AYPE appeared in some manner in five hundred publications with a daily circulation topping fifteen million.[83] When all was said and done, the nation's railroads did much to ensure the success of the West Coast expositions.

Civic and Business Organizations in Promoting the Fairs

Railway companies were not the only commercial entities that helped market the Pacific Coast fairs. Expositions are inherently community endeavors, and civic and business organizations from Seattle to San Diego helped aid fair publicity departments in promoting both their expositions and their cities. Chambers of commerce and similar commercial associations had historically served as the primary boosters of western cities, so it is not surprising that they used their networks and contacts to promote their community's fair. The San Diego Chamber of Commerce, for example, described the publicity work undertaken by the local business organization. Not only did it distribute nearly half a million pieces of advertisement material, but chamber officials also answered approximately twenty-five thousand individual inquiries, provided slides for two hundred lectures, and supplied photographs for innumerable newspaper articles.[84] During the Lewis and Clark Exposition, Portland's chamber of commerce proudly boasted about Oregon's rich timberlands, publishing government data in its monthly bulletin to support its claims.[85] Such support also extended to regional organizations like the Western Development Association, which promised to pool its resources and send a train filled with exhibits, products, and information to more than 250 cities in the East. This promotional tour, officials admitted, "will be more or less . . . an advertisement for the exposition to be held in San Francisco in 1915."[86]

Such ambitious efforts were not the only way local and regional organizations could aid exposition publicity departments. Simple references to the fair included on an organization's letterhead or advertising material could bring needed attention. AYPE director James A. Wood, for example, urged large manufacturers to advertise the Seattle fair in their ads. San Diego officials likewise enlisted the California Hotel Men's Association to print Panama-California Exposition seals on its materials.[87] The innumerable exposition seals, stickers, and stamps produced by publicity departments helped guarantee that easterners did not forget about these distant Pacific Coast expositions. The *Seattle Times* claimed that "[o]ne of the most effective and practical plans for bringing the Alaska-Yukon-Pacific Exposition to the attention of 1,000,000" was the fair's adoption of a colorful stamp that businesses and residents could affix to letters.[88] Likewise, San Diego's chamber of commerce distributed a hundred thousand stickers for mail sent back East.[89] Simple cancellation marks bearing the name of an exposition, as some exploitation departments had initially tried, were not sufficient. With the help of local congressmen, though, San Francisco leaders convinced the nation's postal officials to release upwards of 2.4 million special PPIE stamps to post offices across the country.[90]

Whether official postal stamps or separate stickers affixed to letters and packages, what made this advertising gimmick more effective were the variety of colorful illustrations and images found on these materials. Fair publicity departments often combined nostalgic depictions of their city's past with images of more modern sites. San Diego's chamber of commerce, for example, produced four motifs, including a Spaniard playing a guitar, an image of the exposition's main gate, a view of the city's newly built Cabrillo Bridge, and an outline of the majestic California Tower.[91] AYPE officials likewise included significant exposition buildings and the slogan "Come to Seattle," while the PPIE postal stamps included a likeness of the Spanish explorer Balboa and pictures of the Golden Gate and the discovery of San Francisco Bay.[92] The choice and design of the visual images on fair stamps, historian Bonnie M. Miller has suggested, "sheds light on the struggles of fair organizers and promoters to disseminate and recalibrate the myth of the West to appeal to an increasingly consumer-conscious society."[93]

In short, millions of eye-appealing illustrations and engravings affixed to everyday business mail and personal correspondence helped provide a visual reminder to reinforce the newspaper and magazine articles fair publicity departments churned out each week.

Exploitation directors also devised some novel gimmicks and events that drew additional attention to their respective fairs. Contests and auto races, for example, kept the nation's eyes on Pacific Coast expositions, especially during the weeks leading up to opening day. A Portland manager reported that the General Press Bureau staged popular voting contests in numerous cities across the nation. Promising free trips to the Lewis and Clark Exposition brought a good deal of press coverage: fifty-five newspapers held contests, and then for several months, printed news of the contests nearly every day. The Press Bureau also encouraged department stores to sponsor similar contests in their store ads.[94] Furthermore, exploiting the growing interest in the automobile, publicity departments often organized auto races that started on the Atlantic Coast and ended at the gates of their respective fairs. The *New York Times* reported that Portland officials proposed a race from New York to the LCE Exposition.[95] AYPE officers likewise sponsored a similar contest in 1909, though with a twist. Officials arranged a ceremony where a button was pressed to signal the start of both the auto race and the fair's opening.[96] Exploitation directors recognized the advertising gold mine that such automobile contests provided since cars, covered in signage of the impending expositions, would pass through hundreds of cities on the nearly 4,000- to 5,000-mile transcontinental journey.

Automobiles also figured in one of the most interesting components of fair publicity when individuals made unsolicited and often quite unique offers to publicize western expositions. Portland's Henry Reed, for example, received a letter from Isaac W. Baird and Calvin Heilig offering to don a first-class car with message about the LCE and drive around seven western states for a fee of $150 per week. As part of this fee, they promised to distribute posters and other printed material advertising the Portland fair.[97] In another case, California businessman C. H. Owens announced that he would tour the nation in a Studebaker decorated with banners publicizing the PPIE, as well as present lectures on the economic opportunities available in the San Joaquin Valley.[98] Owens's effort was somewhat unique in that he apparently did not seek any compensation for his publicity campaign. Most unsolicited offers, however, came with requests for employment or stated a fee to provide the particular service. Numerous "lecturers" sent job requests to Portland's Henry Reed highlighting their talent and promising to improve attendance at the LCE.[99]

Novel Publicity Schemes

Sometimes offers to present lectures on behalf of these western fairs included more novel publicity schemes. One couple from Oakland, California, announced that they would hike from the San Francisco fairgrounds to New York City along the "Overland Trail" to advertise the PPIE. Along the way, they would give lectures that included some two hundred color slides illustrating the exposition grounds and buildings.[100] The *San Diego Union* listed some half-dozen walkers who were engaged in long-distance hikes from New York to San Francisco or from San Diego to Seattle in which promoting the PCE was a primary goal.[101] Some offers simply attempted to combine a planned trip with promotion of a city's fair. H. W. Goode, director of Portland's fair, received an offer from one gentleman who was traveling across the country with stops in several large cities, including Salt Lake City; Denver; Chicago; Washington, DC; and New York City. For a fee of $300–$400, he guaranteed "$10,000 worth of advertising by coming in contact with the city editors of many of these papers."[102]

Often these more unique publicity ventures simply offered to advertise the fair by handing out literature or attaching signs and banners to their particular modes of transportation. W. F. Williamson, for example, sent a letter to Reed offering to put together a railroad car with an electric sign to advertise the Portland gathering.[103] Other solicitors suggested more personal touches, including dressing up in a fitting costume in a cross-country walk or pushing a two-wheeled cart from Peoria, Illinois, to Portland.[104] San Diego fair officials rejected an early offer to have "burros equipped to carry an advertisement of the Exposition from San Diego to Kansas City."[105] However, in 1913 a few burros did accompany a San Diego resident on a planned trip through the Pacific Northwest with a final destination in New York. The burros pulled Mr.

Hayes and boxes of postcards advertising the PCE.[106] Recognizing the potential of a captive audience, the Imperial Curtain Company, which constructed theater curtains, proposed to place ads for the LCE on curtains at two Philadelphia theaters.[107] Such innovative publicity schemes did not always come from outside, unsolicited offers. The PPIE Exploitation Department, for example, sent "the Official Herald and his tuba and banner on several distant excursions" to prominently showcase their fair.[108] Though fair officials usually rejected the odd and sometimes bizarre unsolicited proposals, they do nevertheless illustrate the resourcefulness of Americans and how pervasive commercial culture had penetrated the nation by the turn of the century.

WHILE TUBAS AND BURROS MAY HAVE NOT REPRESENTED the most efficient form of advertising, they did reflect the critical importance marketing played in hosting a successful exposition. Pacific Coast fairs faced serious obstacles, from the great distance between the West Coast and potential fairgoers to the relative obscurity of the host cities. Recognizing these challenges, exposition officials understood the crucial role advertising would play in the success of their respective fairs. Fair exploitation departments embraced the new techniques and strategies that national manufacturing firms utilized to sell their products. Resourceful publicity departments exploited the power of the press to spread the word about their expositions. Newspapers and popular national magazines allowed fair officials to target "consumers," all the while providing invaluable coverage of the Pacific slope, replete with pictures of fairs and the surrounding communities. Furthermore, exposition directors cultivated the railway companies' shared interest in developing the Far West. Railroad promotional material put a spotlight on what the West had to offer, while passenger agents helped sell travelers on the wonders of the four fairs. When all was said and done, the Pacific Coast fairs were not only a financial success, but they exposed millions of Americans to the benefits of western living.

3 SELLING THE PROMISE OF THE FAR WEST

PORTLAND, SEATTLE, AND THE PACIFIC NORTHWEST

ON JULY 18, 1909, THE *NEW YORK TIMES* PRINTED A short satirical piece entitled "The Call of the East." This writing lamented the apparent disappearance of the old West, with Sagebush Pete telling a visiting stranger that "There was a time when we had a West, but this doggone East has took th' best O th' Frontier Bunch an' they've heard the Call till there ain't no West out here at all." Sagebrush Pete goes on to explain that there were no more wagon trains and broncos because "th' East's grim cry for things like these has drained us dry!" The stranger learns that if one wanted to experience the West, he should head back East and take in a Wild West show.[1] For exposition executives planning fairs in Portland and Seattle, this conversation no doubt struck a nerve. City leaders and fair directors knew quite well that many Americans still envisioned the West as the stranger did in this tale. A robust and well-defined marketing campaign would be essential to changing or molding popular perceptions of the Far West. A successful exposition, western officials believed, would be measured not just by how many visitors they could attract, but also by how well the fairs could encourage fairgoers to reimagine a new West. To accomplish this feat, westerners would both have to confront their region's mythic past and craft a new image that reflected their own dreams of a West that delivered not just promise but also profit.

Defining the West

From the beginning, exposition directors and local leaders understood that advertising their respective fairs was only one part of hosting a successful event. Little more than a decade following historian Frederick Jackson Turner's announcement that the frontier had closed, many easterners still harbored distorted views of the West. As Richard Slotkin has argued, "For most Americans—to the perpetual dismay of westerners—the West became a landscape known through, and completely identified with, the fictions created about it."[2] These fictions were more often than not born out of representations of the West informed by popular culture, in particular the dime novels and Wild West shows of late nineteenth and early twentieth century. Asserting a more realistic western identity, at least as exposition officials understood it, meant fashioning a promotional strategy that confronted inaccurate representations and replaced them with ones that were more beneficial to the future growth and development of the Far West.

In an address celebrating Seward Day at the Alaska-Yukon-Pacific Exposition in 1909, University of Washington history professor Edmond Meany declared: "How true it is with the people who live out here, where it has been my pleasure to make my home, that the people of the East have scorned at us frequently in their papers and pictures by calling us the wild and woolly West and figuring us in their cartoons with our pants in our boots and our pistols by our sides."[3] Professor Meany's statement expressed a certain frustration shared by western leaders who wished to see their local communities prosper, but faced prospective settlers and businessmen reluctant to relocate to what some still viewed as a less than civilized region. AYPE director-general Ira A. Nadeau similarly noted the popular use of this misinformed idea when defending the Seattle fair's proposal to prohibit the sale of alcohol. "In this respect," he proclaimed, "the so-called 'wild and woolly West' will set an example for the effete East and the entire world."[4] As long as outsiders continued to see the American West as wild and uncivilized, officials saw a dim future for the homeland.

What exactly defined the West as wild and woolly was somewhat fuzzy. For some, it was the region's history of Indian wars and gunfighters, while others noted the West's vast undeveloped lands or its unruly mining communities. The nagging lack of good, trustworthy information about the West only encouraged such simple stereotypes. Travelers, scholar Robert Athearn has argued, "long had found fascination in looking for what they conceived to be the West—a land of cowboys, gunslingers, and 'red' Indians—only to be disappointed when they found black broadcloth suits, real-estate agents, tramways, and gaslit streets."[5] Often when attempting to dispel popular misconceptions of the region, national periodicals reminded readers of these stereotypes. Commenting on the recent transformation of Spokane, Washington, the *World's Work* magazine, for example, sanctioned these views when it suggested Spokane was just a few years before "a pretty tough town, such as you would expect to find in the 'West.'" Whether or not the Washington city had truly changed, the magazine could not help remind readers that just a few hundred miles further east, Indians like Sitting Bull once roamed the range.[6]

The West in Dime Novels

Americans' confusion about the nature of the West was not just due to lack of information or sheer ignorance. Popular culture, especially novels and Wild West shows, effectively filled the knowledge gap.[7] Beginning in the mid-nineteenth century, dime novelists regaled easterners with tales of Indians fighters and gunslingers who operated in the uncivilized frontier west. Emerging mass production techniques by the 1830s helped produce cheap fiction for the masses as the market economy increasingly penetrated the American landscape. Fictional stories about the exploits of western frontiersmen quickly became the "dominant genre of adventure story in the dime format." By the end of the nineteenth century, western-themed dime novels portrayed a West where Manifest Destiny and American ideals stood triumphant.[8]

Central to the framework of western dime novels was the image of "savage" Indians threatening white settlement and control of the frontier. In the wake of the Civil War, the frontier mythic figure Buffalo Bill Cody became one of the most successful subjects of the dime-novel industry. Cody not only scouted the unknown West, but also slaughtered Plains Indians and rescued white women from the clutches of

Advertisement for the Alaska-Yukon-Pacific Exposition using Indian imagery. *University of Washington Libraries, Special Collections, NEG UW 28588z.*

their Native American tormentors. Just as Cody began to bring to life his stories and exploits in the form of Wild West shows, the western outlaw entered the pages of the dime novel. Best exemplifying this new sub-genre were the Deadwood Dick novels, in which the protagonist fled to the West to escape prison and engaged in shootings, robbery, and other illegal activities. Despite the formulaic nature of these writings, easterners gobbled up the dime novels, and in doing so, also consumed rather distorted images of the American West.[9]

By the early twentieth century, the tawdry and sensational western dime novels gave way to the more sophisticated and complicated novels of Zane Grey, B. M. Bower, and Charles Mulford. While the West was still a dangerous, violent, and often unrelenting wilderness, the lonely cowboy emerged as a central figure in the evolving story of the American West. One of the earliest and most successful novels was Owen Wister's *The Virginian,* whose protagonist confronts and later defeats evil rustlers and wins the heart of his lover Molly. By the time 1902 came to close, Wister's novel was the top-selling book in fiction and remained a popular read for many years after. Yet writers were not solely to blame for this regional image. In a time of tremendous social, cultural, and political change, the American audience yearned for stories that spoke to their unease with modern industrial America. Western novelists offered contemporary readers a simpler world where the demarcation between good and evil was clear, and the individual could effect change. As Robert Athearn succinctly put it: "This is not because writers wanted to lie about the West; it was because readers wanted them to."[10]

Wild West Shows

Even the most well-written and rousing literary works could not compete with the visual impact of the Wild West shows that played before American audiences at the turn of the twentieth century. The most famous and influential western show was that produced by Buffalo Bill Cody. Born out of the early dime novels that celebrated the exploits of Cody and several years of theater performances, the famous frontiersman organized his first Wild West show in 1883. For the next three decades, Cody staged shows in dozens of cities throughout the United States as well as numerous others in Europe. Buffalo Bill's Wild West show, historian Richard Slotkin has argued, "was the most important commercial vehicle for the fabrication and transmission of the Myth of the Frontier."[11] Visitors to his show watched reenactments of train robberies and famous Indian–white conflicts, as well as witnessing demonstrations by skilled gunslingers. After a few hours of smelling gunpowder, listening to the crackle of gunshots, and watching

Wild West Show performers, including Nez Perce Indians. The show's use of Native Americans helped add realism to their performances. *University of Washington Libraries, Special Collections, NEG Nowell x2875.*

imposing buffalo and "authentic" Indians, customers left the show thinking that they had relived the conquest of the American West. In other words, as scholar Joy Kasson has suggested, "Buffalo Bill's Wild West became America's Wild West."[12]

Authenticity was central both to Cody's success and the powerful influence his show had on Americans' understanding of the rapidly evolving American West. The showman's desire to entertain was matched only by his dedication to a supposed historical authenticity.[13] Wild West shows achieved this sense of reality by use of prominent western figures, especially Native American performers, and large

painted sceneries deployed as backdrops in the arenas. Moreover, the show's reenactment of real events, like Custer's Last Stand, contributed to the belief that the show was a true representation of the American West. Yet the Wild West show paid scant attention to either fact or truth. What Cody's program included was just as telling as what it ignored. In the end, capturing and maintaining the audience's interest meant that truly authentic western experiences, like farmers plowing the land or miners slogging away in underground mines, were left out. With few competing narratives as compelling as the Wild West show, spectators "realized that it represented an exaggerated and idealized view of frontier life but thought they were seeing 'the real thing.'"[14] For westerners, however, these misrepresentations threatened to stall the progress their homeland had recently achieved.

THE EXPOSITIONS PUT A MODERN SLANT ON THE WEST

Visions of a West brimming with dangerous Indians and gunfighters challenged exposition officials' efforts to redefine the region in the American mind. Seattle newspaper editor Joseph Blethen, for example, declared that the West had developed so much by the opening of Portland's Lewis and Clark fair that names of "Western states no longer suggest vigilantes and Indian uprisings."[15] Similarly, the *World's Work* magazine argued that this "is not the West of prairie or of mining camp, nor of hostile Indians, nor of rough ways."[16] Exposition officials and local leaders insisted that popular conceptions of the West were at best outdated and at worst just wrong. In his speech at the Seattle exposition, historian Edmond Meany simply proclaimed that "the wild and woolly West is a thing of the past."[17] Protestations aside, as long as those east of the Mississippi River viewed the West through the prism of the Wild West show and other fictional representations, westerners would struggle to promote a more positive and attractive image of their region.

Inaccurate representations of the West were not solely a result of Buffalo Bill's visual theater, but also reflected what many western officials believed was a lack of alternative perspectives. One contemporary writer suggested that a true view of the West was one "that the popular understanding does not yet quite know."[18] Commenting on the Pacific Northwest's largest city, the secretary of the Transcontinental Passenger Agents' Association put it more succinctly: "Seattle, in one way, is a great mystery to the people of the East."[19] Pacific Northwest leaders believed that their expositions could go far in educating outsiders about the region as westerners understood it. A 1908 Seattle magazine concluded that the "exposition will do much toward giving the East a proper attitude of appreciation of the West."[20] Rather than inaccurate renderings of the West presented in dime novels and Wild West shows, fair publicity departments wanted visitors to the Far West to "return home with minds cleared of very much haziness that has beclouded them by reason of the acceptance of fictional caricature as gospel fact."[21]

Repackaging the West proved quite challenging to fair promoters. By the early twentieth century, Buffalo Bill Cody faced growing competition from rival Wild West shows and other similar western-themed productions. From Tiger Bill's Wild West to Kit Carson's Buffalo Ranch Wild West, entrepreneurs tapped into the seemingly insatiable interest in the relatively unknown western frontier.[22] No doubt aware of the popularity of these romanticized visions of the old West, exposition directors often undermined their own ambitions by hosting such western-style performances—when all was said and done, these fairs need to cover expenses and encourage visitors from afar to make the long journey to their cities. Whether fair officials liked it or not, easterners had certain expectations, inaccurate as they might be, about the West that had to be met if they hoped to stage a successful event. As historian Elliott West has argued, the "job of advertisers ha[d] been to entice the public with vivid assurances that to the west, the exotic is guaranteed and the remarkable is marked on the map."[23] Publicizing Wild West shows in fair advertisements and handbills both fed these exotic desires and positively affected the bottom line.

Recognizing this reality, Lewis and Clark Exposition directors, for example, planned to set aside sixty acres for "Indian sports and war-dances, Wild West shows and races."[24] In 1905 the *Washington Post* reported that the Portland fair intended to present a production of Custer's Last Stand against the Sioux at Little Big Horn. Employing Native Americans from the nearby Umatilla reservation, the performance promised that "as in the real massacre, the yells of Indians and cracking of their rifles will serve to make the scene thoroughly realistic."[25] Similarly, four years later, Seattle officials included a Wild West show that promised everything: bronco busting, re-creations of Indian attacks on a prairie schooner, the "hanging of the outlaw, the burning at the stake of an Indian," and other attractions "to make the show everything the lover of 'western life' can expect."[26] Staged by a group of local businessmen, Cheyenne Bill's Wild West Show opened in July in nearby Madison Park and was managed by William J. Gabriel, who reportedly was a scout in the 1890 Sioux campaign.[27] The *Seattle Daily*

Times proudly claimed that there "is not faking in Cheyenne Bill's Wild West" and that "[e]very Indian with this show is a full-blooded Sioux or Cheyenne."[28] In July, Gabriel brought his Rosebud Sioux Indians "in full war panoply" to visit the fair, where they encountered a group of Flathead Indians who were performing at the exposition as part of Arthur Dexter's Wild West Show. After eyeing each other for a few moments, they "joined forces and turned loose a war dance."[29] As visitors left these exciting shows, few likely pondered the fair's contradictory messages.

Positive Images of the West

Although mixed messages about the true nature of the American West may have at times undercut efforts to dispel misleading views of the region, the Pacific Northwest expositions nevertheless worked assiduously to promote positive images of the West that would encourage the migration of both capital and people. Boosters, for example, attempted both to "present western places as frontiers of opportunity" and "purge from readers' consciousness the possibility that any of the hardships and dangers, so often associated with the term 'frontier,' existed in those promised lands."[30] Opportunity abounded beyond the Mississippi River, they suggested, which would not only help the nation overcome social and economic strife, but also help it achieve its full potential. Exposition exhibits and advertisements, for example, bragged about the vast swaths of fertile land readily available for new settlers and boasted of large ports offering easy access to the growing Pacific trade with Latin America and Asia.

It was just not economic opportunity that made the West essential to fulfilling the nation's destiny. Exposition exploitation officials produced promotional materials to persuade the public that the significance of the West was more than just beautiful landscapes and open farmland. Less than forty years after the end of the American Civil War, Henry E. Reed, secretary of the Lewis and Clark Exposition, penned an article for a national magazine celebrating the rapid development of the West. While in the first few decades following the war, all eyes were fixed on the East and its fantastic economic growth, Reed claimed it was now the time to shine for the West, which he argued was entering the world stage at a time of American prosperity and peace. Alluding to the infamous sectional struggle, Reed reminded readers that the American West, unlike the South, had always been loyal to the Union and that "instead of proving the destroyer of the nation, [it] has proved its savior."[31]

Equating the American West with the future was a principal marketing theme of the Pacific Coast expositions. Although the region's growth since the Civil War was solid, it was at best uneven and marked by periodic economic downturns.[32] Class conflict afflicted many western communities at the turn of the century. By the early 1900s, the West was home to significant labor strife as well as many noteworthy radical labor organizations.[33] Colorado, for example, suffered from several violent labor conflicts, including the 1894 Cripple Creek mining strike and the 1914 Ludlow Massacre. Further west, Californians witnessed the *Los Angeles Times* bombing in 1910, while the militant Industrial Workers of the World (IWW) engaged in several bloody free-speech fights in Spokane, Fresno, and San Diego.[34] Compared to the industrialized East, historian Carlos Schwantes has argued, the American West was where "volatility of frontier ideals of individualism and personal advancement [clashed] with the dependency inherent in working for wages." This "wageworkers' frontier," as he coined it, helps explain the radicalism of western labor as the region rapidly moved from a frontier to an urban, industrial society.[35] In some ways, workers shared with local elites the belief that the nation's future would be shaped by the Far West. For the working class, however, the region was where labor, not necessarily capital, would help redefine progress.

Boosters, however, seemingly ignored or cast aside industrialization's negative impacts when advertising the promise of the Far West. Whether wishful thinking or simply faith that the region had more upside than the eastern cities, which were plagued by the more profound impact of industrial capitalism, exposition officials asserted that the nation's future would be found in the Far West. Railroad tycoon James J. Hill, for example, claimed that with Seattle's Alaska-Yukon-Pacific Exposition, "we move away from dependence on some past fact, and celebrate instead the general sweep of such forces as make for future progress. The nation faces forward, not backward."[36]

Western People and Western Culture

Portland boosters argued that "civilization has ripened faster than it did in most parts of the Middle West" because early pioneers paid significant attention to forming social clubs, building parks, and establishing schools and colleges.[37] Competing with often misinformed Americans living east of the Mississippi, western leaders and exposition officials had faith that such claims might alleviate any apprehension potential settlers might have about moving to the Far West.

Claims of civilization went beyond simple references to western educational facilities and pretty urban parks. Western living, both Portland and Seattle officials maintained, fostered certain values that both reflected and contributed to this higher civilization. In one promotional piece, Walter H. Page suggested that most western cities were never really frontier settlements, but rather had been settled by eastern men and women who carry with them their eastern sensibilities. These settlers "who set the pace and fashion," he maintained, arrived not in wagons but "came in Pullman cars."[38] In other words, it was recent, more genteel migrants who shaped the culture and lifestyle of western cities, not the stereotypical rough-edged frontiersmen of popular lore. Seattle's Joseph Blethen added that it was more than just the filter of distance and cost, but also the region's unique culture that informed the character of those who now shaped the Far West. "In these men," Blethen wrote, "are now blended the traits of the cowboy and of the real estate man, of the vigilante and the student of law; but added to all these are the conservatism of the capitalist and the responsibilities of success."[39] Western living, boosters concluded, offered more than just material benefits.

Mixing such urbane and sophisticated settlers with the West's sense of opportunity and freedom helped foster a different kind of society. Pacific Northwest leaders suggested that the special character of these colonizers helped them overcome the challenges that the region's untamed environment presented. In other words, the West bred certain qualities that not only insured the region's success but, by extension, also enhanced the nation. "Out of the West," James J. Hill declared, "have come formative impulses that enriched the history of the country. It is the goal of the enterprising and fearless."[40] Walter H. Page simply concluded that the Far West's resources and unique public spirit spawned "a new kind of citizen."[41] The promise held out to future settlers then was that they, too, could partake in and contribute to a new culture emerging on the nation's Pacific Coast.

Responding to larger national concerns and anxieties, exposition publicity directors articulated a shared vision of their homeland as a place to where one could not just escape these conditions but also discover a better kind of life. Public pronouncements, exposition promotional materials, and well-placed articles in national magazines comprised the building blocks of a marketing campaign that wished to redirect the conversation about the Far West. Shamelessly embellishing the superiority of their new Eden reflected boosters' desire to rid one identity associated with popular visions of the wild and woolly West and replace it with something more positive and hopeful.

Pacific Northwest residents' outlook about their homeland resulted as much from what the region had to offer as it did from a kind of rivalry with the East and Midwest. When fair publicity directors and community leaders celebrated the West's supposed happiness and economic opportunity, they came to such conclusions through comparison to social, political, and economic conditions back east.[42] A 1905 *Sunset Magazine* article, for example, claimed that for "a fifth of a century the range of independent chances for young men in the older states has been decreasing."[43] The author argued that upward mobility had diminished significantly, but that the West was still wide open for those seeking to move up in life. Likewise, a Pacific Northwest booster declared that the "Pacific Slope offers more chances in life if you come to seek your fortune. It has richer soil and cheaper land. It has as patriotic as people, too, as energetic, as intelligent; it has less fierce competition; it has fewer social problems." Efforts to promote the West as a place to live or invest, then, reflected popular nervousness about deteriorating conditions back East as much as an emerging regional rivalry.[44]

Celebrating what the West had to offer may have reflected more than just efforts to soothe feelings of inferiority. As David Wrobel has suggested, boosters "were engaging in the most natural and understandable human processes of self-justification. They had taken chances in starting new lives in these locales and wanted to convince those they had left behind of their satisfaction with the momentous decisions they had made."[45] Proud of their new homeland, Portland and Seattle leaders saw their respective expositions as the chance to level the playing field with the East by showcasing the advantages of western living. Exposition brochures and advertisements suggested that successful fairs would deliver more people, capital, and power to the West. However, the West would not be the only beneficiary of such change; the nation would also profit from a more developed and robust region. Northern Pacific Railway's James J. Hill, for example, announced that the AYPE represented the "laying of the last rail, the driving of the last spike, in unity of mind and purpose between the Pacific coast and the country east of the mountains."[46] Railroads may have reduced the distance between East and West, but the nation would not be truly united until all recognized that the future of the United States lay in the West.

Central to this new vision was the belief that the seeds of success had been sown—with just a little cultivation, the Pacific Northwest would soon blossom. During the early twentieth century, Pacific Slope residents proudly identified their region with economic opportunity. First and foremost, western leaders believed that future prosperity depended upon attracting badly needed business investment.[47] Lewis and Clark fair president H. W. Corbett admitted in a 1903 report that Portland leaders had "extended every means within our power to attract immigration and capital, but our progress has been but slow."[48] Even more discouraging was that other regions of the nation continued to surge ahead of Portland. Salvation, Portland officials maintained, would be found in the largely untouched Pacific Ocean trade. Local leaders claimed that the Orient was "the next great development made by this Nation . . . and the Pacific Northwest will be the gateway."[49] The Portland fair, then, would reward the city with settlers, capital, and national prominence.

Four years later, Seattle officials waxed positively about the potential impact of their exposition and how it would clearly demonstrate that the future was now. Seattle newspaperman Joseph Blethen suggested that investors would learn quite quickly that they could make greater profit by investing in western firms. "The West," he claimed, "taught them to take conditions as they find them and make them pay.

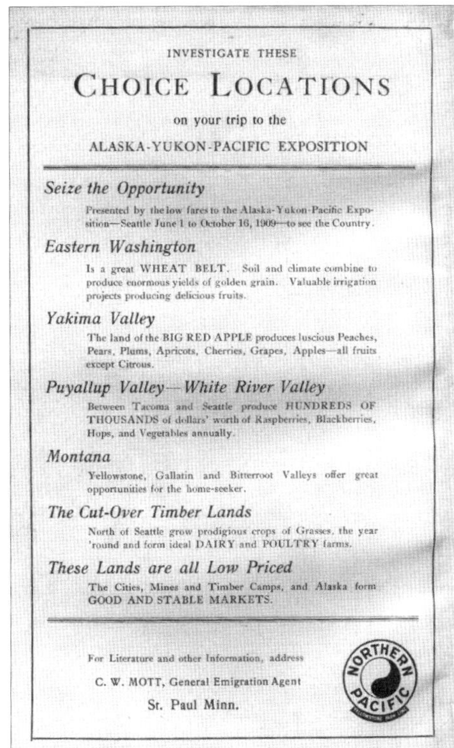

Advertisement to travelers to the Alaska-Yukon-Pacific Exposition regarding available land and economic opportunities in the Far West. *Seattle Public Library Special Collections, spl_ayp_2524191.*

They make money more easily than they save it."[50] After a decade of rapid growth following the Alaska and Yukon gold strikes, Seattle was primed to become the Pacific Northwest's dominant city. Upon passing through the gates, fairgoers would quickly realize "the magnificent energies which are destined to give this section the wealth, magnitude and power, if not sovereignty and independence, of an empire."[51] Portland's modest growth following the LCE, Seattle officials suggested, would pale in comparison to what the Puget Sound would put on display along the shores of Lake Washington.

The Far West's seeds of success—inexhaustible raw materials, transportation networks, favorable climate, and energetic people—ensured a bright future for settler and capitalist alike. James J. Hill contended that the West was "unique in possessing abundantly all of the four great resources of wealth upon which human life depends." Beyond the West's well-known stores of minerals, Hill argued, it also had forests teeming with fine timber, soils that could produce an array of agricultural products, and fisheries that rivaled those of any area in the world.[52] Confirming this claim, both Seattle and Portland exposition publicity departments filled marketing materials and brochures with evidence of the region's natural abundance. The Lewis and Clark Exposition's directors, for example, advertised its fair as an "exposition of natural resources, agricultural, timber, mining, fishing and horticultural."[53] With the opening of the AYPE, Idaho governor James H. Brady concluded that the commercial and economic growth that the Panama Canal—by now nearly completed—promised meant that Seattle residents "shall have as great a city on Puget Sound as New York."[54]

Data

Brash assertions, however, did not go unsubstantiated. Exploitation departments and local chambers of commerce marshaled substantial evidence to support their claims. Moving beyond generalities and empty embellishments, Portland leaders, for example, published brochures and pamphlets that provided detailed production figures illustrating impressive economic activity in Oregon and the Pacific Northwest. One report stated that Oregon cut nearly 900 million feet of lumber in a single year, including a single Portland company that shipped nearly 35 million feet alone.[55] Another lengthy exposition pamphlet cited census data for Portland that listed the value of each major line of manufacturing from lumber and textiles to ship building.[56] In his opening-day speech at the AYPE, James J. Hill stated that the Pacific Coast states produced 17 percent of the nation's lumber output, and that Washington state alone manufactured 60 percent of the nation's shingles.[57] Just months before the city welcomed its first visitors, a Seattle newspaper published a special feature on thirteen consecutive Sundays demonstrating "the city's claim to commercial supremacy on the Pacific Coast."[58] Whether fairgoers toured Portland or Seattle, few could escape guidebooks, newspaper articles, or promotional material advertising the region's promise.

International Commerce

Lumber, mining, and manufacturing aside, Pacific Coast exposition cities never failed to tout their growing role in national and international commerce. All four of them possessed well-developed harbors that had witnessed flourishing trade since the economic downturn of the 1890s. The completion of several transcontinental railroad lines to the Pacific by the dawn of the twentieth century further connected the Pacific Coast states to the nation's flourishing industrial economy. While demand for its valuable natural resources helped fuel the region's early growth, western leaders maintained that the Far West's future would be based on more than an extractive economy. Locations on the Pacific Ocean primed these port cities to capture the lion's share of the growing Asian trade, which one publication claimed totaled six hundred million people.[59] The Lewis and Clark Exposition, for example, helped Portland illustrate the potential of Far East trade ties. "We would advertise our commercial importance to the world," wrote Portland Chamber of Commerce chairman J. M. Long, "and our importance as an Oriental trade port, thereby direct capital from all parts of the Union to our city."[60] Acknowledging the significance of the Orient, a prominent University of Oregon historian expected "peculiar advantages to come to this region in the immediate future from the movements now in operation on the opposite shores of the Pacific."[61] Ample port facilities, railroad lines, and a favorable location on the Pacific could help Portland and Seattle secure the elusive Asian trade, enriching both the Pacific Northwest and the nation.

Businessmen and fair directors backed up such audacious claims with concrete evidence of the Far West's commercial activity. One AYPE promotional guidebook, for example, stated that Puget Sound ports did nearly $69 million in business in 1907.[62] Comparing this trade with other areas of the nation, James J. Hill claimed that in the previous seventeen years, Puget Sound foreign commerce increased 2,184 percent, compared to average of 47 percent for Atlantic Ocean ports and 102 percent for other Pacific Coast ports.[63] Citing its growing trade with the Orient, a Lewis and Clark Exposition publication asserted that foreign commerce shipped through Portland had risen from a little over $10 million in 1899 to $13.5 million in 1903, including more than $3.5 million to Asia.[64] Flourishing trade with Asia combined with the Panama Canal's expected windfall helped fuel business leaders' optimism. If the coastal cities worked together, the *Seattle Post-Intelligencer* declared, there would be plenty of business for all cities to enjoy. If this collective effort succeeded, the paper concluded, "the Pacific coast will become the richest and most powerful trading and business center in the civilized world."[65]

Inland Opportunities

The Far West's economic success, however, hinged on more than the hope that its ports would serve as conduits to Asian markets. Local leaders understood that international trade alone could not sustain the region's growth. Each exposition city possessed a sizable hinterland that, if settled and developed, could ensure the Far West's future. Fair marketing strategies reflected the unlimited possibilities the surrounding territory offered by advertising the West's natural resources and open land to potential settlers.[66] To aid those unfamiliar with the region, the *Los Angeles Times* reported that the land area of Washington, Oregon, and Idaho equaled that of twelve New England states. More importantly, the paper claimed that the Pacific Northwest's ability to "support a large agricultural population is easily demonstrated; but it is just as easily demonstrated that it will also be a section of large cities, created by mining, the manufacturing, and the transportation opportunities."[67] Further illuminating what Oregon had to offer, a promotional book claimed that the state possessed more than twenty-three million acres of land for settlement and even described the process of claiming and purchasing land.[68]

Seattle leaders likewise emphasized the region's abundant resources, including "raw materials of many kinds in almost unlimited quantities, including abundant supplies of fisheries, timber, mineral deposits, and fertile soils."[69] Not to be out done by Portland boosters, a Seattle local paper declared that future settlement of the Far West would eventually produce tens of millions of bushels of wheat, making Seattle the "largest flouring-milling center of the world."[70] Backing up claims that Washington and Oregon possessed sufficient natural resources for millions of settlers, both the LCE and AYPE publicity departments produced reams of pamphlets and brochures outlining the particular opportunities of every individual county, listing official production statistics for the most popular crops, pictures of farms and orchards, and rich descriptions of the fertile land available in each.[71]

Abundant land represented only part of the equation that guaranteed the Far West's success. The two fairs' marketing strategy reminded target audiences that ample terrain signified more space for the next wave of pioneers. Fertile lands and unlimited economic opportunities, Pacific coast leaders suggested, meant that the West could easily absorb millions of new settlers. Somewhat incredulously, a Seattle newspaper, for example, argued that the Rocky Mountain states, the Pacific Coast, and northwestern Canada were "capable of maintaining in comfort a population of more than 300,000,000."[72] To put this in some context, an AYPE promotional booklet explained that Washington, Oregon, Idaho, and parts of Wyoming and Montana were comparable in size to the nation's original thirteen states, which at that moment was home to thirty million people. Simply put, it concluded, "Acre for acre, Washington is capable of supporting as great a population as any state on the Atlantic Coast."[73] Boasting about the fecundity of Oregon's Willamette Valley, Portland leaders likewise claimed that this small sliver of the state alone could support a million people.[74] Mayor George H. Williams added that Portland was best situated to benefit from "a World's Fair because it had room to grow."[75] Such growth, Pacific Northwest leaders maintained, would not only exploit the region's agricultural opportunities, but also push Seattle's population over one million within twenty-five years.[76]

Agricultural Potential

The West's promising future, exposition directors believed, ultimately hinged on its seemingly unlimited agricultural potential. While mining and manufacturing no doubt contributed to the region's economic success, western leaders all agreed that the foundation of future growth and development greatly depended on millions of farmers tilling the soil. That the Pacific Northwest possessed the capability "to support a large agricultural population," one local promoter confidently wrote in 1905, "is easily demonstrated."[77] The Portland Chamber of Commerce put it more bluntly: "Since all wealth comes from the soil, the man who would profitably employ his time must direct his attention to wooing in one way or another the riches of mother earth."[78] AYPE officials encouraged future settlers to develop the region's natural resources and use any farming methods, dry or wet, to exploit the soil. One fair guidebook advertised that "the greatest of all resources of this matchless country are its agricultural interests."[79] Perhaps acknowledging the East's industrial dominance but also the apparent rural crisis outlined by prominent pundits and the recent populist uprising, Pacific Northwest leaders wagered that abundant farmland would best guarantee the region's future.

Putting their trust in the Far West's undeveloped territory, exposition directors concluded that advertising the region's agricultural potential should be a primary focus of their respective fair's promotional campaigns. Persuading potential settlers to consider the Pacific Northwest, however, depended on more than just bold assertions. Brochures, newspaper articles, and public speeches by prominent local officials and businessmen often cited studies and official statistics to support their claims. Detailing the land available out West, Portland's Henry Reed claimed that "[w]hile the West has not quite half the improved acreage of the country, it has 63 percent of unimproved acreage, or 269,000,000 acres out of 426,400,000."[80] Speaking to San Francisco exposition officials several years later, a Portland merchant declared that Oregon alone possessed seventeen million acres of arable land open to cultivation.[81] At times, western leaders even enlisted the support of federal officials and experts to promote what the region had to offer. In a speech before the United States Senate supporting Seattle's exposition, Senator Samuel H. Piles of Washington proclaimed that the Alaska Territory possessed nearly a hundred million acres of agricultural land available for planting.[82] Brochures, thick with detail and exacting figures, could hopefully persuade potential settlers that opportunity awaited them in the Far West.

Vast swaths of open territory might be attractive, but a successful marketing campaign rested on helping customers more precisely visualize farm life in the Far West. Exposition officials understood that more concrete evidence of the region's promise would be more persuasive. The *Lewis and Clark Review*, for example, advertised the apples, strawberries, and a variety of other fruits marketed by Oregon's Hood River farmers, right down to the number of pounds, prices, and profit each farm realized.[83] Precise numbers and statistics added weight to boosters' claims. Describing the Pacific Northwest's abundant opportunities, Walter H. Page, for example, related a story about a preacher from Yakima County in Washington who bought a small tract of land and planted an orchard on it. The preacher nixed plans to sell the land after his first crop brought in $12,500. Page said that owner removed the property from the market and now lived comfortably on the nearly $20,000 a year his farm produced.[84] Similarly, an Oregon newspaper printed a chart entitled "How to Make Money on a Willamette Valley Farm," which broke down the typical investment, expenses, annual crop yields, and livestock values a farmer could expect.[85] Depictions of farmers who did well in the Far West helped demonstrate the region's potential in concrete ways that rural folk in the Midwest and further East could easily identify.

Besides individual production figures, publicity departments published aggregate agricultural values that they hoped would impress potential settlers. Portland leaders, for example, noted the sizable shipments of wheat produced by Oregon and Washington farmers that went through their port.[86] The *Lewis and Clark Journal*, the official bulletin of the Portland exposition, detailed the tremendous growth in Oregon's agricultural market by major product between 1850 and 1900. Besides the nearly 42 million bushels of wheat the state produced, it noted that Oregon farmers harvested more than 15 million bushels of oats and 21 million pounds of hops.[87] Seattle officials likewise touted the fecundity of the Washington's agricultural sector. Products from farms, orchards, and dairies in Washington state, one guidebook stated, topped $100 million. Even in the drier climes east of the Cascade Mountains, the promotional piece stated that "Eastern Washington alone produced more than 40,000,000 bushels of wheat in 1907. Oregon and Idaho together produced 20,000,000 more."[88] Citing more than sheer production levels, one ad for the Yakima Land Company claimed that apples from Washington orchards netted "the highest prices obtainable in the world's markets."[89]

THE NUMEROUS BROCHURES AND NEWSPAPER ARTICLES detailing the Pacific Northwest's rich lands and expected profits only echoed westerners' belief in their region's seemingly untapped potential. Boosters, as they so often did, likely exaggerated or embellished the actual economic opportunities that awaited new settlers, though a worker back east or a struggling farmer in Indiana would be hard pressed to challenge the accuracy of boosters' assertions, especially if coming from government officials. Such bold claims, in some ways, revealed both their optimism and an underlying anxiety. During a time when Americans struggled to cope with the social, cultural, and economic consequences of industrial capitalism, the West, as it had since the heady days of the mid-nineteenth century, promised a better future where economic opportunity was still in the grasp of ordinary people. Yet mind-numbing statistics could perhaps also have masked a certain nervousness among western residents. As this chapter has explained, exposition directors confronted powerful conceptions of the West that the Sagebrush Pete character in the *New York Times* article attempted to dispel. These well-rooted frontier images of the West proved difficult to overcome, especially when Pacific Coast expositions contributed to them through their exhibits and amusement zones. Selling the Far West required fair officials to craft messages and marketing campaigns that not only challenged old stereotypes, but also advertised the numerous benefits of western living. Marshaling data helped lure new settlers and capital and may have helped convince westerners that their choice to reside in the Pacific Northwest was not a mistake. Whatever the motivation, exposition officials wished to share with the American public their belief that the region offered opportunity and hope and that the nation's future was inextricably bound to the Far West's future.

4 ⸎ SELLING NATURE AND LAND(SCAPES) IN THE PACIFIC NORTHWEST

In a special message to Congress presenting the 1909 report of the Country Life Commission, President Theodore Roosevelt wrote that "one of the chief difficulties is the failure of country life, as it exists at present, to satisfy the higher social and intellectual aspirations of country people." He went on to note growing concern with the migration of rural folk to cities and the need for the nation to address this pressing problem, and explained that he had established this commission to explore the causes of the farmers' troubles and determine possible solutions. He warned that this was not just a rural issue, but one that affected the entire country.[1] While securing a sound farm economy was an important step to improve farm life, Roosevelt suggested to the commission's chair that the nation had to find a way to "make country life more gainful, more attractive, and fuller of opportunities, pleasures, and rewards for the men, women, and children of the farms."[2] The antidote to the dangers of which Roosevelt warned, western leaders argued, was western living. By the early twentieth century, the Far West offered a new kind of farming that many believed would attract Americans to the land. Exposition officials promised that irrigation and intensive farming would refashion rural society and permit farmers a lifestyle that blended the best of both the country and city. By highlighting the region's healthy climates, modern urban centers, and majestic western landscapes, exposition publicity departments attempted to sell the Far West as the cradle of redemption and spiritual renewal for a troubled nation.

The formation of the Country Life Commission reflected a larger anxiety in American society at the turn of the twentieth century.[3] Several decades of explosive industrial and urban growth produced serious social, political, and economic problems. New factories and production techniques transformed the nature of work, unleashing labor wars that frightened the American public. Meanwhile farmers confronted changing market forces that left more and more in debt—or worse, landless. While Social Darwinism and political corruption impeded action from the nation's capital and federal courts blocked state legislative responses, farmers and workers turned to more aggressive actions. National labor organizations like the Knights of Labor and rural efforts like the Patrons of Husbandry and the Farmers' Alliance failed to stem the tide of change. Faced with a destructive depression in the mid-1890s, the People's Party, comprised mostly of farmers and a smattering of laborers, nearly toppled the two-party system that dated back to the nation's founding. Undermined by a misguided fusion effort with the Democratic Party in 1896, the People's Party collapsed as the nation entered the twentieth century.

Only a couple years after the tragic assassination of President William McKinley thrust him into the presidency, Theodore Roosevelt emerged as the national leader of what is more commonly known as the progressive movement. Roosevelt demonstrated his leadership and belief in the use of government power by targeting powerful corporate trusts and proposing legislation to regulate big business. Increasingly disturbed by the growing dissatisfaction with rural life, evidenced by farmland-to-city migration patterns, Roosevelt established the Country Life Commission. A quintessential progressive undertaking, the commission would study the problem and suggest reforms that likely would involve government aid or intervention. Scott J. Peters and Paul A. Morgan have argued that the reformers' goals were "either making rural society along urban, industrial lines to meet urban, industrial, and national goals (i.e. an abundance of cheap food), against both the wills and interests of rural people or stopping rural out-migration in order to maintain a romantic dream that was no longer plausible or desirable."[4] In the end, the formation of the Country Life Commission likely reflected a little of both positions. Despite the president's pleas for action, Congress did little more than yawn when presented with the report, even failing to provide funds to print and distribute the commission's findings.[5]

The Country Life Commission failed to spark a national campaign to address the apparent plight of American farmers, but it was not the only effort to lean on rural America to solve the crises that seemingly plagued the nation. While stemming the tide of rural out-migration was a primary goal of Roosevelt's endeavor, an early-twentieth-century back-to-the-land movement aimed to reverse the trend by urging city folk to carve out a new life in America's countryside. Both the commission and the agrarian movement reflected certain anxieties about the nation's trajectory. Economic times may have been better, yet Americans had not forgotten the violent labor conflicts at Andrew Carnegie's Homestead Mill or the political turmoil of populism that marked the 1890s. The crises may have ended, but the associated problems and causes had not. Back-to-the-land proponents, historian Richard White has argued, "proceeded from the assumption that the cities were overpopulated while the rural districts were correspondingly underpopulated. From this fundamental imbalance (in their eyes a development out of step with American history and alien to American institutions) flowed the myriad social problems—unemployment, poverty, disease, moral decline—that they believed would, if unchecked, eventually destroy the nation."[6] Restoring the balance, then, would also restore America.

Marketing Strategies to Encourage Migration

Recognizing the anxiety about the nation's, and for that matter the Far West's, increasingly urban character, exposition publicity departments incorporated the back-to-the-land idea into marketing strategies to encourage more migration to, and settlement in, the Far West. Disturbed by a western rural landscape dominated by large-scale agricultural operations and correspondingly too few small family farms, as well as the rapid growth of cities like Seattle and Los Angeles, state and local leaders believed that encouraging new arrivals to settle the land would enhance both the region's economy and living conditions.[7] Great Northern Railway owner James J. Hill, for example, claimed that the failure to expand the nation's farm population could imperil rapidly growing urban centers. Acknowledging this concern, Seattle businessmen argued that there was ample land for new farmers in not only the less populated eastern part of the state, but also in areas touching Puget Sound. One real estate company executive, for example, explained that there was a market for small farmers that did not exist back East. As he saw it, urging people back to the land was vital because the "city's future depends on the growth of the district which surrounds us and on the welfare of the man who has courage to clear the land and wrest a living from the soil."[8] Intensifying Seattle leaders' unease was the extensive timber activity that had denuded a good deal of city's hinterland. Cries for action appeared to work, for by the time war broke out in Europe, thousands of new farms had begun to appear on these logged-out lands.[9]

By the time Seattle exposition officials closed the AYPE's gates, the back-to-the-land movement had picked up steam in the West. The Salvation Army, for example, had earlier organized a few colonies in Colorado and California, where it placed "poor but worthy families stranded in the cities, as home-owners on the prairies of the West." Rallying support for his plans, the organization's chief officer, Commander Booth Tucker, spoke to a group of Seattle residents in 1904 about a bill before Congress that proposed to fund similar colonies. Booth told the audience that even President Roosevelt stated it was necessary to check growing rural out-migration and "place the landless man on the manless land" in order to defend the nation from the social and political dangers of this trend.[10] A few years later, as the city finished final preparations for the Alaska-Yukon-Pacific Exposition, the *Seattle Times* commented on the steady stream of city dwellers relocating to the open farmlands of the Southwest.[11] The fair's success, however, encouraged local businessmen to promote settlement of the nearby hinterland. In 1910 a Seattle real estate salesman, for example, advertised lands in the nearby community of Riverside that promised to free "prisoners" from the lack of opportunity the current economy offered them. Elsewhere along the Sound, the salesman peddled acreage favorably suited for chicken ranches.[12]

Whether raising chickens or cultivating crops, Seattle leaders founded the future hopes of their city on exploiting something that the region had to offer: ample land. Productive hinterlands plus dynamic ports would ensure a bright future for the Pacific Northwest. While easterners likely understood that the western frontier was a sizable territory, Portland and Seattle fair officials had to persuade them that a good deal of this terrain was unoccupied, fertile land just waiting for eager farmers. On the eve of the opening of the Lewis and Clark Exposition, a 1905 *Sunset Magazine* article, for example, described the "huge, vacant west that lies beyond the Rockies." This "undeveloped country," especially the region beyond the Rockies running between the Mexican border and the Puget Sound, which, the magazine contended, had inspired Horace Greeley's call to "go west," was more attractive than ever, because enough people had settled there by the early 1900s to guarantee success.[13] Boosters believed that with its plentiful unoccupied territory, the Pacific Northwest had the recipe for success.

Irrigation Is King

Empty, unused lands, however, could also evoke images of a desolate frontier. The same novels and Wild West shows that encouraged easterners to imagine a dangerous, uncivilized West could also foster visions of bleak and barren landscapes. Descriptions of uninhabited acreage in exposition advertising material only confirmed what much of the American public had believed since acquiring this territory in the mid-nineteenth century. Painfully aware of the region's "frontier" image, westerners turned this once negative quality on its head and now embraced the West's untouched landscape as what made their region special. While a few decades earlier many westerners would have lamented the region's punishing aridity, irrigation now promised to turn the desert into a garden. The wonders of water engineering now meant that these empty acres would not only provide opportunities for new settlers and perhaps relieve national anxieties, but also help the West purge any vestiges of its frontier legacy and fashion a new regional identity.

Simply claiming that the Far West possessed extensive open lands was not sufficient to change long-held perceptions of the region dominated by pictures of bone-dry deserts. Decades earlier, some boosters attempted to dispel similar views by touting the West as a natural paradise. Drought and extreme temperatures, however, plagued the Great Plains and other parts of the West during the 1890s, which gave "the lie to the promotional insistence of Edenic climates in the new western lands."[14] In light of this reality, westerners turned more aggressively to irrigation as a way to overcome the region's aridity, as John Wesley Powell had advocated in his 1878 *Report on the Lands of the Arid Regions of the United States*. By the 1890s, Californian George H. Maxwell convinced the National Irrigation Congress to support a proposal urging the federal government to fund western irrigation efforts. In 1902, with help of Nevada congressman Francis Newlands, Congress passed the National Reclamation Act, which provided federal funding for large-scale irrigation projects that would open up semiarid lands for new farms.[15]

Maxwell and Newland's efforts aside, it would be William Ellsworth Smythe who would become the heart and soul of the irrigation and back-to-the-land movement in the Far West. After witnessing the devastating impact of drought in Nebraska in the early 1890s, Smythe became a disciple of the potential of irrigation. He joined and later assumed the presidency of the National Irrigation Congress and in 1899 published the widely acclaimed book *The Conquest of Arid America*. Alluding to the national pressure to expand the United States's imperial rule in the Philippines, Smythe urged the conquest of another territory in the introduction to his book, writing, "There is room for one hundred million people in the States and Territories between the Missouri river and the Pacific Ocean."[16] Smythe believed that more aggressive development of "Undeveloped America" would produce significant economic benefits, in addition to saving the republic from the dangers of imperialism. He promised that in the pages that followed, readers "shall then observe what vast resources yet remain to be used, and how the physical conditions of the vacant half-continent in the West mark its future civilization as inevitably different, in important respects, from that of the East."[17] Irrigation, he concluded, would be the primary weapon of this conquest.

By the time the gates of the Lewis and Clark Exposition swung open in 1905, westerners from the rainy climes of the Pacific Northwest to the dry deserts of Southern California believed that irrigation guaranteed a bright future for the Far West. As they crafted their marketing campaigns, Portland and Seattle's fair publicity departments linked irrigation to the agrarian crusade. The *Seattle Sunday Times*, for example, celebrated how the reclamation of thousands of arid acres had encouraged some to coin a new term: "Irrigation is king."[18] The keynote of irrigation, the *Lewis and Clark Journal* announced, is "[i]ndependence of rain or drought."[19] Perhaps needing to dispel misconceptions of the Pacific Northwest, one LCE publicity piece noted that while rainfall fell generously along the coastal regions, that state's eastern half was more arid and benefitted greatly from government irrigation projects.[20] Irrigation was so central to Oregon's future that an Oregon Land & Water Company advertisement promoted a new community called "Irrigon"; a name created by combining the word irrigation with the state's name.[21]

Regional and national publications bolstered Pacific Northwest officials' claims about the impact of water engineering. Just weeks after the gates closed at the LCE, *Sunset Magazine* published a lengthy piece describing the numerous irrigation projects that were transforming the western landscape. Smaller schemes, like one in Honda, New Mexico, reclaimed 10,000 acres, while larger undertakings along the Nevada-California border near the Truckee River promised to open up more than 400,000 acres.[22] According to the *World's Work*, at the present pace of reclamation, the region between the Cascade and Rocky mountain ranges would hold a population that would "soon rival their sister states of the East."[23] In just a few short years, irrigation projects large and small seemed well on the way to conquering the painfully arid West.

Fairgoers traveling through the arid American West to the Alaska-Yukon-Pacific Exposition in 1909 could see the impact of these irrigation projects from the comfort of their trains. Government reclamation efforts significantly expanded both in terms of funding and the range of territory covered. Following the passage of the Newlands Reclamation Act, the Roosevelt administration quickly approved four projects in 1903, and by the end of the decade broke ground on twenty-four additional ventures.[24] Even before easterners reached the

Pacific Ocean, they could see actual examples of how water engineering was transforming the West. The Northern Pacific Railway Company, for example, informed travelers to the AYPE that they could see "striking evidences of the beneficence of irrigation" from train windows as they passed through Yellowstone National Park.[25] In 1909 the *Seattle Sunday Times* crowed about the number of irrigated acres in Washington state. The paper advertised that the U.S. government spent nearly $4 million in the state, which it expected would open up 200,000 productive acres.[26] Illustrating the importance of irrigation to the Pacific Northwest, the AYPE hosted a meeting of irrigation experts where Seattle city engineer Reginald H. Thompson described the watering of arid lands in the southeastern section of the state along the Columbia River. The fair, he argued, would expose visitors to wonderful possibilities of irrigation and the great opportunities it would deliver to new settlers.[27]

During the first two decades of the twentieth century, western officials advertised the wonders of irrigation in newspapers, magazines, and any other forums they could exploit. Although some cautioned promoters to not undermine these efforts by exaggerating the impact of reclamation efforts, government reports and public pronouncements from President Roosevelt and other notable officials encouraged boosters' enthusiasm.[28] When possible, local leaders offered more than just words. In an article entitled "What the Northwest Is," Seattle newspaper editor Joseph Blethen not only described several irrigation projects that farmers had recently settled, but also provided before-and-after pictures illustrating the remarkable transformation of one plot in the Washington state's Yakima Valley.[29] Likewise, a Portland newspaper illustrated how "irrigation transforms the desert" with a photograph of a child standing in sagebrush alongside another image of a corn towering over a farmer.[30] Heeding the adage that a picture is worth a thousand words, fair officials rarely failed to provide visual support for the astonishing marvels of irrigation.

Illustrating the impact of western reclamation projects did not end with printed promotional materials and advertisements. For those lucky enough to visit one of the Pacific Northwest expositions, fair officials provided more concrete demonstrations of the benefits of irrigation. Exposition directors encouraged irrigation advocates to hold meetings and conventions at their respective fairs. Portland, for example, welcomed the National Irrigation Congress to the 1905 Lewis and Clark fair.[31] Discussing his plans before an irrigation convention held in nearby Spokane, Reginald H. Thompson noted that the "coming of the National Irrigation Congress to Washington while the Alaska-Yukon-Pacific Exposition is in progress will result in attention being focused on the irrigation possibilities of this state."[32] Such conventions featured speakers and scholarly papers on irrigation's benefits and often highlighted reclamation efforts in the surrounding region.

Promoting the benefits of irrigation included not just prominent speakers and organizations, but also firsthand demonstrations. Fair publicity bureaus promised visitors to the Far West that they could observe visual displays, models, and miniature exhibits of reclamation projects while touring the four expositions. For example, Lewis and Clark Exposition directors constructed an Irrigation Building where they displayed a miniature model of the Truckee-Carson project, replete with dams, canals, and "topography of a large area of country to be irrigated." Elsewhere in the building, fairgoers could view charts, pictures, and models of other prominent irrigation activities, such as the Salt River and Yuma projects in Arizona.[33] Four years later, the AYPE provided its own education exhibit with pictures and a bioscope to show interested farmers "how to prepare the land, how to run irrigation canals, how to plant" fruit trees.[34] Models and actual demonstrations depicting irrigation in action, fair officials believed, could change perceptions of the region's landscape, allowing both westerners and their visitors to reimagine a new West.

The new West that exposition directors and local leaders envisioned reflected the combination of ample available land and irrigation. Rather than huge, isolated farms that dotted the Midwest, new settlers to Washington or Oregon could live comfortably on as little as ten to twenty acres. In 1904 the *Morning Oregonian*, for example, described settlers who migrated to the Pacific Northwest, where "a farmer can make as much money in a year on a ten-acre tract of irrigated land as on a 320-acre tract of wheat land."[35] In a special LCE issue of the *World's Work*, journalist Walter H. Page wrote about the large number of lucrative fruit, vegetable, and alfalfa farms in Yakima, Washington, that ranged from five to twenty acres.[36] By the time Washington state hosted its own fair, evidence of successful small farms could be found throughout the Pacific Northwest. The *Seattle Sunday Times*, for instance, explained that owners of irrigated land had subdivided their lands into smaller plots of five to ten acres because "it has been demonstrated in the past few years that five acres of bearing orchard is about all that one farmer can successfully and comfortably maintain."[37] No longer was the West the barren, formidable landscape that had greeted migrants just a generation before. Along with the hard evidence, fair publicity departments packaged this new optimism in their quest to sell the Far West. Irrigation now promised to change for the better both land and lives.

Small Farm Lifestyle

Oregon and Washington leaders, however, offered more than broad platitudes when promoting the small farm lifestyle. Boosters explained that the irrigated farming was not just economically viable, but it also eliminated the "drudgery" of American farm life.[38] The *Morning Oregonian*, for example, claimed that greater density of irrigated communities helped rural folk "escape the dreary isolation of farm life under other conditions and enjoy the pleasures of neighborliness which a town affords while living in the country."[39] A Seattle paper likewise advertised the proximity of neighbors, "making possible that social relation which relieves a farmer of the forbidding loneliness of less thickly settled and less fortunate communities."[40] This new lifestyle made possible by small farms meant not just less isolation but implied some more ephemeral happiness. One Seattle paper, for example, described settlers on irrigated lands in eastern Washington as comfortable and "content" with their lives.[41]

In the early twentieth century, westerners trusted that irrigation would compel Americans to return to the land. Despite decades of railroad building and calls to settle its wide-open expanses, the West remained the most urbanized region in the United States.[42] In many ways, Seattle, Portland, San Diego, and San Francisco were urban oases surrounded by sparsely settled hinterlands. Water engineering, however, promised new economic opportunities for farmers and more trade for nearby cities. Exposition publicity departments drew on a wide array of selling techniques, ranging from traditional advertisements to product demonstrations to help change popular misconceptions of the Far West. Irrigation, they promised, would bring smaller farms, greater population density, restore community values, and a new, more satisfying rural lifestyle unknown to those living east of the Rocky Mountains. Exploiting national anxieties resulting from industrialization and urbanization, fair promoters encouraged the American public to reimagine the Far West. Visitors to the Pacific Coast expositions learned that irrigation not only promised a new lifestyle, but also that it would forever transform the landscape of the American West.

As they formulated plans for their respective expositions, fair directors and local leaders in Portland and Seattle were challenged by more than just the region's need for capital and new settlers. The West's climate and landscape also stood as significant obstacles to the promise of a New West. As boosters touted the benefits of irrigation to new settlers, they also recognized how it profoundly transformed the landscape. Exposition officials advertised how reclamation projects not only offered a new rural lifestyle, but also how they changed parched desert lands into gardens. While many Americans might have thought of the Pacific Northwest as a place of tall trees and ample rainfall, upon closer examination they would have learned that swaths of the region east of the Cascade Mountains appeared more like the desert southwest. Irrigation, however, promised to change that. Walter H. Page, for example, stated that the "Yakima Valley is fast coming to be one vast garden."[43] Even visitors who strolled Portland's fairgrounds could take in the lush surrounding landscape, which historian Lisa Blee has argued, "celebrated imperial grandeur and demonstrated that the West was not a great desert but a civilized garden."[44] A few years later, Seattle officials described for those who journeyed to the AYPE that eastern Washington had witnessed "the passing of the desert and the coming of handsome city homes and luxurious verdure of every kind to replace the sage brush and sand."[45] Reclamation, fair leaders proclaimed, promised to rejuvenate both lives and the landscape.

Postcard advertisement for the AYPE showing Seattle street scene juxtaposed with image of snow-capped mountain. *University of Washington Libraries, Special Collections, NEG UW 22327.*

Natural Beauty

While irrigation promised to change deserts into gardens, the Pacific Northwest expositions boasted that the region also possessed natural landscapes that no man-made endeavors could ever replicate. When introducing these scenic surroundings to newcomers, publicity directors and civic leaders proclaimed that the region's natural beauty enhanced both health and spirit. Portland officials, for example, cited the writings of the exposition's namesakes, Meriwether Lewis and William Clark, who described majestic mountain peaks and the impressive Columbia River. One fair publication advertised that visitors would "find a wealth of scenic beauty in and about Portland."[46] In a similar vein, the *Seattle Sunday Times* described what visitors to the Alaska-Yukon-Pacific Exposition could expect when visiting the Puget Sound city: from Seattle's Lake Washington to nearby Mount Rainier, rising 14,526 feet above sea level, there were "a hundred avenues of pleasure and scenic grandeur."[47] Exposition officials crowed that the celebrated western mountain ranges were not only were visibly enchanting, but also provided ample opportunity for the "health and pleasure seeker."[48] In short, fair publicity departments labored to ensure that tourists and settlers alike would discover out West a different and more eye-pleasing America.

By the early twentieth century, the changing attitudes toward leisure, in combination with the extension of railroads and the arrival of the automobile, helped many Americans reconsider where they should vacation. At the same time, early tourists and travel writers increasingly exposed the wonders of the West to the rest of the country, and American nationalism and pride increasingly challenged the belief that leisure was better spent in Europe. In 1905 a Salt Lake City businessman coined the phrase "See Europe If You Will, But See America First." Four years later, a Seattle newspaper stated the "See America First" idea was "awakening public interest in the scenic beauties of the great Pacific Coast."[49] This movement challenged American elites to forego the usual trip to Europe and instead discover what their own country had to offer. The transcontinental railroad lines, of course, quickly embraced this sentiment, with the Great Northern Railway adopting "See America First" as its company motto.[50]

Despite trying to distinguish and elevate the Far West's natural beauty over popular European landscapes, exposition officials and most promotional material nevertheless fell back on comparisons to Europe at times to encourage visitors to attend their fairs. Advertisers knew all too well that familiar associations proved successful in persuading potential customers. The LCE's Henry Reed, for example, suggested that the Columbia River's natural scenery "rivals the Rhine."[51] Urging Americans to visit the AYPE, the *Seattle Sunday Times* explained that tourists who sought "rest and recreation amidst the Alps of Switzerland" would discover that with nearby Mount Rainier and Mount Baker, there were "two natural attractions to one to be found anywhere on the continent of Europe."[52] Even those who might travel to the Alaska frontier would discover "scenery that surpasses the Alps."[53] Whether referencing the Alps or the Rhine River, local leaders understood that such efforts could pay off handsomely if tourists chose to accept the advice of the "See America First" campaign.

What made these superior scenic landscapes unequaled was not just that the American version of the Alps or Rhine were located on the same continent, but how easily accessible they were from the major West Coast cities. Exposition officials advertised that natural wonders like mountains and forests were not located in distant, isolated areas, but visible and within easy reach of Seattle and Portland. Settlers would discover economic and spiritual benefits from lands they farmed in the morning and mountains they climbed in the afternoon. A Seattle newspaper, for example, noted that towering Mount Rainier was located quite near the city and that the Olympic Range, which was "pronounced by globe-trotters more beautiful than the Alps," was just a short steamer ride away. Speaking before a United States House of Representative's exposition committee hearing, John H. McGraw, vice president of the Exposition Company of Seattle, stated that the "Olympic and Cascade ranges of mountains are in plain view from all points of the grounds."[54] Similarly, the *Lewis and Clark Journal* asked: "Is there another city in America that holds within its limits a mountain park in all its ancient, untamed wildness?" Within an easy walk of the fairgrounds, the article explained, a visitor would find the "heart of this Oregon forest."[55] Western living, in short, promised an antidote to the reality of unhealthy and stressful life of most industrial cities.

See Yellowstone

Majestic mountain ranges and deserts may have appealed to many eastern urbanites, yet for others they could also evoke images of untamed wilderness. In the late nineteenth century, tourists were hesitant to visit places like Yellowstone National Park and the Grand Canyon, which seemed too wild and unforgiving. Railroad companies slowly changed such opinions by constructing modern hotels and improving access to the heart of these parks. By the time Portland hosted its exposition, historian Anne Hyde has argued, Americans began to "look at the wilderness as friendly rather than dangerous."[56] As more Americans toured these prominent western landscapes, attitudes about the region also evolved. More importantly, the lure of wonderlands like Yellowstone, Yosemite, and the Grand Canyon helped enhance the attractiveness of less known scenic locales like Mount Hood or California's redwood forests. By encouraging visitors to stop at one or more of these popular parks on the way to the Pacific Coast, exposition directors not only helped foster a more positive image of the western landscape, but also boosted fair attendance.

Recognizing that tourists would have to invest a good deal of money and time to visit the Pacific Northwest expositions, Portland and Seattle leaders exploited the growing interest in the West's natural wonders. Hosting the first fair west of the Rockies, Lewis and Clark Exposition officials urged fairgoers in 1905 to visit Yellowstone Park on their way to Portland. "This marvelous Wonderland in the heart of the Rocky Mountains," a Northern Pacific Railway marketing piece published for the fair declared, "stands unrivaled among globe travelers as the most unusual, strangest, most educative spot on the face of the earth." The booklet went on to describe the park's natural wonders from the famous geysers to the breathtaking landscape.[57] Similarly, an AYPE brochure boldly advertised that "there is no place where Nature has concentrated, on such a lavish and profound scale, the weird and wonderful things to be seen in the Park." The brochure explained that a visit should last up to six days long and that there was no charge for the stopover.[58]

Railway companies' marketing divisions likewise joined with exposition officials to boost the added value of natural treasures like Yellowstone and the Grand Canyon. When advertising excursions to the Pacific Northwest, railroad publicity departments highlighted the wonderful sights and scenic landscapes which riders could experience by visiting Yellowstone en route to the expositions.[59] A Northern Pacific Railway brochure, for example, claimed that with "the stop-over privileges allowed on coast tickets every tourist and traveler to the Northwest and the Exposition during the season of 1905 may be enabled to visit every point of importance and interest in the Pacific Northwest."[60] Photographs of Yellowstone's Old Faithful geyser, maps of the expansive park, and illustrations of the hotels with modern amenities helped fill empty railcar seats as well as aid exposition promotional efforts.[61] Exposition directors and local leaders hoped that fairgoers would find the opportunity to explore western wonderlands too enticing and thus ensure a profitable and productive fair. Moreover, promoting the natural scenery found elsewhere in the Far West helped easterners fathom the range and variety of western landscapes.

Photos

Travelers to the Pacific Coast fairs did not have to wait until they departed to sample the West's natural wonders. Pictures of majestic mountain peaks, glaciers, and expansive forests littered brochures and magazine articles. One AYPE booklet, for example, displayed a picture of the fairgrounds with the snow-covered Olympic mountain range in the background as well as an image of Muir Glacier in Alaska visible from a steamer.[62] Similarly, the *Seattle Sunday Times* prominently brandished a photo of Mount Rainier viewed from the shores of Seattle's Lake Washington.[63] Showcasing the vast wonders of the Far West, the Lewis and Clark fair publicity department authorized publication of a lengthy promotional picture book replete with photographs and illustrations ranging from the Grand Canyon and rock formations in Colorado to Mount Hood outside of Portland.[64] LCE officials also celebrated the Pacific Northwest's forests by featuring an image of the woods from which the logs used to build the exposition's massive Forestry Building were harvested.[65] Whether perusing a magazine or a newspaper in the early twentieth century, exposition publicity departments made certain that those living east of the Mississippi could not escape images of the Far West's scenic beauty.

Copious images of diverse western landscapes both enticed potential tourists to attend the Pacific Coast expositions and helped lure potential settlers who wished to escape crowded, unhealthy urban centers. Just as pictures and well-designed images helped advertisers sell everyday products like soap and canned soup, photographs not only enhanced the fair's marketing efforts, but also provided concrete visual support for written promotional materials. Rather than rejecting the West's natural landscape and sparsely settled lands during a time when rural Americans and immigrants flooded into the nation's major urban centers, westerners embraced them. Even if they toiled in a Seattle factory or in a Portland business office, westerners could find momentary escape on the sandy shores of the Pacific or on the majestic peaks of a Mount Rainier or Mount Hood. Whether these scenic locales were actually in close proximity to, or just visible from, their neighborhoods, Pacific Coast residents nevertheless believed that they contributed to a western lifestyle that was special and superior.

Climate

The Pacific Northwest's salubrious climate only enhanced the profound spiritual and visual impact of western landscapes. Scenic panoramas were pleasant and even uplifting, yet they would not be enough if a punishing climate made daily life too difficult. Exposition officials promoted a western lifestyle that promised potential settlers better work and living conditions. Balmy temperatures, adequate rainfall, and abundant sunshine would not just restore one's vitality, but also enhance daily life. Describing the natural environment to potential visitors to the Lewis and Clark Exposition, Walter H. Page claimed that "[b]esides scenery and climate so mild that no kind of work is interrupted by the weather, you have as many sources of wealth as you have kinds of scenic beauty."[66] In this one short statement, Page summed up the advantages of western living by tying three features together. In addition to beautiful vistas and an agreeable climate making daily life more pleasant, it also promised to enhance work and one's financial future. In the decades following the California gold rush, boosters underscored the West's beneficial climate, playing up "the less humid, more invigorating atmosphere of the West." Settlers, they insisted, would discover mild temperatures and drier air as they took in the beautiful panoramas of the surrounding landscape.[67]

Despite several decades of often exaggerated claims about the West's climate, both Pacific Northwest expositions' promotional campaigns continued to hype the region's superior weather.[68] The *Lewis and Clark Review*, for example, declared that "[f]or scenic grandeur and loveliness, the Northwest is only rivaled by its climate, which is practically equable the whole year 'round."[69] The region suffered from neither extreme cold nor heat, making it "a Paradise under Summer skies, and the Winter one altogether free from the suffering incident to any intensity of cold."[70] Perhaps to drive this point home, one guidebook included a picture of an Oregon home adorned with green foliage but no snow, with the caption "January in Southern Oregon."[71] Alaska-Yukon-Pacific Exposition directors likewise advertised the region's favorable climate. One leader maintained that the Seattle region possessed "the most perfect climate on all the circuit of the globe," while a local newspaper simply stated that they city had a "perfect climate."[72] This perfection, a fair brochure explained, was due to the fact that there were only two seasons—summer and winter—and both were marked by mild temperatures and no snowfall.[73] Even though Washington and Oregon were located along the northern tier of the United States, leaders argued that potential settlers would encounter a pleasant climate throughout the year.

Broad statements of the superior climate in the Far West were advantageous, but exposition publicity departments took additional steps to help potential settlers better understand the region's natural environment. Similar to efforts to promote the region's economy, fair officials borrowed the technique of product comparison, likening the Far West's climatic conditions to various regions throughout the world. Recognizing that some fairgoers often toured Europe during the spring and summer months, exposition publicity department used familiar European locales as reference points to help visitors appreciate the region's climate: Describing the Pacific Northwest's temperatures, Henry Reed, LCE director of exploitation, explained that Oregon's mean temperatures were "slightly higher than that of London or Berlin, but closely agrees with that of Paris and Vienna."[74] References to specific American states and cities also helped visitors better interpret the region's climate. One national magazine, for example, compared Portland's climate to several American cities that shared the same latitude.[75] The *Lewis and Clark Review* similarly advertised that from "Maine to Texas people died by scores, if not by hundreds, of sunstrokes and calorical prostrations. Even in the vaunted 'summer climate' of Minnesota and Dakota, the thermometers boiled over with from 98 to 112 degrees of hideous hotness in the shade."[76] Reminding readers why mild temperatures mattered, exposition leaders believed, went hand-in-hand with concrete evidence of daily mean temperatures and humidity levels.

In an age when Americans marveled at new scientific and technological wonders, exposition directors often turned to statistics and scientific data to support boosters' claims. Like the reams of paper citing economic facts and production figures, fair exploitation bureaus produced charts and graphs demonstrating the West's superior climate. An AYPE brochure, for example, cited an annual mean temperature of 51.4 degrees for Seattle, including the warmest and coldest months, as well as identifying the annual rainfall average of 37.65 inches.[77] Portland officials, too, provided charts comparing the city's maximum and minimum temperatures to leading cities, like St. Louis and Cincinnati, as well as one chart comparing the daily temperatures for July 1904 for Portland and New York City.[78] Confronting the Pacific Northwest's reputation for rain, Oregon's health secretary claimed that most of the rain fell during the winter months. Oregon's yearly precipitation totals, he argued, approximated most northeastern states.[79] Detailed statistics, local officials believed, offered compelling evidence that the Pacific Northwest's climate was unrivaled.

The Pacific Coast expositions presented a perfect opportunity to demonstrate firsthand how the region's climate contributed to a more pleasant natural environment. Fair directors left no stone unturned when it came to landscaping their respective fairgrounds. Portland officials explained that every "temperate-zone grain, grass, fruit, and vegetable grows luxuriantly, and many semi-tropical fruits flourish."[80] One LCE picture book, for example, boasted that while other expositions utilized "landscape artists and designers" to beautify their grounds, in Portland "nature has bestowed attractions unapproachable by the hand of man."[81] Visitors to the fair would not only find roses in full bloom dotting the grounds, but as one writer noted, mild winters permitted roses to bloom in Portland-area gardens throughout much of the year.[82] Seattle leaders similarly crowed about numerous trees, roses, and exotic plants that "will be set out in beautifully arranged beds on the velvety lawns."[83] Descriptions of the Pacific Northwest climate, even if thick with statistics, could not compete with stunning pictures of the fairground's landscape or, of course, the firsthand experience of fairgoers.

Illuminating what nature had to offer future settlers in the Far West was central to exposition marketing campaigns. Newcomers would find good weather and fresh air that, fair promoters maintained, ensured healthier and more enjoyable lives. For those worn down by harsh weather and a punishing lifestyle back East, exposition advertisements professed that the Far West's environment possessed regenerative properties.[84] A pleasant climate, however, meant more than just comfort and beautiful gardens. In an article entitled "Oregon as a Health Resort," a state health officer, for example, described two types of health resorts: those that only offer temporary respite from suffering and prolonged "the feeble existence of the invalid"—and those like Oregon, which offered year-round "health and vigor."[85] Promoting the Pacific Northwest as a healthy environment was directly related to broader claims that the region possessed a superior climate. One AYPE brochure maintained that "Seattle and Western Washington are noted for their healthfulness." Proof of such assertions could be found in health records that revealed low death rates that resulted from the region's mild temperatures, adequate rainfall, and ocean breezes.[86]

Open Space to Play

The Pacific Northwest expositions' marketing strategy seemingly left nothing to chance when it came to exploiting the region's environment. By the early twentieth century, industrialization and urbanization had profoundly reshaped the nature of American life. Being pressed into crowded conditions without the fresh air and open spaces of rural society increasingly troubled many middle-class Americans. Health officials and reformers responded that outdoor physical activity was a central component of a healthy and productive life. By the early Progressive Era, social reformers urged cities to construct playgrounds and parks where residents could find fresh air and room for recreation. In a 1917 history of the playground movement, scholar Henry S. Curtis stated that rural children had plenty of fresh air, trees, and animals to enjoy, but that the city child has "no places where he can play in safety or where he can even be out of doors and establish his health."[87] Similarly, Theodore Roosevelt published a series of essays collectively called *The Strenuous Life*, which—among the numerous references to imperialism and manliness—counseled the nation's youth to engage in more rigorous, physical pursuits. Like the playground advocates, Roosevelt maintained that country boys benefitted from "natural outdoor play" that city life did not offer.[88] Growing national anxiety about the cultural and physical impact of urban, industrial life exemplified by the playground movement and the Boy Scouts spawned efforts to foster recreation and outdoor life.

National nervousness about modern life fit well with the advertised advantages of western living. Boosters reminded easterners that the West's climate and scenic landscapes were unrivaled and that westerners enjoyed the benefits of outdoor life. A national magazine article describing the Pacific Northwest stated that the region "invites to an outdoor life more kindly than any other land of the same altitude or latitude."[89] Similarly, a Northern Pacific Railway booklet produced for the Portland exposition advertised that with Washington state's mountain ranges, "[t]here is no lack of appropriate places for those seeking new and healthful recreation spots anywhere in this beautiful country."[90] The LCE's publicity department also described how visitors could traverse the abundant number of trails in nearby mountains and forests.[91] To help fairgoers understand the real opportunities that the western environment afforded, fair officials and local leaders borrowed the language of the day and equated the Far West's mountains and natural landscapes with playgrounds.

Demonstrating that the Pacific Northwest offered the best of both urban and rural living meant that exposition officials had to convince potential settlers that they would not have to sacrifice modern amenities if they chose to relocate to the Pacific Coast. As J. E. Chilberg, president of the Alaska-Yukon-Pacific Exposition, explained in a letter to President Theodore Roosevelt, the purpose of Seattle's exposition was "to show the transformation of the back-yard into front terraces."[92] In other words, the West would no longer be the nation's wild and unkempt backyard, but now could stand shoulder to shoulder with up-to-date cities back east. As one Seattle businessmen simply stated: "Seattle of today is a modern city."[93] Westerners were quite proud that their fashionable cities allowed them to enjoy equally the benefits of both the region's natural and urban landscapes: western living meant that parents could send their children to fine public schools, drive a car along paved streets, eat at a fine restaurant, transact business at modern banks, and join any number of social club or organizations—all the while gazing at the snow-capped peak of Mount Rainier or the setting sun glistening off the crashing waves of the Pacific Ocean.

Modern Urban Life

Recognizing that tourists and future settlers coveted the benefits of urban life was only the first step in selling the new West. While the Pacific Coast fairs gave ample attention to the potential of their respective rural hinterlands, officials never failed to publicize the modern nature of their cities. Attracting farmers to the Far West might enhance the region's economy, yet fair directors also sought new workers and businessmen who would ensure the future growth and prosperity of the communities that hosted them. Brochures, guidebooks, and other publicity materials depicted the modern amenities that any city dweller would want or expect. Detailing the numerous recent improvements in Portland, the *Morning Oregonian*, for example, concluded that "Portland is now a thoroughly up-to-date city."[94] Similarly, an AYPE guidebook asserted that an examination of Seattle and Tacoma proved that "[m]aterially, educationally, religiously, the region is prospering."[95] The use of words like modern, up-to-date, and civilization signified to those east of the Mississippi River that they would lack nothing if they chose to visit or eventually relocate to one of these Pacific Coast cities.

Descriptions of educational opportunities backed by statistics marked one strategy that exposition publicity directors employed to illustrate that the Pacific Northwest was as progressive as any other place in the country. The growing attention paid to public education in the early twentieth century prompted western leaders to publicize the region's excellent schools. Portland officials demonstrated their commitment to education by comparing the city's number of schoolteachers and pupils to other Pacific Northwest communities.[96] Proof of its success, director of exploitation Henry Reed argued, was that the literacy rate for Oregon's women was the highest in the nation.[97] AYPE directors told fairgoers that "Tacoma boasts a very fine high school" and published a seventy-page report by Washington's Superintendent of Public Instruction that outlined the state's schools, number of students, and public spending on education.[98] Seattle schools, one local businessman claimed, were not only plentiful but "up-to-date in every respect."[99] By advertising the region's educational resources, the Pacific Coast expositions both challenged the notion of the "wild and woolly West" and addressed any qualms potential settlers might have about moving their families to the Far West.

Exposition promotional materials also rarely failed to advertise the host city's social and civil life. AYPE brochures and guidebooks, for example, bragged that Seattle had 225 religious societies and churches, including St. Peter's Church, which cost more than $1 million to build. The city also featured numerous social clubs, such as the Seattle Athletic, Arctic, and Rainier clubs.[100] This cultural investment, city leaders believed, was another sign of the Pacific Northwest's modernity. Describing its own up-to-date city, a Portland newspaper noted that that it had both a historical and a natural history museum, while a souvenir guide published for the Seattle fair provided detailed lists of every one of its theaters, clubs, libraries, and public buildings.[101]

Lists like these helped western leaders defend their claims that the Far West could match the amenities of most eastern cities. Exposition publicity departments and local commercial organizations also believed that the built environment illustrated the modern nature of the host cities. Whether fairgoers visited Portland or Seattle, they would encounter a familiar updated urban environment that had the look and feel of any contemporary American city. Portland officials boasted that their city had more paved streets than any other Pacific Northwest community and by 1904 had constructed 163½ miles of street railway lines.[102] Fairgoers who drove those streets or walked the finished sidewalks would quickly discover impressive, modern hotels, office buildings, and homes that rivaled any comparable American city. Seattle leaders, for example, crowed that their "hotels and cafes are the equal to those of New York" and that the city had built a "modern steel-and-brick skyscraper, fifteen stores high," with four more in the planning stages.[103] Moreover, in an article on the Pacific Northwest, the *World's Work* explained that visitors to the Alaska-Yukon-Pacific Exposition could travel to Spokane, Washington, where they would encounter "good pieces of architecture," including hillside residences that were "improvements over most Eastern residences of the same cost and kind."[104]

Words alone, fair publicity directors understood, would not effectively convey their central message that the Far West was not just as advanced and civilized as the East, but that it was superior. Although exposition officials were confident that visitors from afar would agree with this claim if they chose to attend the Pacific Northwest fairs, they knew quite well that effective advertising could dispel initial reservations that visitors might have about the region. To that end, exposition promotional literature provided ample support with not just words but also pictures. Brochures and guidebooks often included pictures of prominent buildings alongside images of the region's natural wonders or its frontier history. The cover page of one advertising piece published by the *Oregonian*, for example, included a three-part depiction of Portland consisting of a buckskinned pioneer greeting an Indian, a steamship anchored in the city's harbor, and a modern building. The booklet had a multi-page spread with pictures of several business blocks, the dining room of the Hotel Portland, the Bishop Scott Academy, and a local department store.[105] Souvenir books publicizing the Oregon metropolis likewise reflected this duality, where pictures of City Hall, local churches, and prominent business buildings were interspersed among photographs of the Willamette River or nearby Multnomah Falls.[106] A LCE promotional picture book, for example, included a picture of City Hall sandwiched between panoramic images of the Portland cityscape with Mount Hood in the background of one photograph and Mount St. Helens in the other.[107]

Like Portland, Seattle leaders encouraged fairgoers to embrace their modern city by providing images of its urban landscape. A *Chicago Illustrated Review* article on the AYPE, for instance, included photographs of the Hotel Butler and the impressive residence of *Seattle Daily Times* publisher A. J. Blethen.[108] The local Seattle newspaper, *The Argus*, published a special fair edition, which not only contained images of the White office building and the inside of a "Modern Mercantile Establishment," but also a small collage of pictures of the city's past and present transportation systems.[109] Publicity directors, however, never failed to remind visitors of the West's natural wonders. Just a couple of pages following the pictures of Seattle's Hotel Butler, the *Chicago Illustrated Review* provided snapshots of the Snake River's Lower Falls and Lake Mirror at Yosemite National Park.[110]

WHETHER FAIRGOERS OR POTENTIAL SETTLERS READ A brochure or guidebook from either Pacific Northwest exposition, they would be hard pressed to escape the underlying message that western living combined the best of modern urban life with the breathtaking natural landscapes that only the Far West had to offer. While Portland and Seattle fair publicity directors might have embellished, if not exaggerated, the advantages of their respective communities, what they said and how they said it tell us a good deal about how westerners saw themselves and their region. Selling this vision of the new West in a time of profound social and economic dislocation might have seemed simple had exposition publicity departments not faced popular misconceptions of the region. The accuracy of boosters' claims that Pacific Coast cities were just as good as any eastern urban center is perhaps less important than the consensus among westerners that their homeland was special. Informed by this faith, exposition marketing campaigns neatly packaged their understanding of western living to sell to tourists and potential settlers alike. Western landscapes, both natural and urban, combined to provide a new lifestyle that seemingly fit the modern, industrial sensibilities of early twentieth-century America. Irrigation promised a new rural society that was both economically and socially liberating, while nearby natural wonders and scenic landscapes provided emotional and physical health. With its up-to-date amenities, social clubs, and salubrious climate, western cities likewise ensured residents a nourishing lifestyle. Whether a visitor attended a fair in Seattle or Portland, the expositions revealed a shared faith that the Far West offered a new way of living that promised to enrich settlers both materially and spiritually.

Native Americans in ceremonial dress on display at the Lewis and Clark Exposition. *University of Washington Libraries, Special Collections, NEG UW 2142.*

5 ⁜ RACE AND EMPIRE IN THE PACIFIC NORTHWEST

In a nation undergoing profound social, economic, and political change at the turn of the twentieth century, Pacific Coast exposition officials proudly boasted about the region's natural wonders and how they contributed to a healthy and fulfilling lifestyle. Yet western living meant more than just a nice climate and scenic vistas. Westerners could not escape the fact that they also resided in the nation's most racially diverse region. For much of the previous half-century, the United States had struggled to confront slavery and its legacy. For those living east of the Mississippi River, the nation's race relations were largely viewed through the binary lens of white and black. By the time the Lewis and Clark Exposition gates opened, westerners saw a kaleidoscope of colors in the cities and farmlands they called home. Sparked by the California gold rush and subsequent capitalist development of the West, Chinese, Japanese, and Filipino immigrants joined the Native Americans, Mexicans, and Euro-Americans inhabiting the Far West. During the early twentieth century, the Pacific Coast expositions confronted racialist ideas informed by imperialism and southern Jim Crowism, along with cries of race suicide best exemplified by the emerging eugenics movement. The future development and growth of the Far West, western leaders and exposition officials concluded, demanded a marketing strategy that tapped into the appealing exoticism of the region's people of color without exciting deeper racial fears. Striking this balance would prove quite challenging.

Ever since Philadelphia hosted the nation's first international exposition in 1876, fair directors had exploited Americans' fascination with Indians. How Indians were portrayed and the nature of these images would change significantly over the three decades prior to the opening of the Lewis and Clark Fair in 1905. With warfare exploding on the Great Plains in the mid-1870s, Robert Rydell has argued, the Philadelphia exposition presented clear images of Indians as "unassimilable savages."[1] By the early twentieth century, Indian resistance in the West had been eliminated, and the remaining Native Americans struggled to adapt to policies that sought to transform them into little more than white farmers. Americans east of the Mississippi no doubt knew that the military had vanquished or jailed great Indian leaders like Geronimo, Black Kettle, and Sitting Bull, yet western dime novels and the wildly successful Buffalo Bill Cody Wild West Show continued to present contradictory images of the American West.[2] Promoting a civilized West thus would demand careful attention to the treatment and presentation of Native Americans if Pacific Coast exposition officials were going to dispel nagging images of a savage and wild West.[3]

The first Pacific Coast exposition in Portland opened its doors little more than two decades after the passage of the Dawes Act in 1877, which broke up reservation land and allotted plots to individual tribal members in order to facilitate their assimilation into America society. Individual land ownership, along with efforts to bring Christianity and American-style education to reservation lands, was intended to successfully integrate Indians and save them from extinction. By the early twentieth century, the federal government had opened a number of Indian schools whose professed aim was to provide Indian children the knowledge and—more importantly—skills needed to assimilate into mainstream America. To demonstrate their success, reformers turned to expositions to illustrate firsthand how these schools had transformed Native American lives both on and off the reservation.

Just months before LCE directors opened the doors to the Portland fair in 1905, one of the city's newspapers commented on the disillusionment easterners might experience when visiting the exposition later that summer. Expecting to encounter in the Far West "specimens of the blood-thirsty and scalp-hunting aborigine," these visitors would in fact "find mild-mannered and civilized natives. Instead of a scalplock the Indian at the 1905 Exposition will carry an algebra."[4] Fair officials no doubt understood that even though easterners knew that Indians in the American West had been forcefully relocated to reservations, many were uncertain how much this segregated life had changed Native Americans. If a 1901 *New York Times* article is any indication, Americans east of the Mississippi still harbored long-held stereotypes of Indian culture. It noted that Indians traveling with Buffalo Bill Cody's Wild West Show were "mild-mannered, harmless, and as gentle as Mohicans." The paper added that until recently, Indians were "a fierce visage, vindictive, untamable human being"; however, such traits, while no longer evident in Cody's Indians, were not eliminated—only simply "repressed."[5] Despite claims by government officials and western leaders that efforts to assimilate Native Americans had made great strides, visual representations of the West on display at Wild West shows not only contradicted official proclamations, but likely confirmed many Americans' deep-seated stereotypes and prejudices.

Public pronouncements that the Native Americans of Buffalo Bill's show were well along the road to civilization posed a quandary for exposition exploitation departments. Publicity directors knew quite well that Native Americans were a central part of their respective fairs' marketing strategy. Stories of dangerous Indians, however untrue they might be, captivated the American public. Recognizing the importance of Native Americans to the nation's first far western fair, the *Lewis and Clark Journal* attempted to explain to readers the apparent absence of Indians in the region. "The Red Man is vanishing," the journal declared, "partly by absorption of the Caucasian, partly by decay through contact with a civilization whose better side he does not easily accept."[6] Describing an Indian exhibit at the Portland fair, the *Washington Post* added that "the Indian in his war paint is noticeably absent, by reason of the fact that he has ceased to exist as completely in the West as in the East."[7] A year before the Seattle fair opened, the *Seattle Post-Intelligencer* similarly explained that "present day opportunities to see the Indian as he really was a hundred or more years ago are rare indeed."[8] Despite claims that Native Americans were vanishing, indigenous populations, according to historian Nancy Shoemaker, were slowly on the rise in the early twentieth century. Admittedly, western leaders may not have noticed, or cared for that matter, that Indian populations had reached their nadir by 1900.[9] For marketing reasons, the idea of the vanishing Indian served both an ideological and financial purpose.

Although western leaders declared that the region's Indian population had precipitously declined, they still held out the chance for fairgoers to get a glimpse of rapidly disappearing Indian life. Promotional efforts played on this sense of urgency, warning those east of the Mississippi that the Pacific Northwest expositions represented the last chance to experience the rapidly fading old West. Visitors touring the Alaska-Yukon-Pacific Exposition, for example, could explore visual evidence of the reported demise of Indians through the first three volumes of photographer and amateur ethnologist Edward Curtis's multi-volume work *The North American Indian* put on display. Included in the exhibit was one of his most famous pictures, "The Vanishing Race," which a Seattle newspaper claimed "has won so many friends for Mr. Curtis' work from one end of the land to the other."[10] Fairgoers, however, did not have to depend solely on pictures and visual displays. As historian Josh Reid has noted, AYPE officials advertised canoe races, which included Native Americans from Puget Sound and British Columbia, as a final opportunity to see Indians partaking in an important traditional activity.[11]

Explanations for the demise of the nation's Native American population were often glossed over by fair directors. Yet, most could not ignore that the timing of this demographic change was associated with the arrival of whites. A Portland paper, for example, admitted that the vanishing Indian was part of the changing landscape that resulted from white migration. With the arrival of whites, the *Evening Telegram* noted, the Indian disappeared, just like the "gigantic firs among which he roamed."[12] The *Seattle Post-Intelligencer* maintained that "it is only when some great occasion arises when modern man with the everlasting commercial instinct, changes things about and brings the wild tribes to civilization, that the people at large can see and study for themselves."[13] Whatever the reasons for the decline of Native American population, Portland and Seattle leaders believed that their respective expositions offered a unique, and perhaps final, opportunity for visitors to observe and learn about the region's indigenous people.

Despite the effort to dispel Buffalo Bill's Wild West Show's depiction of dangerous Indians populating large swaths of the West, exposition exhibits and advertising materials at times subverted this goal. A good marketing campaign required exposition publicity departments to identify images that would help their customers immediately recognize the special location of the two distant Pacific Northwest fairs. Totem poles and Indian headdresses, for example, were symbols of Indian culture that also had a certain exotic appeal. The Lewis and Clark Exposition's daily program included a drawing of an Indian in full headdress with a spear overlooking what appeared to be the fairgrounds. Similarly, a Union Pacific Railroad pamphlet advertising the Portland gathering depicted two semi-nude Indians with headdresses hunting among tall trees.[14] At the AYPE's Seattle Day in 1909, a picture of Chief Seattle adorned souvenir tickets, while a totem pole appeared on a popular AYPE postcard.[15] Fair officials, like the eastern visitors they wished to attract, could not easily escape the powerful presence Native Americans occupied in the American mind.

Lavishing such attention on the Native American past and present represented more than just an advertising strategy or a nod to the public's fascination with indigenous people of the Far West. Rather than a token exhibit or simple museum display, the Pacific Northwest expositions made Native Americans a central focal point of their respective events. Fair officials, for example, prominently featured Native Americans in exhibits, arts and crafts sales, parades, and academic lectures documenting Native American life and history. One author even published a souvenir edition of a book on Indian legends and poems for the Lewis and Clark Exposition.[16] More than that, Portland and Seattle officials reminded fairgoers that Indians were an important part of their respective cities' histories. However, while Portland commemorated the expedition of two white explorers, Meriwether Lewis and William Clark, few histories of their exploits failed to mention Sacagawea, the Shoshone native woman who helped the two explorers complete their journey. Likewise, AYPE directors explained that Seattle was named after a local Duwamish leader, Chief Seattle, who accommodated white pioneers in the early settlement years. Decades later, the chief remained part of the city's identity and origins. Fair officials even invited his granddaughter Myrtle to participate in the fair.[17] The Pacific Northwest's past and present were inextricably tied to the Native American past.

White Fascination with Indians

Like any good company, exposition publicity departments understood the needs and desires of their customers and labored hard to meet them. The centrality of Native Americans at the Pacific Coast expositions reflected fair officials' conviction that the American public possessed a certain fascination with Indians. Atchison, Topeka, and Santa Fe Railroad officials, for example, recognized this early on and began using images of Southwestern natives in company advertisements by the late 1890s.[18] As Seattle completed the final touches on its exposition, the *Seattle Post-Intelligencer* claimed that "[e]veryone is interested in the study of the American Indian and travelers who visit out-of-the-way places, will unconsciously make a closer study of the inhabitants than they would of their own race." The paper explained that "the romance and tragedy of the real Americans lends zest to the search for information."[19] Fair officials believed that the exposition provided a unique opportunity for those from east of the Mississippi River to see Indians, as well as Siberian Eskimos, who were still a "people unsullied by modernity."[20] Considering the attention to the conquest of the region and the popularity of western novels and Wild West shows, it is not surprising that the American public might have been captivated by the nation's disappearing indigenous population.

Capitalizing on the national fascination with Native Americans meant more than just an exhibit of cultural artifacts or photographs of Indian life. To boost fair attendance, Portland and Seattle leaders understood that the promise of more intimate contact with the region's Native Americans might help lure visitors to their respective fairs. Upholding the exposition's purported educational purpose, officials declared that fairgoers would have the unique opportunity to learn about Indian life by watching and interacting with natives in a natural setting. LCE directors added that their exposition would not neglect "the ethnological matters that interest all who are concerned about the Indian, his past, present, and future."[21] Promising a comprehensive examination of Native Americans, fair officials nevertheless heavily promoted exhibits and live events that presented Indians in ways that emphasized their perceived "primitiveness." Even the United States Department of the Interior noted in a report on its participation in the Seattle exposition that the "American Indian is a subject of perennial interest, and anything that relates to him in his primitive life is always sure to attract attention."[22] Western fairs may have tried to include examples of the "civilized" or assimilated Indians, yet exhibits showcasing Indians in a traditional setting or performing ceremonial dances captured the most attention.

Stories of the conquest of the West and the subsequent founding of reservations meant that fairgoers to the Pacific Northwest might have believed that the Indians resided just a few miles outside the host cities. Exposition directors could not deny—and for tourism reasons did not want to ignore—that a good number of Native Americans still populated the region east of the Mississippi, even if they largely lived on distant reservations. Fair officials, for example, expended large sums of money and often provided ample space for Native American exhibits. The typical museum-like exhibit included everything from Native American artifacts and photos of Indians villages to scholarly papers describing native life and history. Live exhibits, however, captivated fairgoers. Portland fair directors, for example, catered to this fascination by transporting what a local paper called a "band of long-haired, wild Indians" from Idaho to "dance and display the old-time heathenism of the tribe."[23] Later that summer, "The Trail," the exposition's amusement section, added a small group of Nez Perce Indians, including "several squaws with cute papooses," who provided guests "daily performances of war dances and other native ceremonies."[24] Exposition directors ensured that visitors to Portland would leave the fair satisfied that they had the experienced firsthand the frightening Indian war dances and mysterious rites that filled the pages of popular dime novels.

Despite some reservations, local leaders recognized that Wild West shows could enhance the visitor's experience by satisfying the American public's desire to relive this slice of the region's storied past. In

1909 Cheyenne Bill's Wild West Show brought Indian performers to Seattle, where they entertained visitors and locals alike with "weirdly picturesque tribal and ceremonial dances."[25] While the Cheyenne Bill show was held at a nearby park, AYPE directors announced a week before the Seattle fair opened that they had hired the Washington Amusement Company to arrange a show that portrayed "the life of the great frontier in the early days." The company's owner, Jim Gabriel, promised to bring forty Oglala Sioux from Pine Ridge reservation replete with "full regalia of blankets and feathers" to perform at the Seattle exposition.[26] Whether it was Nez Perce "squaws" at the LCE amusement zone or Gabriel's Sioux performance, the line between education and commerce was no doubt blurred.

Authentic Native Life

Ceremonial dances and demonstrations of traditional crafts like basket weaving were only a small part of the more extravagant live exhibits found at the Pacific Northwest fairs. The Lewis and Clark Exposition, for example, offered visitors "a complete and comprehensive illustration of Indian life and progress," including an Indian Village where natives displayed their baskets and other works of art.[27] Seattle fair officials likewise planned to display camps of several different Pacific Northwest tribes, including the Nez Perce.[28]

Attentive to the interest in Alaska, AYPE directors also showcased the region's indigenous peoples in the Eskimo Village exhibit. The *Seattle Daily Times*, for example, advertised that it displayed "Aboriginals of Siberia and Labrador living as they do on their native snow barrens."[29] Housed in a building with a facade depicting a giant log cabin, visitors to Seattle's fair could see natives posing next to an "igloo" and wearing sealskin garments.[30] Announcing plans for the Eskimo Village, the *Seattle Post-Intelligencer* reminded readers that the Siberian natives were largely untouched by modernity, and the fair's exhibit would ensure that visitors saw "these people in their native surroundings, reproduced with exact fidelity to life."[31] For Seattle leaders, these so-called Eskimos shared a similar primitiveness with another indigenous population, the American Indian.

Assimilation

Whether visiting the LCE in 1905 or the AYPE four years later, fairgoers confronted contradictory images of Native American life. Minutes after witnessing Indians slaughter Custer's troops, Portland visitors, for example, could stroll over to the U.S. Department of Interior exhibit and watch moving pictures of Indians performing traditional ceremonies "contrasted with the Indian today at work in the fields and with the Indian children in school."[32] Fair officials, however, struggled to balance images of Native Americans that seemingly portrayed their way of life as static and unchanged with the desire to demonstrate that their supposed primitiveness was quickly giving way to the civilizing efforts of reformers. To help visitors see the progress reformers had made, the LCE included an Indian band playing daily concerts and a girls' basketball team made up of young Indian women who were "cultured, quiet, and refined as any of their white sisters."[33]

Native American exhibits and concert bands reflected Portland leaders' desire to illustrate "the advance that has been made on this continent from savagery to the highest expression of civilization."[34] Fair publicity departments understood that demonstrating this transformation was central to repackaging the Far West for American audiences. "Civilized" Indians were drawn from the nearby Chemawa Indian Training School in Salem, Oregon, and other regional institutions like the Shaw Indian School in Montana. Contrasting the "scalp-hunting" Indians at the Custer Massacre show, Lewis and Clark fair officials wished to show, the *Evening Telegram* indicated, the "first hand results of Uncle Sam's new educational policy with regard to the red man."[35] Government-sponsored exhibits, one LCE publicity program explained, provided the public "the opportunity of examining the character of the training given people in the Government Indian schools."[36] As historian Paige Raibmon has argued, the "exhibitionary opposition between the 'authentic' Aboriginal encampment and the civilized residential school exhibits reproduced the late-nineteenth-century colonial landscape in microcosm."[37] The contradictory images of Native Americans, then, served more than one purpose. If read correctly, they showed that the West was no longer the violent and untamed place that dime novels and Wild West shows so powerfully described. Moreover, the exposition's handling of Indians demonstrated the efficacy of the nation's Indian policy and thus confirmed the legitimacy of the basic tenets of turn-of-the-century manifest destiny.

Nearly three decades after the passage of the Dawes Act, reformers wished to impress upon the public that Native Americans were ready to join mainstream America. Explaining the need for such assimilation strategies, a federal government report on the Bureau of Indian Affair's participation at the Alaska-Yukon-Pacific Exposition noted the persistent interest in the "primitive life" of the American Indian. The Seattle Indian exhibit hoped to replace popular images of Indians donning war paint and riding on horses with depictions of "a brown-skinned plowman in a broad-rimmed hat and blue overalls."[38] To that end, it featured "specimens of tailoring, wagon making, and carpentry," as well as Indian women showcasing their "yards of lace and elaborate pieces of embroidery" rather than fringe and buckskin. Dovetailing quite well with the AYPE's marketing strategy, fair directors added an exhibit of Indians from Metlakatla, an Alaskan town, where for fifty years, the Reverend William Duncan had "lived among tribesmen whom he found in a state of savagery." Under his guidance, the paper claimed, Indians had "prospered and learned industry."[39] In short, fairgoers would leave the exposition confident that the Dawes Act had indeed succeeded.

Education, American officials believed, was essential to the success of Indian assimilation. For decades reformers had argued that it could help civilize Native Americans, resulting in their successful integration into American society. In the wake of the Plains Indian wars, the United States government funded the construction of the Carlisle Indian Industrial School in Pennsylvania. Founded on the belief that Native Americans possessed the social and intellectual abilities to thrive in the country if only immersed in mainstream American culture, the school opened in 1879 with an enrollment of more than one hundred young Native Americans. Within a few years, the Carlisle school would become the model for similar boarding schools throughout the West.[40] Few Americans could visit the Carlisle school; however, a report from the commissioner on Indian Affairs claimed that the Portland fair provided the opportunity to demonstrate the success of federal government schools and how the "results fully repay the labor and expense incurred."[41] In the summer of 1905, the *Washington Post* reported that the Lewis and Clark Exposition furnished "the opportunity to study first hand the results of Uncle Sam's new educational policy with regard to the red man." The paper suggested that both the nine young girls from the Shaw Indian School in Montana who sang and played basketball, and the thirty-seven-piece band from the nearby Chemawa Indian Training School who performed daily concerts at the fair, were "examples of the new sort of red man that Uncle Sam is developing."[42]

Both the Carlisle and Chemawa Indian schools reflected late-nineteenth-century reformers' belief that locating the schools distant from the reservation ensured better prospects for meeting assimilation goals. Such success, the assistant superintendent of Oregon's Chemawa Indian Training School explained, hinged on providing the proper cultural environment to encourage Indian children to see the value of labor and work.[43] Removing young children from tribal homelands would lessen interference by parents and the community and help guarantee that students would fully embrace the "civilizing" instruction they received.

Beginning with the opening of the Oregon Indian school in 1880, nearly all similar institutions would be located in the West. Regional off-reservation schools saved transportation costs, while allowing families and tribal leaders, reformers argued, to see the successful transformation of Indian children. Exposition directors also believed that inviting Indian students from nearby training schools helped demonstrate to visitors afar the great strides Indian education had seemingly made.[44]

Portland and Seattle fair officials may have felt compelled to feature Indian education because of growing disillusionment with federal Indian schools by some political leaders. After a generation of assimilation efforts, a number of politicians and reformers questioned the ability of Native Americans to assimilate fully. Ballooning education budgets and criticism by southern congressmen of the federal government's role in what they saw as local race relations undermined support for Indian schools.[45] Such pessimism seeped into Indian education policy and practice by the early twentieth century. In 1898 Wyoming resident Estelle Reel was appointed superintendent of Indian Education, and over the next decade, she would significantly transform education at the more than two hundred Indian schools. Reel, who rejected the liberal or theoretical approach to Indian education in favor of more practical vocational schooling, organized teaching institutes to promote this view among the two thousand teachers from Pennsylvania to the Pacific Coast. Rather than waste their time on book learning, Reel, who considered Native Americans "too dull" to intellectually succeed, encouraged Indian schools to prepare Native American children for domestic work and the manual trades.[46]

Reel's view reflected racialist ideas, which held that people of color lacked the mental and moral capacity for anything but menial labor. Predicated on the assumption that Native Americans were a "lesser race," white leaders and educators believed that best course for Indians was to maintain segregation, eliminate "savagery," and train and civilize them for industrial work.[47] By the early twentieth century, growing immigration, Jim Crowism, and American imperial endeavors in the Philippines informed deteriorating views of Indian education. As several scholars have noted, Native Americans became one of several "subhuman," "barbarian," "savage," and "backward races" that troubled American leaders. Moreover, contemporary anthropologists and other social scientists seemingly confirmed such views. "Racial formalists," historian Frederick E. Hoxie argues, "seized on the physical differences between native and white Americans to explain social differences. Race alone, these scholars argued, explained the Indians' slow progress and justified their 'speedy extinction.' "[48] Mirroring this shift from the optimism of late nineteenth-century reformers, commissioner of Indian Affairs Francis Leupp explained to the National Education Association in 1907 that "the Indian is an adult child" possessing the mental age of a fourteen-year-old.[49]

Assimilation may have been the goal, but opposition and resistance defined the larger history of federal Indian education efforts. Native American parents, for example, often fought with agents sent to reservations to entice children to attend a training school. They objected to attacks on native language and culture and feared that schools might pose a threat to their children's health. Students likewise resisted school officials by running away, destroying school property, and through more passive resistance, work slowdowns and refusal to participate in class activities. Like any complex event, Native Americans did not speak with one voice. Some parents and children recognized that Indian schools could provide some benefits—new skills and greater economic opportunities might help families and tribes mitigate the bleak future that reservation life seemed to offer—and they struck an accommodation with white educators. At times, Native American children saw the schools as a way to escape harsh conditions and unhappy homes.[50] Given the environment of white–Native American relations at the time, it is understandable how some Native Americans assimilated to a system that at its root sought to eradicate Indian culture. Students, parents, and even tribal leaders may have chosen this course, but they did so in an environment of severely restricted options.

Whether by choice or force, the impact of Indian schools on both students and Native American societies was significant. Indian cultural identity came under assault, and few lives were improved. Whatever the true intentions of federal bureaucrats and white educators, scholar K. Tsianina Lomawaima argues that the Indian schools "did not train Indian youth to assimilate into the American 'melting pot' but trained them to adopt the work discipline of the Protestant ethic and accept their proper place in society as a marginal class."[51] Vocational training left students with limited skills in a labor system segregated by race and class. Separating the best and brightest from tribal homelands also resulted in a brain drain that only undermined future prospects for improving reservations.[52] The seeming failure to fully assimilate and "civilize" Indian children led many whites to conclude that Native Americans could never achieve true equality and citizenship. In the end, historian David Wallace Adams concludes, "the boarding school story constitutes yet another deplorable episode in the long and tragic history of Indian-white relations." Visitors to the Portland or Seattle expositions, however, would likely not agree.[53]

The primary role of education in civilizing and assimilating Native Americans was not lost on the other Pacific Coast expositions. Fair publicity directors and other officials realized that demonstrating the positive impact of education on Native Americans fit well with their larger marketing campaign to sell the new West to the American public. Heralding the Pacific Slope as a modern and rapidly evolving society required that outsiders recognize that the region had moved beyond its less-than-civilized nineteenth-century past. Seattle fair officials, for example, lauded the importance of the Congress of Indian Educators conference held on the fairgrounds, which attracted several prominent national officials, including former Seattle mayor and current U.S. Secretary of the Interior Richard A. Ballinger. The Alaska-Yukon-Pacific Exposition promised to "demonstrate the manner in which the Indian youth is being educated to assume his place in the work-a-day world." Exhibits would contrast traditional Indian camp life with the "modern home of a graduate from one of the government Indian schools."[54] Dr. W. J. McGee—an ethnologist, former president of the American Anthropological Association, and by 1909, anthropologist for the United States Department of Agriculture—told conference attendees that the agency's goal was to move Indians from the "tepee and indolence to modern homes and industry."[55] Fair directors promised that the AYPE would provide direct proof that the government's assimilation policies worked. Not only were some six thousand Indian school employees going to visit the Puget Sound fair, but these educators would present papers, public lectures, and demonstrations highlighting the successful remedies that, according to the *Seattle Times*, helped overcome the "ignorance and degradation among the Indians."[56]

Hosting the Congress of Indian Educators in 1909 was a public relations coup for the AYPE and provided Seattle officials the occasion to dispel popular misconceptions of the American West. Unlike the lurid stories of dangerous, uncivilized Indians who populated the pages of dime novels, fairgoers learned about Indians who lived in modern homes, read Shakespeare, and plied trades like the rest of the American working class. While the AYPE brought a few members of more distant western tribes like the Sioux, Navajo, and Chippewa to demonstrate native arts and crafts, fair directors paid particular attention to the successful assimilation of nearby Washington and Oregon Indians. Washington state's Tulalip Indian School, for example, sent a number of young girls and boys from the school's orchestra to perform at the fair. Young girls from the Chemawa school displayed the skills taught in their domestic-science class by cooking lunch for local dignitaries. These girls, the *Seattle Post-Intelligencer* claimed, showed "that they are being educated to assume a useful place in the world."[57] The national conference of Indian educators allowed Seattle fair directors to provide tangible evidence of a new West where Indians were well on the road to assimilation. Signs of educators' success were quite evident at the Pacific Northwest expositions. Speaking to the Congress of Indian Educators, Superintendent Estelle Reel presented two groups of Native Americans before the audience, stating that "the difference between these primitive Indians on my right and the Indian boys and girls we have brought from Tulalip, Puyallup, and Chemawa Indian schools, most forcefully expresses what the bureau of Indian affairs has accomplished for the Indian people during the last few years."[58] Four years earlier, visitors to the Lewis and Clark Exposition toured a Bureau of Indian Affairs exhibit that included maps with the locations of Indian schools and the "actual work of the pupils from kindergarten to the 8th grade" demonstrating the ability of Indians to assimilate "book knowledge."[59] Fairgoers to these early twentieth-century expositions could not help leave the Pacific Coast impressed by the apparent great strides made by government education efforts to "civilize" native people who once freely roamed the region. Visitors did not have to simply rely on educators' claims: they could see Indian schoolchildren who not only dressed like them, but also wrote papers and sang popular songs like school children from their own home towns.

Sightseers who attended the Portland fair in late August 1905 did not have to wait in lines at the government Indian exhibits or listen to lectures from educators to witness Native American acculturation. The proof, the *Washington Post* proclaimed, was evident when "a band of Indian girls—comely, cultured quiet, and refined as any of their white sisters who have descended from generations of pink-tea devotees—walked through the turnstiles and proceeded to see the fair." Appearance aside, these girls demonstrated the grand achievement of assimilation efforts by playing basketball, performing a dramatic scene from "Hiawatha," and doing a "pantomime, entitled 'The Star Spangled Banner.'" The *Post* added that the girls did not just play basketball, but had soundly defeated "white girl teams" in the several towns they had visited on their journey to Portland. Watching the Indian girls perform and stroll the fairgrounds in their "blue, white polka-dotted gingham dresses and blue caps" no doubt offered a stark contrast to the popular images of Native Americans.[60]

Portland was not the only place where fairgoers encountered ample evidence that the Indians they read about in novels or watched at Wild West shows could indeed be assimilated into American society. Local dignitaries at the AYPE, for example, watched an orchestra comprised of a dozen Native American girls, while attendees at the Congress of Indian Educators listened to a performance by a soprano singer from the nearby Tulalip Indian school.[61] Some local leaders personally vouched for Native Americans. A prominent Seattle judge and his wife, for example, publicly urged fair visitors to recognize the great strides Indians had made and that they "had reason to be proud of their race." During a speech on Indian achievement, Judge Thomas Burke invited his Indian cook and chauffeur to attend the meeting with him.[62] Mrs. Burke similarly defended the use of Indian girls as domestic servants and rejected what she believed were outdated views of "unkempt, barefooted, wrinkle-faced" Indian women.[63] Chief Seattle's own granddaughter Myrtle provided proof by cooking and serving "an appetizing up-to-date luncheon" to the Secretary of the Interior's wife.[64] Illustrating the success of Indian schools, Mrs. Burke hosted a tea during the fair where she invited Flathead Indians regaled in tribal dress and "educated Indian children from various Indian schools in neat uniforms."[65] The Burkes' public testimonials fit quite well with the AYPE's marketing strategy.

"Westward the Course of Empire Takes Its Way"

Reconciling the state of the Native American population with their bold visions of a new West, exposition publicity departments at the Portland and Seattle fairs hoped to show that the Pacific Coast was ready to lead the nation. At the dawn of the twentieth century, Americans celebrated the commercial strides the nation had made since the Civil War, and also basked in the glow of their new commercial empire carved out of the Spanish-American War. In his study of American international expositions, scholar Robert Rydell explained how "expositions offered millions of fairgoers an opportunity to reaffirm their collective national identity in an updated synthesis of progress and white supremacy."[66] Touting the Far West as the launching point of an American empire emerged as a key feature of the Pacific Coast expositions' marketing strategy. As the first of four West Coast cities to host an exposition, Portland officials understood both the commercial and ideological potential the fair offered the Far West. Portland's celebration contained two overlapping visions of empire—the Jeffersonian "Empire of Liberty" undertaken by the early-nineteenth-century Lewis and Clark expedition, and the imperialist thrust represented by American actions in the Orient and Latin America at the turn of the twentieth century. For Portland leaders, the LCE thus offered the unique opportunity to commemorate the former and situate their city at the center of the latter.

Visions of empire clearly occupied the minds of exposition advocates. In a 1903 speech before the United States Senate urging federal appropriations for the proposed Lewis and Clark Exposition, Oregon senator Charles W. Fulton acknowledged the "fact that this government within the last few years has become the most considerable proprietor of the Pacific."[67] The national magazine *Leslie's Weekly* put it more bluntly: "The day when the Pacific shall be transformed into an American lake will come, even earlier than Seward's prophetic vision grasped."[68] Similar claims of a new Pacific empire framed the Seattle fair. At the opening of the AYPE, for example, railroad magnate James J. Hill proclaimed that the conquering spirit that had subdued the American West would continue "across the broad Pacific to remake the Orient."[69] China, Japan, and other Asian nations, fair directors suggested, needed to be remodeled and reformed, and if they not embrace change, they would succumb to the inevitable progress that Americans would bring to their lands.

When visitors approached the gates of the LCE in 1905, they could not escape the fair's marketing slogan, "Westward the course of empire takes its way," prominently featured on the façade above the entrance.[70] To Portland leaders, this motto represented not just the century-long westward expansion of the American people, but also the belief that the nation's new empire looked west across the Pacific. Writing for a national magazine, Robertus Love declared that the LCE told "the story of conquest of the wilds, of the passage of civilized man across the continent," ending in "the constant expansion of American commerce with the Orient."[71] Exposition officials testified that the fair celebrated the culmination of American expansion that had begun with the Louisiana Purchase, continued through the Mexican-American War, and ended with the annexation of Hawai'i and the Philippines. H.W. Scott, president of the Lewis and Clark Exposition, summed up the larger meaning of this expansion for both westerners and the nation at large: "It has faced the United States toward the West, over the Pacific, as hitherto we have faced only toward the East, over the Atlantic."[72]

Reorienting the nation towards the Pacific enabled Portland leaders to boost the importance of the Pacific Northwest to the nation's future and lay claim to the commercial riches the Orient promised. In a letter to Governor R.M. LaFollette of Wisconsin, Henry Reed confidently announced that "time has swung the pendulum around to the West and the great world's market lies across the Pacific."[73] Similarly, the AYPE's publicity department brochure declared that the Pacific Coast states were destined "to replace the Atlantic as the theater of the events which make up the scenario in the drama of world politics."[74] Whether it was Portland or Seattle, officials insisted that their city's proximity to Asia meant that the Pacific, not the Atlantic, would be "the front door of America; that all trade routes of commerce for centuries are to be reversed."[75] The Pacific Northwest expositions, then, promised to connect in the American mind the fortunes of Asian trade with their respective coastal cities, securing for each community new settlers, new businesses, and a triumphant future.

Whether they knew it or not, fair officials were re-imagining the geography of the nation, placing the West, especially the Pacific, not at the periphery but at the center of a new national vision. The Lewis and Clark Exposition's Henry Reed claimed that "geographic lines have been obliterated" by centuries of migration and have "brought the Aryan race face to face on the opposite shores of the great western ocean."[76] Portland, Seattle, and other far western cities now looked west to the less developed frontier of Asia just as New York and Chicago had once looked west to the Pacific Coast states. In other words, the West would no longer define itself simply in relation to the older settled parts of the country. Public speeches and exposition publicity materials consistently sold this vision of empire, with Portland's marketing slogan explicitly declaring the West as central to that of America. At the dawn of a new century, then, the Far West would build on the work of earlier pioneers like Meriwether Lewis, William Clark, and the California forty-niners by leading the nation west, across the Pacific to a new promising frontier.

Tying the future of the nation to the Far West and the Orient, however, further confounded the nature of race in the United States. Exposition officials had to confront their own region's complicated racial past and present, as well as address new issues that came with tighter bonds to Asia and the Pacific. On one hand, fair directors labored to reconcile popular images of violent Indians and exotic Chinese immigrants with the reality of the early-twentieth-century West. Yet opening the gate to the Pacific only further complicated race relations by establishing stronger ties to Japan, China, and the Philippines. As author David Wrobel has suggested, "[i]n the most racially pluralistic parts of the West, in the early twentieth century, promoters, faced with the demographic reality of diversity, increasingly presented wonderlands of whiteness, tinged with a romantic backdrop of cultural color, to prospective settlers."[77] Exposition publicity departments were tasked with striking a balance in their marketing campaigns: recognizing the region's unique color palette without disturbing the racial sensibilities of their target audience. Ironically, at a time when southerners seemingly clarified the binary nature of race in the emerging Jim Crow South, visitors to the Pacific Coast fairs likely left the grounds more confused, uncertain, and perhaps wary about the racial arrangements in the stubbornly diverse American West.[78]

The uncertain racial implications of expanding ties to the Orient took a back seat to the region's economic future when Portland leaders constructed their exposition. Lucrative Far East markets and expanding trans-Pacific trade promised to enrich Portland and the greater Pacific Northwest. Nevertheless, Lewis and Clark Exposition publicity materials often couched economic desires within the larger cultural significance of the emerging Pacific Ocean commerce. One fair souvenir book, for example, claimed that the United States' "commanding influence for higher civilization," combined with Asia's awakened markets, promised a new destiny for the Far West.[79] *Leslie's Weekly* spelled out in racial terms the primary reason why the American people would fulfill this destiny: "The United States is the world's only white power of any consequence which fronts on the Pacific."[80] The LCE, the magazine implied, would mark the beginning of this decades-old dream. With the Pacific as the new American lake, the Far West would soon become the nation's new economic and geographic center.

That Portland shared the vast Pacific Ocean with both China and Japan was not the sole reason that city leaders expressed such confidence. The nation's recent acquisition of the Philippines only enhanced the city's favorable location. In the wake of the American victory in the Spanish-American War, Portland officials recognized the great opportunity Pacific Ocean commerce offered West Coast cities. A 1901 article in the *Lewis and Clark Review and Gazetteer*, a local magazine founded to promote the upcoming exposition, explained why Portland must move quickly: "This is the condition that now confronts us. The war in the Philippines has extended the American flag over isles of the most fertile Pacific. Little Japan, the young giant of the East, now stands ready to trade and exchange her products with the world nearest her. Her ports are nearest to our door."[81] A permanent American presence in the western Pacific seemingly ensured prosperity for Portland and other Pacific Coast ports. With the Philippines firmly in American hands, another fair magazine declared, "Manila will become the financial and commercial center of the Eastern world"[82]—all that was needed to jump start this lucrative trade network was publicity. The acquisition of the Philippines rendered the idea of an America empire less abstract, and fair officials exploited the national debate in their marketing campaign. Portland leaders envisioned the LCE as the instrument to introduce Americans to both their city and the lucrative Asian markets.[83]

Promoting Asia

Dreams that the Far East was central to fulfilling America's destiny did not subside following the closure of the Portland fair. When visitors to the 1909 Alaska-Yukon-Pacific Exposition wandered the streets and pathways of the fairgrounds, they could not escape the central place Asia commanded at the fair. The AYPE's marketing strategy left no stone unturned when it came to promoting Asia. A primary purpose of the exposition, "bridging the Orient and Occident," was evident not only in the numerous exhibits and events, but also in the fair's architecture and official seal. Japanese lanterns, for example, greeted fairgoers as they strolled through the "Pay Streak." When contemplating the fair's official seal, historian Shelley S. Lee has argued, exposition directors settled on a design that "featured three women representing Asia, Alaska, and America seated and facing each other in a gesture of amity."[84] Local officials boasted that the AYPE would serve as an introduction to the Far East and, as the *New York Times* reported, "bring the Asiatic people into personal contact with the Americans by an interchange of the products and manufactures necessary to each."[85] Exhibits of Asian products, celebrations of Asian cultural events, and personal encounters with Chinese and Japanese officials and businessmen promised to break down cultural and geographic barriers and cultivate friendly and productive relations.

Exposing Americans to the culture and art of the Orient, however, was secondary to Seattle's efforts to position itself as the staging point for the lucrative Pacific Ocean trade. James J. Hill heralded the fantastic economic opportunities the Far East offered the nation. "Oriental business," he maintained, "must be studied and cultivated," and the Seattle fair provided such an occasion to do this.[86] One AYPE publicity piece proclaimed that the exposition would not just feature the Oriental trade, but surpass Portland's efforts, which suffered from Japan's engagement in the 1905 Russo-Japanese War. Seattle, the brochure concluded, would increase "the commerce of the Pacific by teaching the merchants and manufacturers of each section the needs of the people of their respective markets."[87] The exposition's efforts and the city's proximity to Asia, local officials declared, meant that Seattle was poised to dominate this profitable trade.

While Pacific Coast leaders all recognized the value of Chinese and Japanese participation in their respective fairs, realizing success proved more difficult. Exhibit halls displaying Asian goods could not alone ensure strong attendance. Exposition publicity directors instead often leaned on the American public's curiosity with the Far East. Fairs offered local leaders the chance to introduce Americans to what many saw as the mysterious Far East.[88] Fairgoers, for example, could meander through exhibits featuring Asian commercial and industrial products, ranging from more well-known indigenous merchandise and agricultural commodities to modern manufactured goods. Like the representation of Native Americans at the expositions, publicists underscored the perceived exotic nature of Chinese and Japanese culture to entice visitors to journey across the country. Playing their part, Asian governments were willing to display the art, architecture, and other popular cultural artifacts and performances of their respective countries, as long as the fairs did not ignore the modern strides that the Far East had made. To achieve their goals, exposition directors also exploited the notoriety of local Chinese and Japanese populations on the nation's western edge. For example, fair officials urged local Chinese and Japanese residents to participate in their city's fair by staging parades, festivals, and cultural performances. Residents helped enhance the fair's exhibits and special Asian days, and also provided city leaders the opportunity to utilize the Far East's exotic appeal by drawing attention to their local Chinese and Japanese communities.

At the outset, Portland officials clearly indicated the importance of Asia when they settled on a title for the 1905 fair. Although widely known by its truncated name, the Lewis and Clark Centennial Exposition, city leaders chose a clumsier title—the Lewis and Clark Centennial and American Pacific Exposition and Oriental Fair. Exposition directors recognized that to internationalize their fair and ensure its success, they would have to encourage participation from Asian nations, so invitations were extended to the governments of Japan, China, Siam, and Korea.[89]

While LCE officials would have been delighted to include several Asian nations, the fair's success hinged on Japan's participation. To entice Japan, director of exhibits Henry Dosch stitched together an

Oregon exhibit and brought it to a 1902 exposition hosted by Japan. He later wrote that he did this because he wanted to be sure to "have this rising and progressive nation" take part in the Lewis and Clark fair.[90] Despite the aggressive campaign to woo the emerging Asian powerhouse, Japan's role at the fair was significantly diminished due to its war with Russia. This distraction was not the sole reason for the reduced Asian presence at the Portland fair, though. As Secretary Dosch explained to the LCE president, Japanese and Chinese exhibitors had experienced rather poor treatment at the 1904 St. Louis exposition and were "thoroughly disgusted with all Expositions."[91] Officials were able to persuade a few private interests to bring their exhibits to Portland and constructed the Oriental Exhibits Building to house largely traditional arts and crafts, like Japanese silks and ebony furniture, teakwood boxes from China, and woven rugs made in India.[92] In addition, the publicity department informed fairgoers that they could enjoy tea at the Japanese Village, a pagoda-style concession sandwiched between a haunted castle and the Siberian Railway exhibit in the fair's amusement area, "The Trail."[93] Taking note of Japan's sinking of the Russian fleet, advertisements for the concession claimed that the exhibit would also show "the habits, customs, and industries of that remarkable and picturesque people."[94] In the end, though, as much as they had hoped to position Portland as the leading economic player in the emerging Asian market, LCE officials failed to deliver. China's reluctance to participate in American expositions and an unfortunate war in 1905 left fairgoers somewhat disappointed and Portland officials frustrated.

Fortunes had changed by the time Seattle officials opened the gates to the Alaska-Yukon-Pacific Exposition four years later. Japan demonstrated its new status as a world power by establishing a strong presence in Seattle, which was quite welcomed by local leaders. By 1909 Japan was Seattle's leading Asian trading partner, and businessmen from both nations wished to cultivate this lucrative relationship. The Far East nation not only built an impressive exhibit, but also sent numerous civic and business leaders and several naval ships to the Puget Sound fair.[95] Exposition directors warmly welcomed Japanese exhibitors, dignitaries, and prominent businessmen, never failing to praise their Asian partners. Washington governor Marion E. Hay, for example, remarked at an opening night banquet that Japan's "marvelous and unprecedented development appeals to us with peculiar force."[96] Similarly, the commissioner general to the AYPE for Japan, Hajime Ota, spoke positively about the fair and the important trade relations between his country and the United States.[97] Describing the visit of Japanese businessmen, the Seattle Chamber of Commerce official journal summed up best the meaning of the exposition:

> TRADE MEANS PEACE
> To see once is worth a thousand hearings
> Let the business men of America and Japan know each other[98]

Kind words were not the only way the Seattle fair demonstrated the importance of Japan to the Far West. When ships from the Japanese navy visited the city in early June, AYPE directors declared "Japanese Navy Day," which featured local children singing Japanese songs and a thirty-piece Japanese concert band.[99] Even the exposition's architecture gave a nod to Japan. One AYPE promotional pamphlet, for example, explained that the fairground's entrance combined "totem poles and a modern adaptation of the architectural style of China and Japan." Japanese lanterns hung from ropes connecting the poles, while at the entrance of the Pay Streak, visitors encountered a pagoda roof in "what might be termed 'Jap-Alaskan' in style of architecture."[100] The AYPE's celebration of everything Japanese culminated in Japan Day in early September, and the fair's publicity department left no stone unturned, spending eight thousand dollars to decorate the grounds with Japanese banners, lanterns, and other artifacts. Japanese dignitaries were paraded through city streets on their way to the fairgrounds, where thousands of Japanese residents from throughout the Pacific Northwest greeted them. Festivities continued well into the night, ending with a "brilliant display of special Japanese fireworks at the foot of the Pay Streak."[101]

The friendly relations with Japan paid off handsomely for the AYPE. A fair publicity piece advertised that "Seattle has been the first friend of Nippon on the Pacific Slope. Japan has reciprocated in some measure by installing at the Alaska-Yukon-Pacific Exposition such an exhibit as it has made nowhere else."[102] In contrast to the Lewis and Clark fair, the Seattle exhibit promised a complete history of Japan from the days of the samurai to the "new Japan the industrial giant."[103] Fairgoers, for example, could explore the nation's feudal era and then see examples of its agricultural and manufactured products alongside models of its warships and contemporary armaments. So impressive was this display that the *New York Times* suggested that it put "all other foreign exhibits combined completely in the shade."[104] Before visitors left the fairgrounds, they could witness another side of Japanese life on the Pay Streak's "Street of Tokio" or at the Japanese Village, where dainty geishas served tea in a beautiful tea garden and "Japanese coolies" labored in a rice field.[105]

Balancing the traditional understanding of Japan, however distorted, with evidence of its emerging economic and political power enabled AYPE publicity directors to realize their goals. Yet these same officials would likely agree that the fair failed to meet the same expectations for China. Still a couple of years shy of its nationalist revolution, China's contributions to the AYPE differed little from the Portland fair four years earlier. "China's representation," one publicity pamphlet acknowledged, "is altogether on the Pay Streak."[106] The Far East government, for example, refused to sponsor an official exhibit, leaving local Chinese residents to raise the funds to construct and operate the fair's Chinese Village. Ah King, a Seattle businessman, traveled to China to collect goods and artifacts to display at the Pay Streak exhibit. Located next to a Ferris wheel, the village included a temple, a tea room, and a theatre.[107] Drawing on traditional Chinese architecture, the exhibit also "reproduced a street of Pekin [*sic*], with its shops, restaurant, theatres, and other features."[108] Seattle's Chinese community also helped stage a China Day at the exposition replete with a parade featuring a Chinese dragon, a luncheon, official speeches, and late-night fireworks display.[109] While the AYPE presented little to help visitors envision the economic opportunities that the Chinese markets offered, local Chinese residents, relying on common exotic tropes, did their best to leave fairgoers with some positive view of China.

Advertisement for the Alaska-Yukon-Pacific Exposition Chinese Village, which was organized by local Chinese-American leader Ah King. The village featured Chinese performers. *Museum of History and Industry, Seattle, Alaska-Yukon-Pacific Exposition Collection, 2006.3.38.*

Local Prejudices

Local elites may have appreciated Ah King's contribution to the AYPE, but many other Seattle residents expressed less charitable opinions of Asians and Asian Americans. Describing what visitors would discover at the Alaska-Yukon-Pacific Exposition, a national magazine revealed the prejudice and racist sentiments that Asian-Americans confronted daily. Explaining the meaning of the fair's official title, the author stated that "Pacific" referred to those peoples inhabiting the far reaches of that great ocean, including the "slant-eyed Chinamen, gazing about always in their childlike innocence of manner[,] . . . the dusky natives of the Pacific Islands," and the "sturdy little brown men of Japan."[110] Racist views like this were not limited to national observers. While awaiting the arrival of a Japanese trade delegation less than two years before the fair opened, AYPE vice president J.H. McGraw declared: "While we all admire the Japanese, we can not [*sic*] for a moment approve of their becoming citizens of the republic."[111] Segregated into racial enclaves, Seattle's Chinese and Japanese residents knew quite well that it would take more than uplifting words and parades to overcome long-held and often virulent anti-Asian feelings.

Seattle's Asian residents witnessed firsthand the damaging impact of such racial hostility. In the early 1880s, Congress passed the Chinese Exclusion Act, severely restricting Chinese immigration to the United States. A few years later, anti-Chinese feelings erupted on the streets of Seattle when a group of white workers marched some three hundred Chinese residents to the docks and put more than half of them on a ship bound for San Francisco.[112] By the early twentieth century, renewed anti-Asian anger fixated on the growing Japanese population on the Pacific Slope. In 1905 San Francisco labor leaders, for example, formed the Japanese and Korean Exclusion League, which later was rechristened the Asiatic Exclusion League (AEL). Mirroring earlier efforts that culminated in the Chinese Exclusion Act, the organization aimed to restrict Asian immigration and further marginalize Asian Americans. Wishing to avoid the humiliation that China experienced when the United States enacted the 1882 immigration act, Japanese officials agreed to restrict the emigration of laborers in the 1907 Gentlemen's Agreement.[113] Despite Japan's action, the international convention of the Asiatic Exclusion League of North America met the following year in Seattle to mobilize against the "Oriental Peril" and call for stronger action.[114] A "Memorial to Congress" demanded "absolute exclusion of Japanese, Koreans, and Chinese from American shores" and threatened to "take the law in their own hands" if Congress failed to act.[115]

Reactions to Prejudice

The decision to host this hostile convention a little more than a year before the opening of the AYPE troubled Seattle officials. Japan's participation in the fair was central to its success, and anything that threatened to derail it could cost the city dearly. City leaders were quick to confront any anti-Japanese activity. The Seattle Commercial Club, for example, passed a resolution urging Seattle citizens to show "their civilization and good manners at all times in dealing with our transpacific neighbors" and avoid "any expression of blind race prejudice."[116] Similarly, in response to a national magazine article that claimed that people on the West Coast hated the Japanese, the *Seattle Post-Intelligencer* stated that while that might the case in San Francisco, there was no Japanese problem in the Pacific Northwest.[117] Besides deflecting anti-Japanese actions, some Seattle leaders publicly praised the Asian nation. Judge Thomas Burke, for example, maintained that when Japan hosted an exposition in 1917, the world would be "taught the arts of industry and commerce." More importantly, he added, the Tokyo exposition "will do what all international expositions do—bring the people of the earth together and wipe out prejudice."[118] Burke and many fair directors believed that the AYPE could be a step in this direction in promoting more tolerance.

Complicating efforts to leave fairgoers with a good impression of the Far East was the fact that Portland and Seattle contained sizable Asian American populations: Chinese and Japanese Americans lived and worked in these cities, shaping their history, economy, politics, and urban distinctiveness. While they may have resided in enclaves separate from whites, unlike Native Americans—who were often housed on reservations many miles from Anglo settlements—Asians lived and worked in close proximity to whites. They shared the same ground and crossed paths nearly every day. Fair directors could not ignore their presence at the expositions, and moreover, they often depended on local Asian residents to help organize the exhibits and festivals that celebrated their ancestral homelands. Furthermore, the use or exploitation of local Asian populations to promote the fairs sometimes extended to their neighborhoods. For those willing to venture beyond the gates and walls of the exposition, publicity officials promised fairgoers the unique opportunity to explore a mysterious and exotic world.

For Lewis and Clark Exposition officials the decision to feature the Orient meant that they had to address both popular opinions of China, as well as the approximately six thousand Chinese residing in the Portland. By the time the exposition's gates swung open, two decades of anti-Asian flare-ups had left the local Chinese population somewhat segregated from the surrounding white community. Publicity officials' advertising campaign mirrored the strategies they crafted for Native Americans. Relying on exotic tropes, promotional materials emphasized the mysterious nature of Portland's Chinatown, yet suggested that its inhabitants, like Indians, could not escape the powerful impulses of Americanization. Descriptions of what visitors could expect if they ventured to the local Chinatown only underscored the strange and the alien, including long queues and "slippered feet."[119] Assuming the inferiority of Chinese culture, fair officials nevertheless intimated that China's future was not hopeless, and thus attempted to temper the exotic images. A souvenir guidebook declared that one only had to visit Chinatown to find proof "the Chinese so varied in condition, so truly heathen and so truly Americanized."[120] While exotic and mysterious, Chinatowns, fair officials suggested, should not be feared but better viewed as laboratories of Americanization.

Hawai'i and the Philippines

Whether it was local Asian American populations or trade opportunities in the Far East, Pacific Northwest officials tried to promote the positive while undercutting more negative impressions of Asia. As America's new lake, the Pacific Ocean seemingly bestowed unmatched economic opportunities as well as contact with new and different peoples. While China and Japan had rather prominent roles at the two Pacific Northwest expositions, two lesser-known Pacific locales, the Philippines and Hawai'i, also proved popular with visitors. Unlike the Far East powers, the two island nations were American possessions. Lacking political independence and with little obvious economic allure, fair publicity departments nonetheless lavished some attention on the inhabitants of the nation's newest possessions. Connecting these American imperial holdings with the Far West helped fair officials remind the public how important these host cities were to national imperial designs in the Pacific. Exposition brochures, guidebooks, and advertisements underscored in very different ways the primitiveness of the Philippines and Hawai'i. Passive and exotic, Hawaiians presented a simpler and nostalgic lifestyle in contrast to the energetic and frenetic pace of modern, industrial America. Filipino primitiveness, however, was quite different and marked by supposed savagery and barbarism.

Hawaiian villages were a staple at the Pacific Coast expositions. Acquired at the end of the nineteenth century, Hawai'i often served as an antidote to the chaotic lifestyle of modern, urban society: the land of pineapples, hula dancing, and the ukulele, the Pacific island territory offered an escape for those looking for a less complicated existence. National leaders, however, saw Hawai'i as instrumental in the growing American influence in the Pacific. Speaking at the opening day of the Lewis and Clark Exposition, Vice President Charles Fairbanks told the large gathering that Hawai'i was "acquired for strategic purposes and demanded in the interest of expanding commerce."[121] National leaders likewise recognized its strategic importance. In announcing its support for Seattle's fair, the House Committee on Industrial Arts and Expositions stated that the Pacific Ocean would have a significant impact on the nation's commercial future, and the acquisition of Hawai'i had made the Pacific "become of vital importance to the nation."[122] Despite its place in the nation's imperial designs, exposition directors included Hawaiian exhibits less for their martial importance and more for their exotic appeal.

Just weeks before their city's fair opened, Seattle officials announced plans for a large Hawaiian exhibit. Island natives, the *Seattle Times* stated, would be "transplanted in Seattle with all their romantic customs, their homes and their everyday manner of life . . . for the education of the hundreds of thousands who have never tasted of the delights of a tour of the 'Cannibal Isles.' "[123] Whatever fair they attended, tourists could visit concessions surrounded by lush tropical gardens and see "Dark-skinned beauties from the Cannibal Isles serve delicious tropical fruits" accompanied by "singing and music day and night by island musicians."[124] Exposition directors assured visitors an island experience that was as educational as it was relaxing.

As fairgoers sipped sweet tropical drinks to the sounds of ukuleles, they may have pondered the educational message that fair officials promised. At first blush, visitors to the Lewis and Clark Exposition may have concluded that little distinguished native Hawaiians from

Indians, Filipinos, and Alaskan Eskimos, since exposition officials had placed their exhibits in the United States government display located on a peninsula on the fairground's lake. Concentrating these ethnic groups together in this manner reflected not only the darker skin color they shared, but also that they possessed a different relationship to the nation as wards of the government.[125] However, government and exposition officials also recognized that Americanization efforts had succeeded in many ways with both Indians and Hawaiians. Declaring Hawaiians "robust and happy as a race," Smithsonian exhibits at the AYPE provided evidence of American "civilizing" success following the nation's expansion westward to and then across the Pacific.[126]

Hula dancers and young Native American girls playing basketball and singing patriotic songs at the Pacific Coast expositions likely helped Americans accept the racial implications of American imperialism. However, not all those under American sway were apparently as ready or prepared to join the "civilized" world. Despite the relatively easy capture of the Philippines from Spain, the United States quickly faced a defiant independence movement in their new island possession. Resistance to American rule seemed only to confirm to many that the Filipinos were too primitive and backward to rule themselves. Moreover, the strategic importance of the Philippines in the Asia-Pacific region demanded a more permanent American presence. By the time Portland opened its fair in 1905, the United States had firmly established itself as an imperial power. Whereas Hawaiians and Native Americans appeared to show much promise in terms of civilization, fairgoers would encounter a starkly different depiction of Filipinos.

THE PHILIPPINE VILLAGE

The Lewis and Clark Exposition not only permitted visitors to reflect upon the larger significance of America's influence in the Pacific, but it also afforded them the unique opportunity to confirm and justify American rule over its new imperial possession. Success in Asia, however, hinged on the United States' control of the Philippines, which would serve as a "stepping-stone" to China.[127] American goals in the Pacific further enhanced the growing importance of the Far West.

Exposition publicity departments paid particular attention to the Philippines, yet in doing so left a troubling image of the new American territory. Unlike the exhibit constructed by the new world power Japan, which the *Evening Telegram* referred to as a "rising and progressive nation," the Philippine Village displayed not artifacts and industrial goods—but people.[128]

First introduced at the 1898 Omaha Fair, the Philippine Village attempted to reconstruct a "typical" Filipino settlement on the fairgrounds inhabited by indigenous tribes brought directly from the new American possession. Philippine territorial governor William Howard Taft urged Louisiana Purchase Exposition officials in 1904 to include a display of Filipinos so as to introduce the new possession to the American public and expose Filipinos to American customs and culture.[129] Before the gates closed at St. Louis, Portland's director of exhibits, Henry Dosch, impressed by the financial windfall of its Philippine display, wrote to LCE president H. W. Goode that "we must have the Philippine Exhibit and the villages."[130] After months of political and logistical intrigue, Portland officials proudly welcomed the opening of their own Philippine Village in September 1905.

As originally conceived, exposition officials planned to display five Filipino villages encompassing some three hundred inhabitants. Each settlement would represent different indigenous tribes from the "artistic" Visayans to "dog-eating" Igorots. After finding it difficult to secure so many villagers, fair directors settled on fifty Igorots. Immediately press releases and newspaper reports sensationalized the arrival of the "band of head-hunting, dog-eating Igorrotes [*sic*] from the Island of Luzon."[131] The *Washington Post*, for example, highlighted the head hunting and dog eating associated with the Igorots, referring to them as the "lowest in civilization of the inhabitants of Uncle Sam's domain."[132] Readers were hard pressed to find articles or brochures about the Igorots that did not refer to dog eating, head hunting, or nudity. The *Evening Telegram* simply concluded that Igorots were "repulsive, sickening and disgusting."[133]

The Philippine Village represented more than just a sensational and voyeuristic exhibit assembled to titillate visitors and secure a tidy profit for the fair corporation. As Rydell has suggested, exhibits like these

Postcard picture of the entrance to the Igorrote Village, which housed tribal members of the Igorote people of the Philippines. The concession aimed to show the Igorote as primitive and needing American supervision. *University of Washington Libraries, Special Collections, NEG UW 40293.*

helped "world's fairs provide a partial but crucial explanation for the interpenetration and popularization of evolutionary ideas about race and progress."[134] Fair publicity materials may not have offered such a sophisticated interpretation of these exhibits, but they did help ensure that audiences recognize the need for an American presence in the Philippines. From a safe distance, visitors watched the "head-hunters and dog-eaters from Uncle Sam's island domain" and confirmed their inherent belief in the superiority of American civilization. More importantly, the image of half-clothed, dark-skinned Filipinos provided powerful evidence that American control of the Philippines was not only beneficial but an outright necessity.[135] Standing outside the village, American visitors witnessed firsthand proof of the nation's manifest destiny and confirmation of its imperial designs.

Juxtaposed against the Philippine Village "dog-eaters" at the Lewis and Clark Exposition, images of "tamed" Indians performing concerts provided unvarnished evidence of how Americanization efforts could propel the uncivilized up the evolutionary ladder. In this case, the Portland fair suggested that the conquest of the American West was complete. Yet fair publicity materials did not present the Filipinos in the same way. The Philippine Village now reminded white Americans of the tepees and huts of Indian villages they had read about in dime novels; the uncultured Filipino replaced the once uncivilized but now reformed Indian.[136] Describing the nation's new wards and their place in the prevailing racial hierarchy, one reporter suggested that Filipinos "look as intelligent as the average Indian."[137] Visitors could turn their eyes from the half-dressed Filipinos and look to Indian girls playing basketball and behold the future of the new territory. Holding onto the Philippines, then, was not as dangerous or risky as anti-imperialists argued.[138] For Portland and other West Coast port cities, such conclusions would ensure that they assume a more significant role in fulfilling American policy in the Pacific.

After the LCE gates were locked and the Igorrote Village dismantled, fair president H. W. Goode explained the value of the exhibit: "The representation of primitive man as exhibited in the Igorrote Village has not only been a distinct drawing card at this Exposition, but has justly regarded as a fine anthropology and ethnological display, of a high educative and scientific value."[139] Recognizing the economic and educational potential of the Igorots, the exhibit organizers took the village on the road in the following year to Los Angeles and Chicago before returning to the Pacific Coast in 1909 to operate their concession at the Seattle fair.[140]

AYPE leaders likewise embraced the Igorrote Village for its educational qualities. Admitting that the American public possessed little knowledge of the "little brown brother," one exposition guidebook stated that the exhibit allowed visitors to "observe their social, civic, and domestic life, and that they, in turn, may absorb the atmosphere of enlightened civilization." The publicity piece added that the U.S. Government Building displayed other features of the Philippines that would demonstrate the political and industrial promise of Filipinos and encouraged Americans to support the government's "benevolent policies."[141] In June 1909 the former governor of the Bontoc Province, home to the Igorote tribe, visited the AYPE and spoke about the concrete efforts undertaken by the United States to civilize the remote region of the Philippines.[142] Seattle residents did not have to rely on government officials alone to confirm the benefits of American imperial policy. Upon returning from a tour of Asia, prominent Seattle leader Judge Thomas Burke defended U.S. colonialism, claiming that "[t]here is not another colonizing nation in the world dealing with the people in the disinterested, enlightened and statesmanlike manner which the United States treats the Philippines."[143] Seattle leaders confidently believed that after a trip to the AYPE, visitors would agree that after nearly a decade, the nation's new possession was making strides but still needed American guidance and governance.

Exposition officials made sure that fairgoers could witness directly how Filipinos benefitted from American rule, rather than depending solely on the opinions of prominent leaders or the press. Displaying the products and industries of the nation's new possession, the Philippines Exhibit showed "the evolution of the islands from the 'dark days' to present, marked by the introduction of American customs and American devices."[144] One section, for example, included a map accompanied by statistics indicating the growth in railroad mileage, while another housed minerals, textiles, and other products indigenous to the Philippines.[145] The *Coast* magazine described how visitors could also learn about the different tribes inhabiting the island possession, from the more "primitive" Negritos and Igorots to the more advanced and Christianized Tagalog tribe.[146] A few years earlier, the Portland fair also included exhibits demonstrating the Philippines' commercial potential and evidence that the American education efforts produced results, yet the sensational publicity surrounding the Igorrote Village drowned out the fair's rather meager attempt to expose another side of the Philippines.[147] The AYPE might have tried to provide a more balanced perspective, but in the end it likewise struggled to overcome the lurid fascination with dog eaters and headhunters.

Looking back, one should not be surprised if fairgoers failed to see or appreciate the complexity of life and society in the Philippines. Publicity officials could not ignore the paying public's fascination with stories and pictures of "dog eaters." The AYPE *Official Guide*, for example, featured a section on the exhibit of "Wild People" from the island possession. Along the fair's "Pay Streak" loomed an attraction of "these strange head-hunting, dog-eating people" who were in "the childhood of a race, a wild, uncultured people."[148] Likewise, a local paper printed an eight-page advertisement announcing the display of "Fifty Barbaric Wild People" at the Igorrote Village, while another published a story about Igorots eating a dog left at the exhibit.[149] During the summer, a controversy arose when AYPE directors debated whether to force the Igorot men to wear pants. Some residents, complaining that the Igorrote Village was indecent and immoral, demanded that fair directors address the matter. Local newspapers poked fun at the request, including one cartoon that depicted an Igorot male appearing like a monkey in a tree resisting AYPE president J. E. Chilberg's attempt to hand him a pair of pants while screaming, "Here, Be Decent." If the pants issue did not remind readers of the Igorots' primitiveness, the image of a dog in a pot hung above a fire imprinted with the word "Dinner" no doubt confirmed the villagers' barbarity.[150]

Not all of those who hailed from the island possession objected to the Igorot exhibit. Writing to a local Seattle newspaper, one Filipino high school student challenged opponents of the Igorot Village, arguing that the exhibit offered Filipino residents the rare opportunity to see a tribe that even few native Filipinos had laid eyes on, since the Igorots hailed from a very remote region of the Philippines. The student claimed that he and his family visited the exhibit weekly, that "it is an education to us" and an "interesting place for students of science."[151] Exposition directors seconded the Igorot Village's educational value and likely welcomed the student's public support. More importantly, the controversy brought a great deal of attention to what Chilberg called "the Exposition's more valuable and interesting assets."[152] The village was indeed an asset. Attracting customers helped secure the fair's bottom line, while its larger message helped ensure Seattle's place in fulfilling America's role in the world.

⁜ RECOGNIZING THE GROWING IMPORTANCE OF THEIR region, westerners labored to articulate a clear and effective identity that would help ensure a prosperous future for the Far West. Already challenged by popular images of the West as "wild and woolly," fair publicity departments had to overcome another more complicate obstacle: race. Exposition directors understood that Native Americans were inextricably linked to the region in the public mind, yet they could be a double-edged sword. Selling the Far West meant catering to the exotic desires of eastern consumers, but without further contributing to popular representations of a rough and savage West. Showcasing Indian progress allowed exposition officials to include "primitive Indians," all the while demonstrating that they posed no threat by offering competing stories of success from government Indian schools. Mysterious and exotic Asian peoples may have also tantalized eastern visitors; however, their place at the Pacific Coast fairs was complicated by the needs of American foreign policy. The fortunes of the Japanese and Chinese at these expositions shifted as their status in the world and their potential as trading partners evolved during the first two decades of the twentieth century. Filipinos, however, emerged as pawns in a larger national debate about the United States' imperial aspirations. While the expositions may have embraced—or at least acknowledged—the region's racial diversity, in the end, their inability to present a clear and effective view of the Far West's complex social relations may have only confounded the American public's perceptions of the Pacific West.

Panama-California Exposition controversial concession located in "The Isthmus" fun zone commemorating the colorful and bawdy side of the California gold rush. *San Diego History Center, Photo ID #79_111.*

6 ⊱ SELLING THE PROMISE OF THE FAR WEST

SAN DIEGO, SAN FRANCISCO, AND THE AMERICAN SOUTHWEST

By the time San Diego and San Francisco opened the gates to their fairs in early 1915, perceptions of the Far West had improved little since the closure of the Alaska-Yukon-Pacific Exposition five years earlier. No doubt the two Pacific Northwest fairs had introduced much of the nation to the wonders and opportunities on the Pacific slope. Millions of Americans, by personal visits or by reading literature about the two earlier expositions, had learned about the rapidly growing region. Yet despite these efforts, novels and Wild West shows still contributed to popular misconceptions about the West. City leaders and fair directors in the two California cities believed that a sound marketing campaign that highlighted the economic, social, and cultural advantages of western living might finally help change popular notions of the Far West. Demonstrating that it was as progressive and sophisticated as the rest of the country, California officials believed, would encourage fairgoers to reimagine a new West.

⊱ Mixed Messages

More than a decade into the twentieth century, many Americans still had a rather fuzzy understanding of the area. The two Pacific Northwest fairs tried to educate the public that the region was not what they might read in a Zane Grey novel or what they saw at Buffalo Bill Cody's Wild West Show. Nevertheless, negative opinions about the West still plagued the region on the eve of World War I. As a San Diego newspaper explained, there "were many things associated with the city by the bay that needed explaining, and other things that called for suggestion, in order that the world might know the truth, not concerning the San Diego of the past, but more especially the city of the present."[1] Why "things" needed explaining could be summed up by a 1914 *Sunset Magazine* article, which claimed that "Heretofore the Southwest has been considered a kind of national sand pile especially designed for invalids, *pueblo* Indians [original italics], cowpunchers and prospectors, a parched waste aggravated by copper smelters and punctuated by an occasional green oasis."[2] If true, this assessment of how the rest of the nation viewed the Far West required California leaders to design their expositions carefully. Fair directors wisely chose exhibits and advertising messages that indicated that the Southwest represented future opportunity and growth and not where one lived their last days.

Removing the haziness that masked the real West was difficult enough, yet the Pacific Coast fairs also contributed to it by the mixed messages they presented to visitors in the fairs' programs, displays, and exhibits. Historian Robert G. Athearn has suggested that at times, western cities did not want to relinquish completely their colorful frontier image. *Sunset Magazine*, the Far West's premier promotional publication, contributed to the contradictory image when commenting on an infamous Utah manhunt for a notorious outlaw named Raphael "Red" Lopez, who murdered a miner in a Utah copper mine.[3] The well-known manhunt, the magazine claimed, "shows that the Wild West has not yet been wholly tamed." While at first confirming this popular view of the region, the article then refuted this misconception when stating that tourists did not have to worry about encountering the Wild West because "Outside the moving-picture show it takes time, money and effort to reach the untamed remnants of the Far West."[4] Consciously or unconsciously, western boosters sometimes undercut their own marketing campaigns.

Like the coastal cities to the north, San Francisco and San Diego could not help but contribute to this distorted view of the West.

Exposition officials' efforts to cast the Far West as modern and safe sometimes acquiesced to the profits that the bygone days of cowboys, Indians, and gunfights generated. A few months before the Panama-California fair's opening, for example, the Wells Fargo Express Company announced its plans for an exhibit that would spotlight the company's role in the "history of the conquering and winning of the West."[5] Fair officials later finalized an agreement to bring a Wild West show to "The Isthmus," the exposition's amusement area. The show not only shared this fun zone with restaurants, novelty exhibits, and dancing girls, but also the Painted Desert exhibit, a large display of Native Americans living in what officials portrayed as their natural surroundings.[6] Even Buffalo Bill Cody himself visited the PCE in the spring of 1915, accompanied by a few Indians from his show. The showman and "a befeathered allotment from the north," as the *Santa Fe Magazine* described his Indian colleagues, toured the Painted Desert, where they learned about Pueblo Indian culture.[7]

Despite an exposition that purported to celebrate the height of the civilized world, San Francisco's Panama-Pacific International fair similarly advertised shows that evoked images of a wild and untamed West. In late April, Buffalo Bill Cody, for example, brought his Wild West show to downtown San Francisco. Wanting to ensure that fairgoers did not miss out, PPIE directors invited a competing company, the Miller Brothers' 101 Ranch, to perform its western-themed show at the fair.[8] Hailing from Oklahoma, the Miller brothers toured the nation entertaining audiences with a variety of acts, ranging from stagecoach hold-ups and horse thefts to spectacular Indian battles. Advertisements for the 101 Ranch alleged that it possessed the "World's Greatest Indian Village" and that fairgoers could watch special performances of "Indian War Dances" and "The Attack by the Indians."[9] Attendance at the 101 Ranch show was so strong that, according to the PPIE's official historian, fair directors paid the Miller brothers to stage the show for free "to relieve the rather serious aspect of the more ambitious and educational features along the joy street."[10] Whether gunfights or Indian battles actually balanced the serious, educational exhibits, the popular shows nevertheless were inconsistent with the fairs' marketing strategy of presenting a modern, civilized American West.

Besides the two California expositions exploiting the popular images of the cowboy and Indian West, they also reached back into the state's colorful and unruly past by including gold rush–era performances. Without a doubt, one of the most controversial exhibits or acts that entertained fairgoers at both the San Diego and San Francisco fairs was the '49 Camp. First created for the 1894 California Midwinter Exposition, the concession sought to re-create a typical mining camp replete with dance hall girls, gambling saloons, and frontier gunfights.[11] The '49 Camp, historian Barbara Berglund has argued, "presented the fair-going public with a nostalgic version of California history" that played on "already familiar tropes about 'the wild west.'"[12] Twenty years later, little had changed, as the same elements went on to dominate the scenery at the recreated gold-rush camps.[13] The rather unsavory climate of the PPIE '49 Camp, however, quickly attracted the attention of local reformers who expressed concern with the fair's promotion of such immorality. Debate over the concession's future would occupy fair directors for several months.

San Francisco officials struggled mightily to tame the '49 Camp, forcing it to close several times during the fair's run. A 1915 article in the journal *Social Hygiene* claimed that women were hired to dance with male customers and that prostitutes frequented the camp's dance halls. It likened the activities at the camp to the "pattern of the Barbary Coast," San Francisco's notorious red-light district.[14] In late February, the *San Francisco Chronicle* reported that the '49 Camp had been indefinitely closed until it could provide an environment that did not offend visitors. Referring to the venue as the "real bad boy of the Zone," the exposition's official historian stated that gambling likely took place on its grounds, admitting that it would not be a realistic re-creation if games of chance were not present. Unable or unwilling to portray gold-rush California without the lucrative vice offerings, the '49 Camp closed and reopened several times during the fair's run until it was permanently shut down in October.[15]

Down the coast, San Diego's '49 Camp sparked a similar conflict with local authorities. Dubbed by its operator "The Torrid Zone of Pleasure," the '49 Camp opened its door in April 1915 and quickly became one of the more popular concessions on "The Isthmus."[16]

According to the *Santa Fe Magazine,* the camp "was jammed until early morning with curious easterners participating in the dancing, the gaming and other activities of the frontier display of early western life."[17] Within weeks San Diego's district attorney, D. V. Mahoney, arrested the camp's manger on gambling charges, and the following month, local officials closed the bank that supplied the scrip used at the gaming tables. The venue continued to offer other amusements, including the dance halls, yet without the gambling, attendance declined. Camp operators challenged the city's action in court seeking an injunction to prohibit the city from interfering with its gambling operations, but in September a local judge denied their request.[18]

The Future of the American Republic

Wild West shows and gold rush camp exhibits that drew upon the region's past may have provided entertainment that fairgoers could not resist, yet San Francisco and San Diego leaders never forgot that their expositions' primary purpose was to help visitors reimagine a new and modern West. As the president of the California Society of New York told an audience in 1913, California "is the best place on earth . . . because it offers to all an opportunity of bettering one's position in life, no matter be he laborer, tradesman, or manufacturer."[19] In short, boosters claimed that only the Far West offered every class of citizen the necessities for a successful life. Spurred by a sense of regional rivalry, San Diego leaders went a step further declaring that the West, not the East, represented the future of the American republic: "There is an old theory that civilization and education of all sorts move westward, and the west must learn from the east. Next year it will be found that the far west has produced an idea which the east must learn."[20] The Panama-California Exposition thus promised to usher in a new "empire in the making, and tomorrow must be an empire in reality."[21] Like Portland and Seattle, California officials concluded that the Far West represented nothing less than a new stage in history, which promised hope and opportunity for those seeking a new start or wishing to fulfill unrealized dreams.

Tying the American West to the nation's future was a central theme of both California fairs' marketing campaigns. One Pacific-Panama

International Exposition publication, for example, declared that the completion of the Panama Canal would transform global trade routes and ensure that the Pacific Coast would command a greater place in the nation.[22] Describing how the PPIE would reshape trade and commerce, one San Francisco attorney concluded that "[w]hat is true of San Francisco, in a larger sense is true of California, and in a greater degree, of the entire West."[23] Americans, however, would not have to wait years or decades to realize the region's power. As the *San Diego Union* put it, the West was assuming "its part in the leading role, during the generation now already upon us, in making this Twentieth Century the brightest of all centuries since civilization began."[24] Evidence that the Far West was ready and able to shoulder its new status, some leaders believed, was undeniable.

Illustrating that the Far West's future was bright, PCE director of exploitation Winfield Hogaboom penned an article for *Sunset Magazine* entitled, "Looking Into The Future." In it, he noted that only seven million people inhabited the greater southwest portion of the United States. That region, Hogaboom boldly proclaimed, could easily embrace twenty-five million people and expand business by fivefold.[25] To this end, San Diego fair directors devised an advertising strategy around the concept of "processes, not finished products," which emphasized how things were produced rather than just shelves of finished products.[26] As one pamphlet put it: "It will present human life, not in repose, but in action—gripping, throbbing human activities."[27] Describing the larger purpose of this approach, an *Overland Monthly* article suggested that San Diego fair directors were committed to "showing progress still to be made."[28] Whether it was large swaths of undeveloped farmland or the exciting trade potential of Asia, Pacific Coast leaders believed that their region would no doubt command the next stage in the American narrative.

While economic opportunity was central to the Far West's optimistic outlook, boosters and residents bragged that the region also offered a more civilized lifestyle. Like Portland and Seattle, California leaders believed that it was more than just economic opportunity that guaranteed a better life in the Far West. Speaking about the impending Panama-California Exposition, fair president G. A. Davidson averred that the new population attracted by the San Diego event would "inaugurate a new kind of civilization on the shores of the Pacific."[29] Davidson and other fair officials suggested that the recipe for this unique "civilization" resulted from combining the distinctive culture of the Far West with the special breed of people who would choose to settle in California. Remoteness and the prohibitive cost of transportation to the Pacific Coast meant that only those with "high plane of intelligence and financial ability" contributed to the region's "select population."[30] The opening of the Panama Canal and the superior character of western residents, San Francisco attorney Gavin McNab concluded, would bring to the West "new life, hope, a new world, a higher civilization, rich in usefulness and happiness."[31]

Public speeches and fair marketing materials confirmed boosters' belief that their new homeland encouraged and rewarded boldness. The recent settlement of the Far West meant that residents were freed from deep-seated political and cultural institutions, which often dampened innovation or novel ideas in the long-settled region east of the Mississippi River. A San Francisco water engineer explained that "the splendid class of pioneers who settled the West have built up social and political institutions which are attractive to thinking people."[32] For many Californians, this was more than mere boasting. Spurning traditionally conservative leadership, residents elected Hiram Johnson to be California governor in 1911, making California one of the leading progressive states in the nation.[33] Far from being a handicap, fair officials proposed that the Far West's recent settlement and relative youth cultivated a distinctive regional culture that offered newcomers a more promising future.

The upshot of the West's unique values and citizenship was something even more ephemeral: happiness. The *San Diego Union*, for example, declared that eastern visitors to the city's fair would leave with the "conviction in their own mind that this is the place in all the world where they can live easiest and best, attain the highest culture and the most happiness."[34] State leaders were not shy in identifying the source of the region's apparent bliss. *California Magazine* claimed that the "influence of the Western atmosphere, the broadness of the land, the freedom of life, and the health and vigor imparted by the air and by the cleanly lives of the inhabitants" helped ensure the region's state of happiness.[35] Encouraging Americans to visit the San Francisco fair, noted educator David Starr Jordan likened California to springtime.[36] Whether the West was truly a happier place is impossible to measure. No doubt not all westerners shared such sentiments, especially Japanese farmers in California encountering anti-alien legislation or Colorado coal miners facing off against Rockefeller's mining operations. Nevertheless, a nation wracked by social and economic conflict, growing bureaucratization, and by 1915, cries of war, seemed primed for messages of hope and happiness emanating from the California expositions.

The Panama Canal

Like the earlier Pacific Northwest fairs, San Diego and San Francisco officials suggested that their expositions would help unify a divided nation and help bridge the gap between West and East. Railroads may have helped promote national unity by overcoming the daunting distance that separated the two coasts, but it was the Panama Canal that promised to deliver that most perfect union Americans had sought since the birth of their nation. The completion of Panama's big ditch in 1914 would do more than just lessen the time of ocean travel. Western leaders argued that the canal would forge stronger ties between the Atlantic and the Pacific, improving trade and communication between the two coasts. As the PPIE welcome its first visitors, University of California president Benjamin Ide Wheeler maintained that the East and West were different and "wide apart," but that with the completion of the Panama Canal, the two "would be drawn closer together."[37] Hosting their respective fairs only months after the first ships passed through the new waterway, both PPIE and the PCE promotional campaigns rarely failed to highlight the canal's significance to the nation. Reminding readers that the Far West was central to reaping the canal's benefits, *California Magazine*, for example, explained that the Panama Canal meant that "America's position on the Pacific depends on the West."[38] If successful, the California expositions, with the aid of the Panama Canal, would help finish tying the knot of national unity.

The Panama Canal's completion guaranteed more concrete benefits beyond aspirations of national unity. By the second decade of the twentieth century, the Far West's future seemingly hinged on the material dreams the canal promised to deliver to the up-and-coming region. The canal, *California Magazine* averred, marked "one of the greatest movements of civilization—a mighty shifting of the world's commerce." The magazine added that if the grand waterway fulfilled the "world's hopes, the West will come into its own, and there will evolve a commerce, wealth, and prosperity, creating an empire second to none."[39] More specifically, explained J. E. Caine, secretary of the Commercial Club of Salt Lake, the canal's opening would "mean a great development to all the west" by delivering thousands of new European immigrants who would "develop idle acres" throughout the Far West.[40] Nearly a century after the Erie Canal ushered in a market revolution that made the Northeast the nation's economic powerhouse, it would be another canal located thousands of miles south of the United States that promised a new empire in the Far West.

That a new commercial empire would emerge on the Pacific Coast seemed a fait accompli to most western leaders. As historian Carl Abbott has argued, western cities and states, unlike the East, "have been differently placed, looking in four directions: still eastward to be sure but also westward across the Pacific, north to the Artic, and southward to Hispanic America."[41] The idea of an American empire looking east from the Pacific Coast was a key part of both California fairs' marketing campaigns. Homer S. King, a San Francisco banker and fair executive, explained that the Panama Canal's completion marked the beginning of an "era of progress that will make the Pacific the 'Twentieth Century Ocean.'" King also suggested that the new waterway signified the "realization of dreams of conquest" of the West and the beginning of the dominance of the Pacific.[42] PPIE's publicity chief went further, claiming that the West was a "great empire" that rivaled many of Europe's past kingdoms.[43] Perhaps less grandiose but no less bold, San Diego leaders predicted that the Panama Canal would insure that their city became an entrepôt for a larger "southwestern empire."[44] As the first American port north of Panama, San Diegans believed that new railroad lines would allow the city to capture the growing trade from the territory, extending in a semi-circle from the eastern border of New Mexico to as far north as central California.[45]

California officials may have shared the idea of a Pacific empire, but San Diego had much farther to go if the city was to achieve it. As the metropolis of the Pacific Coast, San Francisco, unlike the southern California exposition city, possessed the capital and commercial connections to exploit the windfall from the Panama Canal. Like Portland and Seattle, San Diego was smaller and less well known. Fair directors had to overcome these disadvantages by aggressively advertising the unique possibilities available to potential outside investors. One PCE official, for example, claimed that the Southern California fair would "present the golden opportunities for profitable investment awaiting the man with financial resources who will come from 'back East.'"[46] San Diego officials even nicknamed their event the "Opportunity Exposition," which aimed to point out the "limitless future opportunities of this great 'American Southwest.'" Visitors to the PCE, fair directors declared, would discover "this great 'Empire of Opportunity'" whose mineral holdings reportedly rivaled what the Spanish found when they encountered the Aztecs four centuries earlier.[47]

"Another 'Go West' Period"

Such bold embellishments from exposition promoters were an essential feature of booster strategies. Exploiting California's early history, *Sunset Magazine*, for example, likened the energy and opportunity of what it called "Another 'Go West' Period" to the 1849 California gold rush and the subsequent Comstock lode discovery.[48] Likewise, *California Magazine* concluded that the "golden opportunity of the Now is more alluring than any which beckoned men in the old days."[49] Cashing in on these opportunities apparently demanded little. Newspaper articles, exposition brochures, and speeches by prominent local leaders identified certain factors that would guarantee success. Speaking before Kern and Tulare county boosters, PCE president G. A. Davidson, for example, stated that California offered "unusually liberal chances to the man who is willing to build his happiness by an honest application of brain and brawn."[50] Like the stories of simple farmers awash in gold after a few days panning California streams, the California expositions pinpointed the unlimited opportunities awaiting capitalist and laborer alike if they chose to snatch the brass ring that was the Far West.

Exposition boosters, however, recognized the need to provide more than broad, amorphous promises of wealth and fortune. Central to the West's future success was the diversity of economic pursuits available to settlers, whatever their background or skill. California governor James N. Gillett, for example, announced that visitors would discover "millions of fertile acres, rich mineral lands, magnificent forests, and healthful climate."[51] More specifically, San Diego officials professed that its fair would demonstrate the "definite opportunity for the settler. That settler may be a farmer, or a merchant, or a manufacturer, or an artisan. Whatever he be, he can find in the Western Empire work for him to do." Pressing their case, Panama-California Exposition publicity directors advertised that the region's prospects extended beyond raw materials and offered "extraordinary advantages" in nearly every economic endeavor imaginable."[52] Whether a small businessman, farmer, or wealthy investor, the Far West promised opportunity and wealth, for all backgrounds or abilities.

California exposition officials provided ample evidence of economic activity to substantiate these bold assertions. Both San Diego and San Francisco's exposition publicity departments joined local chambers of commerce to present concrete proof that new settlers could achieve success. The Southern California Panama Expositions Commission, for example, published a sizable book detailing everything from the acreage of citrus production in Los Angeles County to manufacturing production in San Diego. The commission stated that more than forty thousand acres of orange, lemon, and grapefruit acreage together produced more than $10 million worth of fruit. Similarly, San Diego's 216 manufacturing firms had a total output that exceeded $14 million.[53] Furthermore, while most Americans likely recognized San Francisco's preeminence in the Far West, PPIE directors nevertheless reminded visitors of this regional powerhouse. One publication, for example, advertised that San Francisco's bank clearings nearly equaled the combined clearings of the next five largest coast cities. California's leading city, it declared, was "the wealthiest city on the Pacific Coast and the fifth wealthiest in the country."[54] Just like the earlier Pacific Northwest expositions, whether fairgoers toured the California fairs or just read about them in magazines and exposition brochures, they learned much about the economic opportunities awaiting them if they chose to relocate to the nation's western edge.

Farms and factories were not the only economic activities that western leaders referenced when celebrating the region's bright future. By the time the two California fairs opened their gates in 1915, the Pacific Ocean trade had assumed greater importance with the completion of the Panama Canal. Home to two of the best natural harbors on the West Coast, San Diego and San Francisco leaders believed their cities would benefit most from the new trade routes. Noting the timing and location of the San Francisco fair, a PPIE advertisement proclaimed that "the Exposition is fittingly placed on the shores of the Pacific, because of the new and immense importance which the nations of the Pacific area, under the stimulus of the Panama Canal, will now assume in the eyes of commerce."[55] Describing trade between the Atlantic and Pacific coasts that traveled across the Isthmus of Panama before the completion of the canal, *California Magazine* valued the various products—from iron and steel to fruits and canned salmon—at more than $131 million. By the end of the Panama Canal's first year of use, the magazine expected this trade to reach at least $150 million.[56]

Geography, San Diego leaders believed, favored their city in the competition for the expected increase in trade. Due to the city's proximity to the canal, San Diego businessmen asserted that if "the Pacific was going to be the theater of commerce," their harbor would emerge as one of the "principal ports of the world."[57] A *San Diego Union* editorial added that the Panama-California Exposition would help visitors recognize the commercial possibilities of the city's port by showcasing the economic potential of the surrounding hinterland that the harbor would serve. Fairgoers would leave with knowledge that San Diego possessed an "important seaport; an out port and entry port to rival any other on the Pacific coast."[58] The lucrative Pacific Ocean trade only bolstered Californians' confidence that the Far West offered nothing but promise and rewards for those who called it home.

Well-developed harbors and a new canal would have limited benefit if the Pacific Coast cities had little to trade. Local officials wanted to be more than just a transit site between Asia and the rest of the United States. To that end, California exposition officials advertised their sizable hinterlands that, if settled, could ensure the Far West's future. A PCE publicity piece, for example, stated that fair's purpose was to "direct to the manless land of the Great West the landless man."[59] Such abundance and fertility were essential to westerners' visions of their region. Yet the "immense resources of the West," especially the "vast acreage of unused lands," only needed settlers to realize the limitless opportunities and wealth the region had to offer.[60] The *San Francisco Chronicle* bluntly declared that the "commodity that California has to sell is land."[61] What made this marketing pitch that much more alluring was the belief that the vast western acreage was empty, virgin land just waiting for enterprising hands. PCE president G. A. Davidson, for example, identified "millions of acres of undeveloped territory" along the Pacific Slope that "have been peculiarly blessed by nature and that have awaited through the centuries the touch that will transform them in the paradises of the Western hemisphere."[62] Thriving urban centers aside, exposition officials and city leaders equated the promise of the Far West with its alleged unused hinterlands.

Space for More People

Like Portland and Seattle, California exposition officials were similarly confident that their vast hinterlands guaranteed long-term growth. Buoyed by the promise of the Panama Canal, San Diego and San Francisco predicted that the Southwest region's vast productive lands were "capable of sustaining an immense population."[63] Recalling the state's recent robust growth, the *San Francisco Chronicle*, for example, compared California's population density with that of New York and concluded that the "opportunity for larger gains is apparent."[64] More specifically, one periodical boldly advertised that the greater southwest could hold twenty-five million people "without straining it a particle," while the *San Diego Union* believed that California alone had room for twenty million "happy, prosperous people."[65] The state's urban centers would likewise benefit from this expected growth. Describing future plans laid out by California cities, *Sunset Magazine* detailed the numerous skyscrapers Los Angeles had recently built and how the city already "absorbs hundreds of new residents yearly and yet seems to have occupation for them all."[66]

Beyond providing refuge and a better life for Americans, California and the Far West also promised to help the nation deal with its thorny "immigrant problem." Decades of industrial expansion had attracted millions of immigrants to the United States, leading some American politicians and intellectuals to raise concerns about the threat immigrants posed to the nation. As early as the 1890s, David Wrobel has shown, the West figured prominently in the national immigration debate. The frontier and its open lands, a former superintendent of the census declared, had once acted as an assimilative force, transforming and Americanizing the millions of downtrodden masses. The rising anxiety over the reported demise of the frontier following the famous 1893 speech by historian Frederick Jackson Turner sparked demands for immigration-restriction laws.[67] While numerous eastern politicians and intellectuals continued to decry the threat of immigration well into the twentieth century, some western leaders began to challenge this line of thought, arguing instead that the West could help solve the immigrant problem.

By the early 1910s, the impending completion of the Panama Canal encouraged some western officials to insert themselves directly into the national immigration debate. For example, in 1913 Robert Lynch, a San Francisco businessman and former member of the California Commission on Immigration and Housing, penned an article for *Sunset Magazine* suggesting that the West was ready and able to handle the expected increase in European immigration. When ships sail directly from Europe to San Francisco following the opening of the canal, Lynch declared, "the disembarking immigrant will meet a different experience from that which faced his less fortunate brother who in years past entered the United States through the port of New York."[68] The author argued that the immigrant was not to blame, but rather that poor planning and exploitive social and economic conditions largely explained the alleged immigrant problem. Western states, especially California, had learned from eastern failures and were prepared to handle the wave of new immigration. Not only had Washington, Oregon, and California recently held meetings and conferences to study the issue, but California, Lynch noted, had established a state commission designed to address any possible pitfalls or obstacles.[69] Thoughtful preparation and government intervention, the author concluded, could both solve the immigration dilemma and ensure a better future for new arrivals.

Lynch's optimism no doubt reflected the progressive spirit of the early twentieth century, as well as westerners' unwavering belief that their region had much untapped potential. Despite Turner's earlier proclamation, western boosters maintained that the door had not yet fully closed on the western frontier.[70] In a 1911 congressional hearing held to discuss whether New Orleans or San Francisco would host the international exposition, Theodore A. Bell, a former representative from California, argued that his state "shall in the future take care of the great immigration of Europe."[71] As the *San Francisco Chronicle* explained, the West had the capacity to absorb more settlers and would benefit from immigration. "California needs people," the paper declared, and the state "will get them through the immigration that will set in to the Pacific Coast by way of the canal."[72] San Diego exposition directors likewise shared this belief. A PCE fair advertisement, for example, concluded that the greater Southwest would "become the focusing point of the world's immigration, the new land of opportunity next to be conquered by peaceful settlement."[73] The Far West, then, would help the nation solve one of its most vexing problems.

Agriculture

Despite the fact that the nation's industrial cities had absorbed the lion's share of new immigration, California exposition directors strongly believed it would be the Pacific Slope's unlimited agricultural potential that would soak up most of those who ventured west, including new immigrants. Mining, manufacturing, and international trade were no doubt important, but the region's economic success hinged on millions of farmers tilling the soil. Working from this conviction, exposition publicity directors assembled marketing campaigns to promote farming and rural living. Writing about the San Diego fair for *Sunset Magazine*, Walter Woehlke suggested that new "business does not fall from the sky. Quite the reverse; it grows out of the soil."[74] In a similar vein, an official Panama-California Exposition guidebook explained that "[b]efore the cities and manufacturing industries of the western states can reach their full growth, it will be necessary for the agricultural industries of the states to be fully developed." San Francisco leaders agreed that California depended on the state's capacity to help farmers find the best land to succeed.[75] By providing ample evidence and designing effective exhibits, the San Diego and San Francisco fairs could help persuade potential settlers to choose the Far West.

Underscoring what California specifically had to offer, the *San Francisco Chronicle* incredulously announced that there were ten million acres of prime farmland in the Central Valley region awaiting hard working hands.[76] PCE president G. A. Davidson claimed that new settlers "will look toward the west for agricultural comfort and fortune as the pioneers turned to California in the '40's in the mad romantic quest for gold." Rather than rely on simple platitudes or bold comparisons, Davidson identified "44,000,000 acres of arable land in the southwest that can be converted into rich farm lands." Perhaps to illustrate its potential, he noted that some eight million acres already in use had produced farm products valued at $143 million per year.[77] Believing that a new railroad line and the completion of the Panama Canal would allow the city to extend its hinterland as far east as New Mexico, San Diego's marketing efforts focused on the potential of the entire Southwest. Fair officials readily admitted that while the city hoped to help itself, "San Diego seeks to help the West far more."[78]

Publicizing the aggregate amount of open lands might be impressive; however, this was not necessarily persuasive on its own. After hiring a "corp of statisticians" to survey the southwest and collect data on available acreage, rainfall amounts, and transportation networks, San Diego fair officials erected a large map of the Southwest illustrating what each state and county had to offer. The exposition's director-general believed that marshaling such detailed evidence would reverse the tide of American farmers who moved to western Canada, despite its shorter growing season and tough winters, to cultivate its sizable farmlands.[79]

San Francisco officials likewise believed that more detailed information was needed to meet the different needs of farmers. The *San Francisco Chronicle* described how the California Development Board, the Colonization Bureau of the Southern Pacific Railroad, and staff from a state agriculture college helped newcomers find the best location to suit their needs. A settler from Holland or France, the paper maintained, might not fare as well in some areas of the state as a farmer from Michigan would. Drawing on the comprehensive information provided by these experts, the PPIE could help ensure that there was "no excuse for the newcomer failing to find the kind of land he wants, and that he can handle profitably."[80]

Profits, however, were only one part of the equation. California leaders understood that to entice farmers to the Far West, they needed to provide more specific data on the cost of farming and the value of crops produced in the region to persuade easterners that relocating was a sound decision. One San Francisco leader, for example, outlined the start-up costs a typical settler might expect to encounter. "Many men," local journalist C. A. Horne stated, "with a good team, hard muscle and not more than $1000 have been successful. After the land is paid for, twenty acres means independence, and forty acres a comfortable fortune." Outfitting a brand new twenty-acre farm, he indicated, could run upwards of $5000, though after the first year the crops should cover the cost of land, which averaged between $100 and $200 per acre with water rights.[81] Precise costs and detailed information of what a settler could expect were a key part of exposition marketing campaigns.

Similarly, publicity departments published state and regional agricultural production data, which they hoped would impress potential settlers. In promotional material published for the two California expositions, Los Angeles County officials advertised the acreage dedicated to citrus and deciduous fruits in the county, while Imperial Valley officers indicated that their county produced 60,000 bales of cotton valued at $5.5 million.[82] Statewide, California farmers exported 47,839 railroad car loads of citrus, while fruit canners produced 5.5 million cases of canned fruit valued at $15 million.[83] For those eyeing the fertile territory of the Central Valley, the *San Francisco Chronicle* stated that based on current production, the value of ten million acres could top more than $1.3 billion.[84] Summing up the unlimited opportunities for farmers in the Far West, PCE president G. A. Davidson calculated that undeveloped land could produce an income of $743 million.[85] Guidebooks and exposition exhibits chock full of production and profit data, exposition officials hoped, could not help but impress potential settlers.

WHILE THE TWO PACIFIC NORTHWEST EXPOSITIONS had exposed Americans living beyond the Rockies to the opportunities available in the Far West, stubborn misconceptions of the region continued to trouble California leaders when they announced their decision to host not one but two fairs in 1915. The Panama-California and Panama-Pacific International expositions hoped not just to confirm the positive image presented by the earlier fairs, but also to persuade Americans that the West promised a brighter future for both the nation and new settlers who chose to relocate to the Pacific Coast. Selling the Far West required fair officials to devise marketing campaigns that simultaneously challenged old stereotypes and advertised the unique advantages of western living. Five years after the Seattle exposition closed its gates, San Diego and San Francisco exposition officials built upon some of the good work done by the two earlier fairs. The growing significance of Asian markets and the excellent prospects for new farmers remained central to boosting the Far West in 1915. However, California officials possessed something that neither Portland nor Seattle had: a newly completed Panama Canal and the tremendous lure of San Francisco. Anointed the nation's official international exposition, the Pacific Coast metropolis commanded the American public's attention both in the press and at the gate. Moreover, the canal's expected impact on world trade promised to usher in a new era where the Pacific Ocean would rival the Atlantic. The California expositions, then, would finally facilitate American's reimaging of the West.

7 ⇜ SELLING NATURE AND LAND(SCAPES) IN THE AMERICAN SOUTHWEST

When San Diego officials welcomed the first guests to the Panama-California Exposition in January 1915, Americans' anxiety about the impact of industrialization had subsided little. Socialist movements continued to attract new followers as many workers grew restive despite the efforts of progressive reformers. Booming factories lured poor immigrants and failed farmers to cities increasingly plagued by congestion, filth, and foul air. Tapping into growing discontent, California officials believed that their two fairs could showcase a better way of life available in the Far West. Like the Pacific Northwest fairs before them, land remained a central part of the San Diego and San Francisco marketing campaigns. Western leaders, however, articulated a vision of the region where land offered not only economic opportunity, but also a unique lifestyle that satisfied both the stomach and the soul. Just as with popular misconceptions of a wild and woolly West, fair directors confronted widespread images of the region as a painfully dry and desolate frontier. Defying these notions, California fair officials instead encouraged fairgoers to exit the expositions picturing the Far West as a place of small, irrigated farms bounded by fresh air and beautiful mountain vistas.

By the time the Alaska-Yukon-Pacific Exposition closed in late 1909, Americans were just learning about President Roosevelt's Country Life Commission. Established to address what many perceived as a crisis in rural America, the commission aimed to improve rural life and reduce farmland-to-city migration patterns. Seattle leaders may have not had time to exploit the attention produced by the formation of the commission, but they did heed the call to action by back-to-the-land advocates. Businessmen advertised plots of land available in the city's hinterland, while public officials proclaimed that settling the hinterland would fill the holes—physically and economically—left behind by the once-dominant timber industry. Seattle, however, was not the only Pacific Coast city to embrace the back-to-the-land movement. In 1914 San Francisco officials announced that two California congressmen had secured for the Panama-Pacific International Exposition the 1915 convention of the American Congestion League, which was "devoted to promoting the 'back to the land' movement."[1] Part and parcel of exposition marketing campaigns, hosting prominent conferences generated national attention both to the issue and the region, which further helped officials advertise the virtues of the Far West.

Those advocating a rural revival, however, seemingly ignored the reality of California's countryside at the dawn of the twentieth century. Farming in the state was increasingly corporate and mechanized, and the future of the family farm appeared rather dim.[2] What distinguished San Francisco's excitement from Pacific Northwest cities was the impending completion of the Panama Canal. New trade routes, officials predicted, would produce an agricultural boom for the West Coast, and port cities like San Francisco and San Diego stood ready to benefit from increased commercial activity. A San Francisco banker visiting New York described the canal's benefits and explained that "the land of the Western states is ready for the American boy." Once he recognized this "golden opportunity, he will turn his back on the cities, their intense competition, and bitter disappointments and face toward the farms."[3] Farm life in California could provide more than just a better standard of living. As the *San Diego Union* explained, the city's fair presented not only "something better," but also "free out-of-door life" where children could enjoy fresh air and "grow up under the beneficent influence of unspoiled nature."[4] Poised to profit from the state's bountiful countryside, California fair officials looked forward to the chance to sell California's wares to disgruntled city dwellers.

⁜ Irrigation and Ample Open Territory

Timing, as they say, is everything. The back-to-the-land movement's growing momentum by the time San Diego welcomed its first visitor resulted from a combination of timely factors, including the opening of the Panama Canal, the apparent national economic crisis, and the outbreak of war in Europe. The global conflict, the *Los Angeles Examiner* concluded, would decrease European farm exports and help further stimulate the back-to-the-land movement.[5] The confluence of these events helps explain why San Diego leaders felt confident about the region's untapped potential. Yet the back-to-the-land movement continued to languish, San Diego leaders argued, because poor education and advertising failed to explain to easterners how conditions had changed. The PCE would rectify this by reversing the common belief that the West always learned from the East. "Next year," officials proclaimed, "it will be found that the far west has produced an idea which the east must learn."[6]

Successful education and advertising, San Diego officials understood, meant convincing potential settlers that there was ample land to go back to, and it could be easily farmed. Despite Portland's undertaking to publicize vacant land open for settlement in 1905, nearly ten years later, *Sunset Magazine* reminded readers that there were "still unproductive arable lands in the Southwest."[7] California boosters and fair officials, for example, consistently advertised their state's "vast acreage of unused lands,"[8] "unoccupied land,"[9] "empty acres of the Southwest,"[10] and the immense acreage that "have never been tickled by the plough."[11] Substantial plots of land ready to be tilled might have been persuasive had not the Southwest evoked images of dry and forbidding deserts. Fair officials, however, had prepared for this. For more than a decade, western leaders had labored to address the region's aridity. As a PCE brochure advertised, merely diverting a river turned a plot of sagebrush and cactus into productive soil. Simply put, irrigation "made possible the unrivaled production of the Land of Opportunity."[12] For those who wished to return to the land, San Diego and San Francisco leaders offered the recipe for success—irrigation and ample open territory.

By the time California welcomed visitors to the two 1915 expositions, western leaders could point to concrete examples of how irrigation could transform the landscape. Government-funded reclamation projects, for example, had opened up hundreds of thousands of acres of western territory for farming in New Mexico, California, and the Pacific Northwest. Moreover, national magazines like *Sunset Magazine*, along with the Portland and Seattle fairs, had introduced Americans to the wonders of irrigation. California boosters likewise celebrated how it could change not only the land but lives. "Irrigation," the *San Francisco Chronicle* declared, "allows man's energy to meet and overcome the shortcomings of nature."[13] Western residents would no longer be at the mercy of nature. After years of oppressive droughts and a natural environment that limited opportunity at best and produced misery at worst, irrigation seemingly promised westerners the chance to control their destiny.[14] Selling the Far West, then, hinged on convincing outsiders that irrigation would transform both the landscape and their lives.

Whether or not irrigation signified humankind's conquest of nature, most westerners did believe that it guaranteed a prosperous future for their homeland. Exposition publicity departments devised marketing strategies that built upon the growing public interest in irrigation and the attention given to several prominent Bureau of Reclamation projects. For example, a fair brochure described what visitors to the Panama-California Exposition would discover, advertising that the "future of the West is bound up in the development of her irrigation resources, and the cry of the arid lands is for men and capital to conserve the waters and then blossom into rich productivity."[15] More specifically, San Diego officials maintained that millions of acres of untapped land waited for "water and labor to make it produce as abundantly as the vast developed lands of today."[16] Yet western leaders did not simply rely on rosy predictions when discussing the promise of irrigation. Even as they continued to plan and build their two expositions, California officials publicized irrigation projects that promised to remake the Southwest. Two of the largest and more challenging western reclamation projects were located along the nation's southern border. After nearly eight years of planning and construction, the Roosevelt Dam opened its gates in 1911, providing water for 250,000 acres and the residents of Phoenix, Arizona. Farther west, another project

Postcard featuring irrigation of a typical orange grove at the Panama-California Exposition. *Author's possession.*

tapped into the Colorado River and opened up a swath of territory in southwest Arizona, which when added to earlier private efforts in the Imperial Valley, San Diego officials argued, provided "700,000 acres of land as fertile as the Nile Valley."[17]

As the two 1915 California expositions neared, state and local leaders continued to highlight reclamation projects, plus the tens of thousands of acres in the Central Valley and San Diego County's backcountry groomed for irrigation.[18] To illustrate the agricultural bounty that irrigation guaranteed to new farmers, fair brochures and other promotional materials typically included pictures of fertile farms and lush fields. A lengthy treatise published by the Southern California Panama Expositions Commission, for example, featured several photographs from farms in the newly irrigated Imperial Valley, including a healthy cornfield, a full-page picture of a sizable cotton plant, and even images of some date trees.[19] Powerful visual images provided clear evidence of the astonishing marvels of irrigation.

The Model Farm

Advertisements, magazine articles, and brochures may have helped fair directors encourage Americans to imagine a new West, but visitors who traveled to San Francisco or San Diego could see with their own eyes the virtues of irrigation. The Panama-Pacific International Exposition, for example, hosted the International Irrigation Congress meeting in September 1915. On the way to San Francisco, the organization held sessions in three other California cities, where attendees learned about successful developments.[20] The PPIE also provided a U.S. Reclamation Service diorama of the Shoshone irrigation project in Wyoming and transparencies of numerous irrigation scenes.[21] PCE directors went a step further, providing an actual five-acre farm where fairgoers could tour a typical citrus orchard with "a complete irrigation system in actual operation"[22]—an ambitious undertaking and an important step towards helping Americans reimagine a new West.

The PCE's Model Farm was a clear manifestation of how westerners believed that irrigated farming could not just change the region, but also remedy national urban anxieties. Within months of deciding to host the 1915 exposition, San Diego exposition directors advertised plans to demonstrate how "the small farm is the solution of the economic difficulties in which millions of city-penned men find themselves in the United States."[23] Realizing that the back-to-the-land movement had not reached the levels that many expected, fair officials believed that a firsthand example of such a farm would help stimulate the effort. Providing this unique exhibit to visitors was in many ways akin to product demonstrations popular in many consumer-marketing campaigns. The Model Farm would provide immediate evidence of irrigation's impact, which the usual speeches and newspaper articles could not do. Fairgoers could walk through the five acres of fields, plus the adjacent citrus orchard and observe its working irrigation system and the latest agricultural machinery perfectly fitted for smaller farms. After visitors inhaled the fragrance of orange and lemon trees, touched the freshly sprouted plants, and (if lucky) tasted a ripe berry, exposition directors believed that potential settlers would recognize the tremendous opportunity that awaited them in the Far West.[24]

The Model Farm's most important lesson was that farmers no longer had to labor on tracts of lands hundreds of acres in size. Irrigation and intensive agriculture, instead, could turn the dry western soils into productive and profitable farmland. Officials claimed that those people who "couldn't afford the usual 320 acre tract" could succeed on much smaller plots in both San Diego and the greater Far West.[25] A decade of reclamation projects, along with developers and local politicians, had enlarged the amount of available farmland. Several years after the AYPE closed its gates, Washington voters, for example, were asked to consider a referendum measure in 1914 that would irrigate nearly 450,000 acres in Quincy Valley.[26] In California, the *San Francisco Chronicle* reported that new irrigation projects had subdivided tens of thousands of acres of former wheat fields into small irrigated farms ready for new settlers.[27] Likewise, San Diego officials alleged that the state had "room for 100,000 more forty-acre farms."[28] Governments were not the only champions of western agriculture. International Harvester sponsored an impressive model farm exhibit divided into four parts, each representing what one would experience in each season of the year.[29] Visitors to the Bay Area exposition could easily see illustrations and exhibits of how irrigation could produce viable small farms.

The emphasis on small farms, best exemplified by the Panama-California fair's Model Farm, reflected the visions of irrigation proponents like William E. Smythe. In his turn-of-the-century study, *The Conquest of Arid America*, Smythe explained how irrigation could transform both the land and rural life. He detailed how San Joaquin farm sizes had shrunk with irrigation and that the large, bonanza wheat farms had given way to holdings a tenth the size. California, he argued, was "destined to be the land of the common people . . . because, owing to its peculiar climatic conditions, it requires less land to sustain a family in generous comfort." Recognizing the nation's growing urban population, Smythe believed that it would be the "surplus population" that would settle the newly open lands. What made the West ripe for new growth, he suggested, was that smaller farms demanded less capital and once easterners overcame the "[p]opular ignorance of the West," the region would finally reach its full potential.[30]

In Smythe's eyes, irrigation promised more than just smaller farms and new opportunities for eastern migrants. Bringing water to arid lands would usher in profound changes to rural society, including crop diversification, greater productivity, and the need for less farmland. Because farmers could thrive on smaller plots, the countryside's population density would increase, helping mitigate the isolation of a typical farming district. This irrigated landscape also promised to engender a sense of community and spawn a cooperative culture that would enrich the farmers' lives. In short, Smythe declared, "[i]nstead of crowded cities festering with vice and poverty, throughout Arid America are farms that blend into beautiful towns, and towns that shade almost imperceptibly into peaceful farms. Here are country people who enjoy all the advantages of the country."[31] Irrigation, then, promised to alter the look and feel of the countryside as well as enhance both individual lives and the nation's social, political, and cultural wellbeing.

That the PCE's Model Farm should so closely resemble Smythe's vision was no coincidence. Soon after publishing *The Conquest of Arid America*, Smythe moved to Southern California to work on Charles Fletcher Lummis's booster magazine *Land of Sunshine*. Heeding the calls of the San Diego Chamber of Commerce that ample open lands awaited development, Smythe announced on August 1, 1908, the formation of the Little Landers Colony. Premised on the belief that one could live well on a "little land," he located the colony less than twenty miles south of San Diego along the border with Mexico. Small, irrigated farms practicing intensive agriculture, along with a vibrant cooperative community, represented the foundation of the colony. In its first few years, the Little Landers Colony struggled from a lack of sufficient capital, undeveloped irrigation facilities, and political violence stemming from the Mexican Revolution, but by the time the exposition opened, it was a small and modestly successful agricultural colony. During the fair's run, it remained a popular example of what irrigated farming could produce in the West. In 1916, however, a devastating flood destroyed much of the utopian settlement, and it limped along for a few more years before finally collapsing.[32]

Inspired by Smythe's successful colony, the first issue of the *Panama-California Exposition News*, published by the fair's publicity department, announced the inclusion of a "Little Landers' Colony" in the upcoming San Diego celebration. The periodical noted the growing attraction of small farms where the owner "is living well, raising a family, enjoying good health and happiness, and filling his place as a useful and beneficial member of society."[33] The *San Diego Union* put it more bluntly: "The farm in California is more nearly the ideal place on which to spend a life of usefulness and happiness than can be found elsewhere in the world."[34] Central to this blissful lifestyle was the apparent sense of community that, as Smythe had articulated in his book and public speeches, offered the best of both city and country. Western boosters thus identified their new West with happiness and a vibrant sense of community that was seemingly disappearing in the increasing fragmented urban society of the industrial East.

Boosters, in fact, often spent as much time and space publicizing the social and cultural advantages of small farms as they did their economic potential. San Diego leaders, scholar Matthew Bokovoy has argued, "created a rhetoric of egalitarian economic and social possibilities, while hiding their purely economic motivations."[35] Fair officials believed that selling this version of the new Southwest—or at least San Diego—would also pay off for new settlers, land developers, and the city itself. Acknowledging the findings of the Country Life Commission, western leaders underscored the common urban amenities farmers would find in these new agricultural colonies. The *San Francisco Chronicle*, for example, claimed that "the telephone, the daily mail, and even electric light and power, are at the service of the family on the twenty-acre irrigation farm in California."[36] PCE's publicity department added that the "little lander" had "better schools, better churches, better roads" compared to the punishing loneliness of life on a large ranch.[37]

Visitors to the San Diego fair did not have to travel twenty miles south to the Little Landers Colony to see how small farming worked, but instead could walk just a few yards northeast of the fairground's main plaza to explore the Model Farm. More than just a field with crops, the exhibit included a five-acre citrus grove, a three-acre demonstration field, and a model bungalow in addition to the six-acre fully functioning farm. Whatever the time of the year fairgoers toured the Model Farm, they could see the cultivation of berries, vegetables, citrus, and even alfalfa.[38] The *San Diego Union* noted that flowers were also added to the area around the farmhouse "to show the possibility of combining the artistic and beautiful with the commercial in a home on a small farm."[39] Much like the City Beautiful movement, which attempted to re-make the urban environment at the turn of the century, exposition officials wished to demonstrate that farm living could be both aesthetically pleasing and profitable. Fairgoers could not only stroll around the fields and orchards, they could wander through the impressive International Harvester outdoor exhibit to see the latest labor-saving devices, such as an orchard tractor that spread manure, which promised to nearly eliminate the back-breaking farm work of old. To help visitors remember this image of western farming—and to perhaps help them share it with their friends and family back East—the PCE publicity bureau produced postcards that depicted San Diego's back country with an orange orchard and a pleasant house surrounded by a eucalyptus grove.[40]

The Panama-California Exposition directors' decision to add a model bungalow to the Model Farm exhibit was an attempt to demonstrate that the new style of agriculture promoted by the Pacific Coast fairs represented the best of both city and country life. The *San Diego Union* declared that the bungalow's popularity rivaled that of the farm itself.[41] The inclusion of the home illustrated clearly that new settlers risked little in terms of lifestyle when taking up farming in the Far West. PCE publicity director Mark S. Watson explained that the bungalow proved that "the farmhouse can be as comfortable, under modern conditions, as the city residence."[42] Writing on the quality of rural life in California, *California's Magazine*'s editor claimed "that California country homes are of very high excellence."[43] This reflected not only the intelligence of the owners, evidenced by the fact that "greater per capita consumption of periodical literature in California country homes that in other rural communities," but also the greater number of homes with running water and modern plumbing. Whether it was aesthetics, housing, or the relative ease of farm labor, the PCE's Model Farm promised new rural settlers financial rewards and a better quality of life.

Selling the Lifestyle

The benefits of this new western suburban-like farm life also extended to women and children. San Diego fair officials prominently advertised how western rural life would relieve the farm wife of the isolation and "arduous labors she had feared."[44] One PCE brochure advertised that the greater density of small farm living was the "feature that appeals to the woman, the realization that in leaving the city she is not losing the chance to mingle with neighbors, that her children can still go to school, that the health of life is waiting."[45] Moreover, the new western bungalow, replete with the latest machinery for the kitchen and household, promised to "cut down the drudgery which her grandmother had to bear," just as tractors eased the work of farmers.[46] Women who settled on an irrigated farm would soon learn that "the comforts of the city apartment have been transferred to the farm," because irrigation dams often produced the electricity that would light farmhouses and power common household items.[47] Summing up the powerful impact the Model Farm could have on visitors to the Panama-California Exposition, one fair publicity official described how a husband and wife "can observe and study the demonstration of facts that no amount of reading would ever make clear; and there is born the irresistible desire to go back to the land."[48]

Both the PCE's Model Farm and Smythe's Little Landers Colony harkened back to a simpler time. As industrialization transformed the nation, many westerners trusted that irrigation would compel Americans to return to the land, but not as isolated poor farmers of old. Rather, boosters envisioned a blurring of country and city by promoting a more modern suburban, middle-class lifestyle.[49] Advertisements and actual demonstrations helped publicized the promise that water engineering could provide a daily routine that combined the best of urban and rural living. Those living east of the Rockies could read about the economic potential of irrigated lands and peruse pictures of small farms in magazines and newspapers. The ones who visited San Diego could touch the moist soil, take in the aroma of oranges, and view the city's lights from the window of a modern bungalow. If they gazed beyond the orchard, they could see that irrigation not only change their lives but also the landscape of the American West.

Fairgoers who walked the streets and pathways on the opening January day of the Panama-California Exposition might have been fooled by the green trees and lush gardens that enveloped them. Had they hiked a few miles east, they might have instead discovered dry, brown chaparral covering San Diego's hillsides. For decades, the American West evoked images of desolate deserts interrupted only by imposing rocky peaks and deep canyons. However accurate, images like this challenged westerners who wished to see their homeland grow and prosper. Even in the rainy climes of the Pacific Northwest, Portland and Seattle leaders had to overcome similar views of the eastern parts of their states, trumpeting how irrigation could change the sense of the landscape and transform these parched wastelands into gardens. California governor George C. Pardee, for example, claimed that the Colorado River—"the Nile of the arid west"—had turned Imperial County from a desert to a flourishing farming community.[50] Describing the transformation of the West, *Sunset Magazine* explained that with irrigation, "ornamental trees are grown and the comfortable home and prosperous ranch replaces the old sod house and the desert."[51] Few officials outwardly rejected descriptions of a desert West, but instead they simply alleged that irrigation had altered that landscape—Governor Pardee and other western leaders declared that the desert was no more.

PCE officials tackled head-on the lingering perceptions of the western landscape by constructing the Model Farm and redeeming the dry landscape of the city's park. Like much of the Southwest, the small plot where the Model Farm stood, one San Diego fair brochure stated, had lain empty for centuries covered by little more than "cactus and sagebrush."[52] However, by the time the exposition opened, change was in the air. San Diego fair president G. A. Davidson, for example, urged settlers to "make a teeming garden of the now wasted places of the southwest."[53] Visitors only had to stroll over to the Model Farm to see how irrigation could convert arid lands into productive farmland replete with green shrubs and colorful flowers. However impressive a five-acre plot might be, California leaders also pointed to large-scale efforts that dramatically altered the landscape. University of California president Benjamin Ide Wheeler rejoiced that irrigation had "turned miles of desert into garden."[54] The *San Diego Union* likewise pointed to eight million irrigated acres "being cultivated, to turn the desert into a garden."[55] Ensuring the region's growth and prosperity, then, hung on officials' ability to convince outsiders to see the Far West as a place of beautiful gardens, not forsaken deserts.

Unmatched Natural Scenic Landscapes

At the same time westerners altered the West's topography through irrigation, they also celebrated the region's unmatched natural scenic landscapes. Sagebrush and chaparral seemingly marred the terra firma, but the hand of man and the wonders of water engineering could redeem it. The West, however, offered other breathtaking landscapes, which many believed revealed the handiwork of God that no man could enhance. As historian Susan Rhoades Neel has suggested, "Out West, it is said, nature has worked some kind of wonder, transforming the ordinary into the remarkable, the old into the new."[56] The region's natural landscapes were not only unmatched by anything the East could offer, they also possessed redemptive properties. By the dawn of the twentieth century, the wonders of the West's natural environment distinguished the region from the rest of the country as much as—if not more than—its purported economic potential.

Like the Pacific Northwest cities to the north, San Francisco and San Diego exposition directors touted the blessings and wonders of the region's unique landscapes. San Francisco fair president Homer S. King, for example, argued that the region's "thousand wonders and natural marvels," including its giant trees, beaches, and orange groves, was proof that "the West has a charm no other part of the United States possesses."[57] As King suggested, it was not just the sheer beauty of these landscapes, but also the diversity of accessible scenic wonders located in the Far West that impressed visitors and settlers alike. A PCE guidebook proclaimed that there "is not a state exhibiting which has not some mighty display of mountain or valley, lake, sea or desert, or forest to show to the wondering world."[58] Summing up the region's scenic beauty, a San Diego newspaper declared that fairgoers would discover a city situated in "a land of snow-capped peaks and fertile valleys, and the vast rolling sea," which "is in crystal form, the loveliness and grandeur of the West."[59]

Fair promoters drew on a variety of strategies to induce Americans to embrace the West's natural wonders. For those who struggled to imagine this new California, boosters exploited more familiar European aesthetics when possible. Since the 1870s, Southern California promoters had compared the climate and scenery of the region to the Mediterranean. In his 1891 book *Our Italy*, writer Charles Dudley Warner explained that the region's landscape and balmy climate resembled Italy and encouraged an outdoor lifestyle. Visitors to San Diego could experience this firsthand by staying at the Hotel Del Coronado, which opened in 1888 with lush plants, statuary, and courtyards that evoked thoughts of Italy.[60] Besides the region's European milieu, the outbreak of war in Europe provided California leaders another reason for easterners to visit the California expositions. The Panama-California Exposition Information Bureau, noting the impact of the "See America First" movement, claimed that the "Easterner has only a faint idea of the wonders offered in the West. The year of 1915 will be a year of discovery."[61] Fair officials insisted that visitors would discover that "the American West has mightier peaks and more fertile valleys, fairer lakes and bolder crags than has any country of Europe."[62] Brimming with confidence, exposition directors believed that western landscapes not only resembled those in Europe, but in fact were superior to them.

When travelers arrived in either San Francisco or San Diego in 1915, they would quickly discover that the region's natural wonders were visible and often easily accessible from the city's hotels. San Francisco officials, for example, noted the proximity of "Mount Shasta, Lake Tahoe, [and] the Big Trees."[63] Describing the wonders of the city's exposition, a PPIE guidebook included a picture of the nearby Marin Hills visible from the fair's concession district.[64] Even in the more arid regions of the Southwest, tourists could encounter fantastic natural scenery within a day's travel. A promotional guidebook on Southern California cities produced for the PCE praised Los Angeles's "incomparable climate, between mountains and the sea."[65] More specifically, a Union Pacific Railway brochure described orange groves near Los Angeles within sight of the beautiful San Bernardino foothills. Living

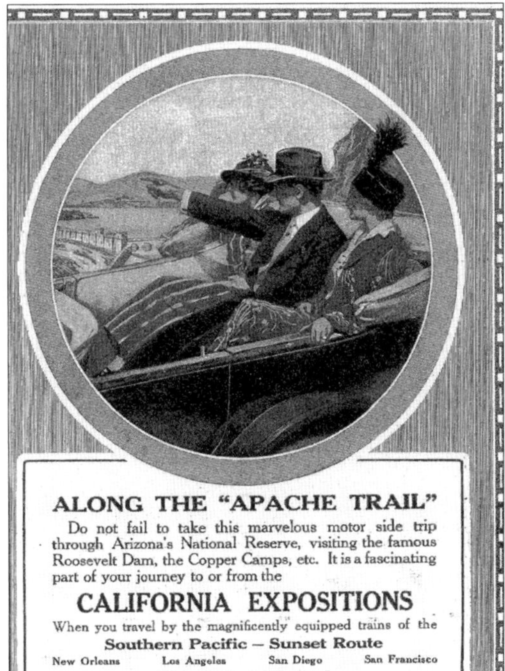

Southern Pacific Railroad ad highlighting destinations that travelers to California could see on their way to the two expositions. *Author's possession.*

along the Southern California coast meant that residents could glance east to see nearby mountain ranges as they wet their toes on the sandy beaches during a magnificent Pacific Ocean sunset.[66]

Fairgoers and prospective settlers, however, did not have to wait until they arrived at exposition cities to experience the wonders of the western landscape. Whether traveling west to Portland in 1905 or San Francisco in 1915, visitors could spy the mountain vistas and beautiful canyons from the window of a railroad car. A PPIE brochure advertised that the trip west would not disappoint. Tourists could expect to "cross the great American desert, now a land of cultivated farms; to climb the Rockies and the Great Sierra Mountains and feast your eyes upon their rugged grandeur; to visit California and the Pacific slope and delight in their sun-clad beauty and blooming fertility" before even passing through the exposition gates.[67] Marketing their westward lines, railway companies likewise provided descriptions for travelers who rode the rails to each of the fairs. The Union Pacific explained that whatever route—north, south, or central—visitors took to California in 1915, they would encounter exciting adventures along the way. One brochure, for example, detailed the mountains, deserts, and exotic scenery in Colorado, Utah, and other western states through which riders would pass.[68] Even before visitors reached the exposition cities, they likely had witnessed scenic landscapes and wide-open spaces like few had ever seen. By whetting travelers' appetite, railroad advertisements dovetailed well with fair publicity campaigns that promised such scenic views to prospective settlers.

Brochures and railroad marketing materials encouraged travelers to enjoy the journey west as much as they looked forward to their final destination. Like the earlier fairs, California exposition directors saw the advantages of promoting stopovers at popular national parks. Panama-Pacific International Exposition president Charles C. Moore, for example, wrote in *Sunset Magazine* that San Francisco would alone attract tens of thousands to the fair. In addition, he stated, "[j]ust think what the visitor will have thrown in for good measure. The Yellowstone National Park, the Grand Canon of the Colorado, [and] the Yosemite" offered a great opportunity to explore the West.[69] A 1915 Union Pacific brochure explained to tourists what they could expect if they included a stopover at Yellowstone: "Picture such an area consecrated to Nature and man's enjoyment thereof; barred to shrieking locomotive, and popping motorcycle, and chugging automobile"[70]—perhaps exploiting growing anxiety with urban life. San Diego and San Francisco officials also reminded fairgoers that California had its own "national 'play grounds,'" in particular Yosemite National Park, with its stunning waterfalls and inspirational peaks.[71] Exposition directors and local leaders hoped that fairgoers would find the added opportunity to explore western wonderlands too enticing and thus ensure a profitable and productive fair.

Since not all of the nearly nineteen million visitors to the PPIE could drop by Yellowstone National Park or the Grand Canyon, San Francisco fair officials constructed massive exhibits in "The Zone," which permitted fairgoers to experience "Nature's grandest awe-inspiring attractions."[72] Like irrigation demonstrations and San Diego's Model

Farm, these amusement district exhibits allowed fairgoers to experience in a different manner these natural wonders. The Santa Fe Railway, for example, built a six-acre exhibit that included a model of the Grand Canyon where visitors could ride miniature cars along a constructed canyon rim and see the most important canyon locations.[73] Not to be outdone, the Northern Pacific Railway assembled a four-acre reproduction of Yellowstone, which it claimed was the largest single exhibit ever constructed at a world's fair. PPIE advertisements noted that the display also included a "great Spectatorium seating 1000 people" with a large stage where some important sites were reproduced, including an Old Faithful Geyser that spewed water and steam and a scale model of the Old Faithful Inn that served as a restaurant.[74] The two impressive re-creations of these western natural wonders, historian Sarah J. Moore has suggested, were "a marketing strategy of the respective railroad companies to encourage the tourist to visit both the virtual and real landscape."[75] Through re-creations and firsthand visits, the four Pacific Coast expositions regaled visitors with the natural wonders that helped define the American West.

Recognizing the numerous scenic attractions located along the Pacific Coast, exposition directors lauded other nearby and perhaps less well-known natural vistas, which fairgoers could visit on the way to or from the fairs. Promoting the natural scenery found elsewhere in the Far West would help easterners grasp the diversity of western landscapes. Again, railroad companies often collaborated with exposition officials to advertise side trips to nearby nature spots. The Union Pacific marketing department, for example, urged visitors to the San Francisco exposition to take rail lines or steamships to Puget Sound and the Columbia River, where they could see Washington's Mount Rainier or Oregon's Mount Hood.[76] San Francisco officials also implored fairgoers to take side trips to visit the "Redwoods" and the "Calaveras Big Trees."[77] To whet travelers' appetites, exposition publicity bureaus peppered brochures and magazine articles with images of California's scenic wonders. PPIE guidebooks, for example, provided numerous illustrations of the state's mountains, big trees, and deserts, while a Union Pacific brochure featured a photograph of a crowded stretch of a southern California beach that allowed "Surf-bathing all the Year."[78] True to its goal of promoting the West, *Sunset Magazine* even published color images of prominent California natural settings, including Lake Tahoe and Yosemite Park's El Capitan.[79]

Whether it was the majestic peaks of the Sierra Mountain range or the irrigated fields of the Panama-California Exposition's Model Farm, fair publicity departments attempted to refashion how Americans saw and understood the Far West. The hand of God in shaping the mountains and the hand of man through water engineering now made possible a new and better lifestyle on the Pacific Coast. Relocating to the region promised both to enhance new settlers' economic prospects and improve daily life by offering a more healthy alternative to industrial cities back east. By confronting popular misconceptions of the land, western leaders encouraged those unfamiliar with the Far West to conceive of the territory west of the Rockies differently.

Climate

Farming and scenic vistas alone, California fair officials understood, might not be sufficient to guarantee the region's success. Beautiful mountains and sandy beaches belied the fact that to many, the Southwest was little more than a hot, dry desert. Blistering heat could potentially undermine any benefits that irrigation and scenic landscapes offered to settlers. Success, therefore, meant challenging false impressions of the region's climate. As they had since Charles Nordhoff published his famous guidebook *California: For Health, Pleasure, and Residence* in 1873, California leaders rejoiced at the state's weather.[80] PPIE fair president Charles C. Moore, for example, declared that "California's climate is recognized as her greatest asset," while the state's university president argued that "[o]ne of the chief resources of California is its climate."[81] Boosters for both expositions emphasized their cities' year-round mild temperatures. A San Francisco fair guidebook claimed the city's climate "is delightfully cool in summer and spring-like in winter."[82] Competing with the much larger metropolis to the North, San Diego leaders touted Southern California's superior climate. A PCE brochure, for example, advertised that "San Diego is fair and balmy and altogether lovely the year round."[83] Perhaps a more

Postcard featuring the Yellowstone National Park exhibit at the Panama-Pacific International Exposition. *Special Collections Research Center, California State University, Fresno.*

A postcard from the Panama-California Exposition showing a San Diego residential neighborhood during the winter. *San Diego State University Special Collections, John and Jane Adams Postcard Collection.*

novel approach that San Diego officials undertook was celebrating "Straw Hat Day," when residents were encouraged to wear straw hats in January to highlight the city's nice climate. A cartoon accompanying a 1915 *San Diego Union* article included a drawing of "Mr. Back Easterner" dressed in a coat and scarf beside a photograph of a San Diego resident in a nice suit and straw hat.[84] While the other three Pacific Coast exposition cities maintained that each possessed favorable climates, San Diego trumpeted that its natural environment allowed it alone to host a year-round fair.[85]

Hosting a year-round exposition was powerful evidence of southern California's mild climate, yet San Francisco and San Diego exposition publicity departments found other methods to promote the region's natural environment. Just as the two Pacific Northwest fairs did, California officials often compared their climatic conditions to other places in the United States. The *San Diego Union* averred that San Diego was a "garden spot of the world, in contrast to the snow, ice, and winter desolation of other parts of the country."[86] Promotional materials specifically identified the "East" or "the Atlantic" when praising the superior climate of the Pacific Coast. A PPIE article, for example, contended that San Franciscans "may cry for blankets, while the East swelters in dog-day heat."[87] In a 1915 *California Magazine* article, a University of California climatology instructor even cited weather bureau records when describing temperature ranges between California cities and several Atlantic Coast and Mississippi Valley urban centers.[88] Juxtaposing the West Coast climate to New York or New Orleans, in short, helped fair officials differentiate what they believed was their region's superior weather.

California's pleasant temperatures and fresh air promised more than just comfortable living conditions. Exposition publicity directors wrapped the region's climate into their larger marketing strategy by arguing that the Far West's weather also made work easier and more productive. Benjamin Ide Wheeler, for example, claimed that California's climate "cancels the perpetual struggle of life against weather. It is an economic factor and cancels the waste time spent in shivering and wiping perspiration."[89] The region's environment, he noted, permitted full days of labor all year round. Similarly, the *Panama-California*

Exposition News explained that it was easier to earn a living in Southern California by farming small plots than wage work back East, where "the rigors of winter follow the withering heat of summer year and year, in paralyzing, disenergizing [*sic*], succession."[90] The paper intimated that milder temperatures and fewer winter snow days meant that farmers could enjoy a better life and economic future. Not only would labor be less demanding, but the favorable climate insured a better variety of crops and enhanced yields. Throughout the Pacific Slope, boosters believed that western living promised a more meaningful and productive life, or as one PPIE guide advertised, a "more livable and lovable country."[91]

Demonstrating that the Pacific Coast was a more livable country remained a central goal of exposition directors at both California fairs. One method was to bathe the exposition grounds in greenery and flowers that only could grow and thrive year-round in Pacific Coast cities. San Diego boosters, for example, reminded fairgoers that pictures of earlier fairs in Chicago, St. Louis, and Buffalo showed buildings of bare walls with an "utter lack of a green cover except along the very base" with "puny bushes" and few shade trees.[92] San Francisco officials similarly advertised the Bay Area's exposition's 3,000-foot South Garden and "its grand esplanade, with its floricultural splendors."[93] Perhaps no West Coast fair was more proud of its landscape than the Panama-California Exposition. *Collier's Magazine* stated that the San Diego fair showcased what was possible with a "full twelve-month growing period, with veritable wildernesses of roses always in bloom and evergreen groves of palms and acacias."[94] Promotional guidebooks and brochures overflowed with claims that San Diego's climate permitted "extraordinary feats of landscape architecture," so that visitors could expect to see the grounds "covered with a thick growth of foliage, from the tropical palm to the hard pine."[95] After a day at either California fair, local leaders firmly believed that few would return home and look at the Far West's natural environment the same ever again.

Claims that the Pacific Northwest's climate was the truly the healthiest in nation had greeted visitors to the earlier Portland and Seattle fairs. California leaders, however, refused to let such assertions go unchallenged. For more than four decades, boosters had unfailingly protected the Golden State's reputation as a health resort.[96] California's standing as a place of health and vigor, exposition officials advertised, was due to its superior climate and scenic landscapes. A PCE fair brochure, for example, included a section entitled "Climate, Health, Location," in which it claimed that "San Diego is a paradise for the healthseeker."[97] Similarly, the University of California's Benjamin Ide Wheeler maintained that due to the region's agreeable climate, "[o]ld age will be prolonged five years or more by coming here."[98] The state's weather and natural scenery, however, offered more than just an antidote to disease and malnutrition. The healthy climate, fair marketing materials insisted, enhanced both the body and mind. A San Diego County Board of Supervisor's exposition guidebook, for example, advertised that it was the city's "almost perfect climatic conditions that make for the comfort, zest and joy obtainable nowhere else."[99] Even more than emotional health, a PPIE booklet boasted that to "the salubrity of the climate can be attributed the virility and versatility of her native and adopted sons and daughters—writers, artists, sculptors, engineers, architects, scholars—who have brought fame to themselves and their beloved state in all parts of the earth."[100] Western living, with its pleasant climate and mild temperatures, yielded all the benefits of a good and productive life.

Lifestyle

The Far West's natural environment offered more than just an agreeable climate where visitors and residents could breathe fresh air. In contrast to more sterile and passive experiences with nature, the region's mountains, forests, and beaches inspired physical activity. During a time when progressive reformers urged big cities to construct playgrounds to improve young children's health, California leaders touted the region's natural settings within easy reach of local residents. Claiming that his state offered the best of both urban and rural life, San Francisco Board of Works president Timothy A. Reardon stated that "[w]e of the West have much to be thankful for, whether our lot be cast in city or country, since we are always in touch with both." He insisted that city residents were just a "short ride" from the "most delightful of natural surroundings."[101] It was not just the proximity of mountains, waterways, and national parks that made outdoor life possible, but also the Far West's favorable climate. A PPIE guidebook, for example, praised the region's "out-of-doors-all-the-year-round climate" that aided westerners' health and enjoyment, while San Diego officials emphasized Southern California's "perpetual sunshine."[102] California boosters insisted that the mountains and beaches did more than just soothe the eyes. Leisure was fine, but these places encouraged more energetic pursuits. San Diego might be "a paradise for the pleasure seeker," a local newspaper argued, but it also provided vigorous activities like fishing, hunting, and swimming in the Pacific Ocean.[103]

Like any good marketing campaign, exposition leaders were quick to employ the words and ideas of the national playground movement to bolster their case. A San Diego newspaper, for example, claimed that the Southern California city's natural wonders and fine climate made "this little corner of the United States the playground of the world."[104] More importantly, it was not exclusive to the well-heeled. As Benjamin Ide Wheeler claimed, California's climate made "the great outdoors available all the time in luscious abundance to ordinary men." The university president asserted that the Golden State was not just a good place to work, but also "the natural playground of the nation." He described a place that included climbing in the Sierra Nevada Mountains, fishing in the state's streams, and tennis and golf in seashore resorts.[105] As Americans journeyed to the Pacific Coast in 1915, *California's Magazine* summed up the state's special lifestyle with "California: Playground of the World," an article that described numerous outdoor activities replete with pictures.[106] Western living, with its pleasing weather, breathtaking views, and outdoor lifestyle, exposition officials concluded, promised to cure the ills that plagued a modern, industrial nation.

Just as Portland and Seattle fair officials had advertised a few years earlier, the two California expositions also touted the Far West's modern amenities and lifestyle. If easterners chose to relocate to San Diego or San Francisco, they would discover fine schools, churches, and progressive social clubs. With the growing attention paid to public education, California leaders publicized the region's excellent schools: a PCE brochure noted that San Diego's "good educational facilities" included twenty-four public schools valued at more than $1.5 million.[107] Advertising what their county had to offer, the Ventura County Board of Supervisors likewise claimed that there "are fine schools in all the cities and in all the county," while Oakland stated that it had built nineteen new schools during the previous decade.[108] Taking advantage of the great interest in their exposition, PPIE officials invited the National Education Association (NEA) to host its meeting at the fair, giving educational leaders the opportunity to highlight the state's accomplishments. California educator David Starr Jordan, NEA president in 1915, wrote in his message to visitors that "the pressure of higher education is greater in California than anywhere else in the world." Fairgoers could also tour exhibits with models of public school buildings, films of classroom teaching, and other examples of the state's modern educational system.[109] Descriptions of educational opportunities and facilities signified one strategy fair publicity directors employed to illustrate that the Far West was as progressive as any other place in the country.

Fine schools were not the only features of modern life that settlers would discover in the Far West. Exploitation departments boasted that California cities had ample religious, social, and cultural clubs that further enhanced urban living. The *San Francisco Chronicle*, for example, explained that the "opportunities for religious instruction and worship are the same here as in other states." The paper described the city's impressive churches and cathedrals, as well as prominent social clubs, like the Bohemian Club, which hosted distinguished guests from around the world.[110] Though a significantly smaller community than the other Pacific Coast exposition cities, San Diego leaders proudly proclaimed that it was "a church-going city" with its fifty-two churches and headquarters for the International Theosophical Society. The city was also home to two business clubs and two "ladies' literary clubs."[111] Churches, clubs, and social organizations, fair publicity bureaus believed, demonstrated that these Far West cities promoted an active and vibrant lifestyle that was matched only by that provided by the scenic vistas of the surrounding natural environment.

Clubs and religious institutions aside, West Coast urban centers also cultivated the arts and literature. Exposition marketing materials confronted images of the "wild and woolly West" by advertising the remarkable, refined lifestyle visitors would encounter in Pacific Coast cities. Despite the region's recent settlement, local leaders maintained that the West's cultural development was on par with cities like Chicago and New York. Panama-California Exposition publicity directors, for example, proudly professed that San Diego was building the "[f]inest theater west of Chicago" at a cost of $600,000.[112] After a visit to exhibits on artwork at the San Diego fair, the *Los Angeles Times* suggested that the western art on display was also quite good. A prominent artist told the paper that "we of the Big West have at last attained to an art of native expression, and that our message need not be—and indeed is not—delivered in an apologetic whisper."[113] Sensitive to their city's size, San Diego officials, like Portland and Seattle before it, put particular emphasis on its theaters, arts, and civic offerings in order to persuade the nation that it, too, was a worthy destination.

No western city, however, could match San Francisco's cultural and artistic offerings. As the metropolis of the Pacific Coast, the Bay Area city was home to numerous theaters and museums. One guide to the exposition host city noted the city's twelve-month-long theatrical season as well as the impressive Institute of Art.[114] A 1915 article in the *Nation* maintained that easterners did not truly appreciate San Francisco, stating, "What has only slowly been perceived, however, what for the older American East has as yet hardly been perceived at all, is that underneath this energetic pursuit of wealth, lavish expenditure, and moral relaxation lay a profound and strenuous concern for art, for music, for literature; for everything, in fact, which embodied intellectual interest or the spirit of beauty."[115] Proud of the state's artistic accomplishments, the *San Francisco Chronicle* described the cultural production by prominent Californians, such as William Keith's landscapes paintings and the literature produced by renowned writers like Mark Twain and Bret Harte.[116] What the newspaper and exposition art exhibits indicated was that the Far West not only produced prominent artists and writers, but that the region itself served as an inspiration for their artistic creations.

A typical bungalow residence at the Panama-California Exposition illustrating a unique southern California lifestyle available to settlers. *San Diego History Center, Photo ID #1457-A.*

Prominent writers, impressive museums, and a vibrant civic life helped California leaders prove that newcomers would give up little if they moved to the Golden State. Promising the best of both rural and urban life, exposition publicity departments and local commercial organizations proclaimed that the built environment likewise illustrated the host cities' modern qualities. Gone were the dusty streets and poorly constructed wooden buildings of frontier days. Whether fairgoers visited San Diego or San Francisco, they would encounter a familiar, up-to-date urban environment that had the look and feel of any contemporary American city. Travelers to California in 1915, one writer noted, "learned to their surprise that there were good roads . . . beyond the Mississippi."[117] Putting this into context, the *San Diego Union* stated that "San Diego is a county of roads" that stretch throughout a county slightly larger in area than Massachusetts.[118] The PCE advertised that the county had spent two million dollars to construct "between five and six hundred miles of wonderful contour roadways."[119] Even a natural disaster could not deter San Francisco from celebrating its built environment. Opening its gates less than a decade after the devastating earthquake, a PPIE guidebook claimed that on the city's "broad streets and amid her stately buildings she proffers the best conditions of life which civilization has to offer."[120] Whether one sought eye-pleasing mountain landscapes or the clean streets and splendid new buildings of urban landscapes, exposition publicity departments promised that new residents would discover better living along the Pacific slope.

Fairgoers who drove the paved streets or walked the finished sidewalks of San Francisco, San Diego, or most Far West cities would quickly discover impressive, modern hotels, office buildings, and homes that rivaled any comparable American city. Exposition directors promoted their respective cities' urban environment as another way to illustrate the modern qualities of western life. A 1914 *San Francisco Chronicle* article described the city's expansive Civic Center currently under construction with its $5 million steel-framed city hall.[121] Nearby visitors could gaze at the Institute of Art at the corner of California and Mason Streets or impressive business buildings in the Mercantile District.[122]

The Bay Area city was not the only locale of note. The rapidly growing metropolis of Los Angeles attracted the attention of *Sunset Magazine*, which stated that the Southern California city "builds skyscrapers until its business streets are almost like the canyons of New York."[123] While San Diego's urban landscape might not have been comparable to New York or Los Angeles, local officials noted that the city had spent $500,000 in 1910 to erect several "smaller modern hotels."[124] Moreover, San Diego possessed impressive business buildings and hotels in addition to, as one Panama-California Exposition brochure advertised, "private residences that are as fine as those of any eastern city twice the size."[125] Whether it was a personal home, government building, or commercial shop, tourists and settlers alike would discover modern facilities that rivaled anything an eastern city could offer.

Like other exposition publicity ventures, both California host cities provided ample photographs in brochures, guidebooks, and newspapers to illustrate their cities' modern built environment. Not as well-known to the rest of the nation, San Diego—as Portland and Seattle had before—felt compelled to demonstrate that its urban landscape compared favorably to cities east of the Mississippi. One brochure, for example, displayed photographs of several impressive homes surrounded by palm trees and greenery.[126] The San Diego Chamber of Commerce's PCE brochure likewise included a collage of "typical" San Diego homes alongside photographs of high schools, a state Normal school, several downtown business buildings, and a couple of churches. Reminding readers that California offered the best of both urban and rural living, promotional materials often interspersed among these photos of modern buildings pictures of nearby mountains, idyllic orange groves, and, in the case of San Diego, a beach snapshot from the nearby community of La Jolla.[127] San Diego might not be familiar to those back east, but rest assured, fair officials asserted, newcomers would discover a modern city.

San Francisco officials, however, faced a different challenge. As one of the largest cities in the nation and the premier metropolis in the Far West, most Americans recognized that San Francisco was a modern city. Yet the Panama-Pacific International Exposition opened its gates less than a decade after a devastating earthquake nearly destroyed the city. Bay Area officials thus had to assure fairgoers and visitors that the city had overcome this tragedy. Acknowledging the earthquake's impact, one brochure explained that San Francisco had been rebuilt and provided a picture of Market Street occupied by several prominent business buildings, a bird's-eye view of the city, and a photograph of the St. Francis Hotel.[128] A PPIE fair guidebook also featured panoramic pictures of the San Francisco cityscape and images of bustling Market and Kearney streets interspersed among photographs of Ocean Beach, Yosemite National Park, and Lake Tahoe.[129] Despite residing in the most famous and oldest state west of the Rockies, California exposition officials nevertheless felt it necessary to challenge any false impressions that their cities were any less modern and urbane than other American cities.

⊧ DURING A TIME WHEN RAPID URBANIZATION AND industrialization profoundly transformed American society, Pacific Coast cities encouraged those less familiar with their region to reimagine the Far West. Seeking to grow and prosper along with the rest of the nation, California promised a new kind of living that combined the best of modern urban life with breathtaking scenic landscapes. Whether visiting San Francisco or San Diego or perusing an exposition brochure, outsiders confronted different images of the region than those they might have found in a Zane Grey novel or a traveling Wild West show. The West may still have possessed wide-open and desolate landscapes, yet the fair host cities wished instead to feature landscapes that offered a more fulfilling life. Moreover, despite differences between the Pacific Northwest and the Southwest, westerners shared the belief that nature uniquely blessed the Pacific slope. Scenic landscapes and a salubrious climate ensured better physical and even emotional health. Yet even where nature fell short, irrigation permitted a new rural lifestyle that all envied, one that offered with a stone's throw the comforts and conveniences of urban living. The California fairs, like their predecessors to the north, carefully crafted marketing campaigns that promised a new lifestyle that seemingly fit the modern, industrial sensibilities of early twentieth-century America.

The Panama-California Exposition's Painted Desert Pueblo Indian Village. *San Diego History Center, Photo ID #18028-4.*

8 ⊧ RACE AND EMPIRE IN THE AMERICAN SOUTHWEST

When the Panama-California Exposition opened its gates in January 1915, the nature of race and race relations in the Far West had seemingly changed little since the Seattle fair had ended its run. California exposition directors, like their brethren at the two Pacific Northwest fairs, had to walk a tightrope when formulating a marketing strategy that acknowledged the appealing exoticism of the region's diverse populations but that did not further animate racial anxieties. Both the Panama-Pacific International and Panama-California expositions continued to play on familiar tropes when addressing Native Americans. San Diego's desire to become the entrepôt of the Southwest, a region with a large and diverse Native American population, encouraged officials to confront its Indian past and present, yet in a rather confusing and contradictory manner. By 1915 geopolitical changes, both in Asia and at home, moderated how the California fairs handled Asia-Pacific nations. Defending America's imperial role abroad, the changing place of the Far East in the world, and lingering anti-Asian sentiments in California steered exposition officials' efforts to balance the region's economic aspirations with popular racialist ideas of early-twentieth-century America.

⊧ "The Life of the Vanishing Race"

As San Diego and San Francisco officials planned their expositions following the Alaska-Yukon-Pacific Exposition's successful run, they had to carefully considered how best to feature Native Americans in their respective fairs. The two Pacific Northwest celebrations recognized that the region's Indian past would help attract visitors to their fairs. Dime novels portrayed a version of western history that, though warped and inauthentic, fascinated much of the American public. Rather than ignoring the region's Native American population, Seattle and Portland officials had tried to dispel any misunderstanding of them by celebrating Indians as examples of successful Americanization. Yet whether consciously or unconsciously, the two fairs undermined this effort by sometimes perpetuating popular stereotypes. From Wild West shows to exhibits highlighting "primitive" Indians, exposition directors offered contradictory images of Native Americans that likely did little to eradicate popular misconceptions. However, the history of the Spanish missions and the Southwest's larger, more diverse Native American populations meant that San Diego and San Francisco fair officials could not similarly disregard Native Americans.

Desires to boost fair attendance and satiate fairgoers' appetites for exotic Indians immediately shaped exposition publicity campaigns. Like Portland and Seattle, the two California fairs publicized the opportunity to encounter Native Americans up close in their advertising. Western leaders admitted that the region's Indian population had precipitously declined by the dawn of the twentieth century. Symbolic of the apparent demise of Indians was James Earle Fraser's famous statue *The End of the Trail*, which one PPIE guidebook described as the "dying Indian, astride his exhausted cayuse, express[ing] the hopelessness of the Red Man's battle against civilization."[1] Promotional efforts played on this sense of urgency, warning those living east of the Mississippi that the California expositions represented the last chance to experience the rapidly fading old West. San Francisco's fair, for example, included a small southwest Indian village titled "The Life of the Vanishing Race" in the amusement zone's Grand Canyon exhibit.[2] Similarly, PCE directors constructed a live exhibit that offered visitors the opportunity to "see a restoration of the life of the vanished or vanishing tribes."[3] Dr. Edgar L. Hewett, founder of the School of American Archaeology and director of exhibits for the Panama-California Exposition rejected the premise that Indians were vanishing, yet he acknowledged that Native American cultures were at risk because "the white man [had] pushed them onto the limited reservations they now occupy."[4] Indian lives might not be disappearing, Hewett suggested, but the reservation system the white man imposed on them no doubt threatened their traditional way of life.

The opportunity to see Native Americans in "realistic" exhibits was only one example of the central role Native Americans played at West Coast expositions. Fair officials also included parades, arts and crafts displays, and photographic exhibits to help quench the thirst of those fascinated with Native American life and history. San Diego officials hitched their city's Indian past to the city's exposition more than San Francisco—since the PPIE was the official national exposition, San Francisco leaders instead emphasized the global nature of their fair compared to the smaller regional San Diego celebration. Visitors to the PCE, however, could not escape the central place that Father Junípero Serra, California Indians, and the missions played in the region's history. Guidebooks and other promotional materials, for example, often began with romanticized histories of the mission era. Like the Indian imagery used by Pacific Northwest expositions, San Diego fair directors riddled exposition guidebooks and publicity publications with images of Spanish missions. Few readers, especially those who read fair publicity material, would be unfamiliar with the story of Spanish friars attempting to "civilize" California Indians.[5] Even the exposition's architecture featured Spanish Colonial revival and Mission-style influences. The Southwest's past and present, then, was inextricably tied to the Native American past.

Appreciating the American public's fascination with Native Americans, PCE directors advertised that visitors would enjoy the rare opportunity to see Indians in their native setting. The success of both the Portland and Seattle fairs confirmed that the public's interest in Indian life had not waned. San Diego officials commented that "visitors from the far corners of the world" were captivated by the fair's impressive exhibit of Native American life.[6] Since the Columbian Exposition in 1893, exhibits of Native Americans in so-called "natural" settings had been a staple of most American expositions. California leaders witnessed this interest firsthand when they borrowed the "Sioux Village" from the Chicago fair and featured it at the California Midwinter International Exposition in 1894.[7] Like the earlier fairs, the California expositions benefited from their location in the region of the nation most associated with American Indians.

With the western Indian wars fresh in Americans' minds, fairgoers may have expected to find Native Americans residing near the exposition host cities. Pacific Coast leaders seemingly did little to refute this because Native Americans' exotic appeal could help increase traffic to their expensive expositions. Instead, exposition directors urged the public to travel west to see the rapidly disappearing Indian. Commissioners from New Mexico, for example, had high expectations for their state's exhibit at the Panama-California Exposition. By the time San Diego closed its gates, they hoped that the "public will know that New Mexico is not a place where Indian tribes war and hunt," but instead see the state as place with good schools and "where Indians live peaceably on government reservations."[8] State officials only had to look to the similar displays of Indian life in the Southwest staged by the Fred Harvey Company and the Santa Fe Railway, which Leah Dilworth has argued, "presented a region that was peaceful and fully domesticated."[9] Fair officials believed that academic presentations and well-crafted Indian villages could help dispel misconceptions and stereotypes that haunted many western states and cities.

Indian Villages

Like the earlier Pacific Northwest fairs, the California expositions prominently featured Indian villages and Native American cultural ceremonies. Visitors to San Francisco's fair had ample opportunity to see and learn about Indians. The Great Northern Railway, for example, staged a powwow of Blackfoot Indians at the Panama-Pacific International Exposition where they reportedly performed the medicine lodge rites for the first time outside the boundaries of a reservation.[10] That a prominent railway company sponsored or presented Indian performances was not uncommon or unexpected; railroads and Indians went hand-in-hand in popular representations of the West. Dances and other performances were not the only occasion for fairgoers to encounter exotic Indians. At "The Zone," the San Francisco fair's amusement area, the Grand Canyon exhibit included a Pueblo Indian Village housing twenty Zuni and Hopi families, as well as a Mexican-style Tehuantepec Village, which promised visitors a "typical reproduction of an aboriginal community."[11] After touring the impressive Grand Canyon reproduction, fairgoers could head to the rooftop, where they could visit the Pueblo Indian Village to watch the Zuni and Hopi residents prepare meals, make silver jewelry, and weave blankets.[12] Live performances, interactive villages, and arts and crafts demonstrations, PPIE officials believed, would leave potential settlers assured that Native Americans were domesticated.

Not to be outdone, the directors of the Panama-California Exposition constructed an impressive six-acre southwest Native American village. The Painted Desert, as it was called, aimed to "reproduce a true representation of Indian life and to depict their mode of living at home." Home to some three hundred Indians, the *San Diego Union* claimed that a portion of the fairgrounds were "made into perfect imitations of Arizona and New Mexico."[13] San Diego fair officials asserted that the six-acre exhibit "gathered real scenes of life in a dozen sections of the southwest, where the red man once ruled."[14] Like San Francisco's Grand Canyon exhibit or the AYPE's Alaskan Village, visitors to the Far West expositions could thus immerse themselves in reproductions of Indian villages occupied by Native Americans transported not from thousands of miles away as in previous fairs, but rather from nearby pueblos and reservations. As the PCE's publicity department proposed, the region's Native American population was not yet extinct, but could be found on a sliver of San Diego's city park.

Less than two weeks after the opening of the PCE, the *San Diego Union* published a front-page article with a headline that declared "Indians Great Attraction, Exhibit Declared Wonderful." The paper included pictures of the "wonderful" Painted Desert exhibit, which also attracted numerous artists who could "sketch from real life" southwestern Indians in surroundings that imitated their native lands. Here, the *Union* maintained, "[e]very phase of Indian life is depicted. There are no delusions. Only those things, which enter in the real life of Indians are allowed."[15] Originally hoping to gather some eight hundred Indians from the areas through which the Santa Fe Railway line traveled on its way to the Pacific, fair officials had to settle for a smaller and slightly narrower exhibit. As historian Richard Amero has argued, Santa Fe Railway president Edward Ripley agreed to sponsor the proposed display at the San Diego fair, believing that "the picture of handsome, dignified, taciturn, and exotic Indians, in colorful robes, backdropped by the blue skies, multi-hued hills and vast spaces of the Southwest could be converted into a magnet to draw tourists."[16] By early 1914 the railway company displayed models for its planned Indian village at its local headquarters, as well as in several other cities the railroad served.

Deriving profit, however, was only one reason for such an ambitious project. Exposition directors also touted the exhibit's educational value. One important feature of the Painted Desert was that "the great colony of Indians who are inhabiting their desert are not idle, and are not in white men's clothes, but are living just as they lived and their ancestors have lived for centuries. . . . They are reproducing life so that the white man can understand it. In other word, within the space of a few acres is reproduced with startling accuracy the life of the various Indian tribes throughout the whole southwest."[17] Recognizing this opportunity to help the American public better understand Native American societies, the president of the School of American Archaeology, Edgar L. Hewett, accepted PCE president David Collier's offer to serve as director of exhibits. The negative impact that the conquest of the West had on the region's indigenous people deeply concerned Hewett. He hoped to design a display that showed southwest tribes as they lived so that white Americans might learn about and better appreciate Indians and, if possible, help save their culture.[18]

Hewett and Collier's lofty goals aside, the Painted Desert exhibit was as impressive as it was ambitious. Located at the northern end of the exposition, the exhibit was divided into two sections. On the west side, visitors encountered Apaches; the Havasupais, with a replica of a cave where the cliff dwellers once resided; and Navajos living in their traditional hogans. The eastern section housed a Pueblo-style village, which included members of the Taos, Hopi, and Tewa tribes. Exposition officials transported nearly two dozen Native Americans from the San

Ildefonso Pueblo in New Mexico to San Diego to help construct the $100,000 exhibit. At its peak, nearly three hundred Indians lived and worked in the village, performing traditional dances, making pottery and other crafts, and, at times, posing for visiting artists. By locating the Painted Desert next to the exposition's Model Farm, fair officials believed visitors could not escape the Southwest's remarkable progress from the "primitive agricultural methods" of the Pueblo Indians to the "tract where the methods of the white man are being shown."[19] A testimony to its widespread appeal, the Painted Desert was without a doubt the most photographed and advertised exhibit at the 1915 San Diego exposition.[20]

Central to San Diego fair directors' vision of the Painted Desert was its perceived authenticity. Brochures, marketing materials, newspaper reports, and public comments by Panama-California Exposition officials consistently heralded the exhibit's realism. Collier, for example, explained to a contingent of congressmen during a visit to Washington, DC, that there "will be primitive men from all parts living as their fathers lived, practicing pursuits their fathers practiced." Herman Schweizer, an official with the Fred Harvey Company (a chain of hotels and restaurants built alongside rail lines in the Southwest), claimed that his goal was to "reproduce a true representation of Indian life and to depict their mode of living at home."[21] The exhibit's authenticity extended beyond the buildings and grounds. The *San Diego Union* explained that visitors could observe Indian women preparing corn "in the primitive manner of years ago" and baking their bread in traditional ovens, and even watch Indian families eat their meals.[22]

Reproducing an authentic experience for fairgoers hinged on making the exhibit appear as natural as possible. The *Los Angeles Times*, for example, alleged the Painted Desert display is "[s]o natural . . . that the Indians themselves are quite at home in it."[23] A Santa Fe Railway Company representative emphasized that the exhibit was not a show. Visitors instead watched Indians "doing any number of things that may have looked strange to you, but it is all in the life of the Indian. We just want them to be natural while in San Diego. And, being natural, is the easiest thing they do."[24] Fair guidebooks and brochures advertised that "natural" meant more than just an imitation of the landscape and buildings. Commenting on the educational value of the Painted Desert, the *Journal of Education* explained that the "Indian does not strive to make something different from that which his people commonly make. He tries to make what he makes just as his ancestors made it."[25] The exhibit's authenticity stemmed from the false belief that what fairgoers witnessed was timeless and unchanged. Whatever day of the week one toured the Indian village, visitors believed that they not only saw Native Americans as they had inhabited the Southwest centuries ago, but also as they still lived in the new states of New Mexico and Arizona.

Balancing entertainment against authenticity proved to be difficult for San Diego officials. Besides largely ignoring the fact that many of the Native Americans residing at the Painted Desert exhibit came from government reservations, even some of the dances performed at the San Diego fair were less than genuine. While the audience at a special performance thought they had witnessed "tribal dances that had been handed down through generations of redmen," an exposition official admitted that these dances were not indigenous to the San Ildefonso Pueblo Indians who performed them but had been borrowed from other tribes.[26] Moreover, since fair directors wished to stage such performances at night, exhibit designer Herman Schweizer had to find a way to light the Painted Desert village without undermining the authentic look he desired. Less than a month before the PCE opened its gates, he explained to the *San Diego Union* that "we contemplate using electric lights which cannot be seen. If large glowing lights were to be seen the whole atmosphere would be changed. Four large poles with lights will appear as four moons hovering over the village."[27] While no doubt an ingenious solution, many fairgoers must have wondered how an Indian village could have four moons.

Four moons hovering over an Indian village signified the importance of these live Indian exhibits to western leaders. The commercial demands of expositions necessitated the inclusion of Native Americans, while larger ideological and political goals required authenticity. The popularity of native dances and the Pueblo villages promised profit, as well as the opportunity to demonstrate that Native Americans no longer posed a threat to white settlers. Fair publicity directors understood that these exhibits' apparent realism was central to promoting their respective expositions and crafting a new image for the Far West. Such staged authenticity gave the appearance of "natural" because it was primitive—in stark contrast to white American life.[28] As one scholar has argued, "the pueblo village provided an ostensibly stable reference point for visitors to gauge the differences between savage and civilized and for the inhabitants' vanishing state to be the inevitable result of the former."[29] The discourse of authenticity insisted that authentic items and exhibits were not of the present, but rather fading into the past, just like the vanishing tribes.[30] Exposition officials ensured that visitors left the fairgrounds confident that the new West still possessed the charm of its Indian past—but not its danger.

The Civilizing Efforts of Reformers

Fair directors, however, struggled to balance images of Native American life as static and unchanged with desires to demonstrate that supposed primitiveness was quickly giving way to the civilizing efforts of reformers. Like most expositions, San Francisco's PPIE hosted national meetings of prominent academic and government organizations, including the Congress on Indian Progress, where experts discussed the current state of Native Americans. Similarly, the Palace of Liberal Arts featured a lecture entitled "Progress of the Indian" by a special agent of the United States Indian Office, while films sponsored by Rodman Wanamaker's department store described Americanization campaigns to help Indians achieve a better life.[31] San Diego leaders likewise advertised that the array of Indian exhibits at the Panama-California Exposition "will emphasize in a most uniquely practical way the well nigh unbelievable progress made by the descendants of these first inhabitants."[32] While Director Hewett may have objected to the Bureau of Indian Affairs' assimilationist objectives, a fair brochure nevertheless advertised that the Painted Desert exhibit would show Southwest Indians grazing their animals and "bringing their wares into the trading post, and exchanging them for food and white man's clothing."[33] While perhaps a minor aspect of the Indian village exhibit, a pair of trousers or a muslin shirt symbolized a first step towards eventual integration.

Trading woven baskets for a pair of pants was not the only purported evidence that Native Americans were on the path to assimilation. Four Hopi women who resided at the Painted Desert exhibit explained that they had attended a U.S. government school in Arizona, where teachers had Americanized their names to make it easier for school employees.[34] Praising the achievements of Indian schools, the *San Diego Union* claimed that a group of Indians from a Yuma, Arizona school, did not need an interpreter when they listened to the "voice of their 'Great White Father' "—President Woodrow Wilson—who had recorded a message to them on a phonograph.[35] Native Americans' command of the English language was not the only sign of acculturation. A PCE *Daily Program*, for example, advertised a concert by a group of Indians from Yuma, while visitors to the PPIE '49 Camp could listen to Native Americans from a Nevada Indian school perform opera and popular music numbers.[36] Fairgoers could not help being impressed by the apparent great strides made by government education efforts to "civilize" Native Americans who once freely roamed the region.

Following the efforts of the earlier Pacific Northwest expositions, fair officials often identified Indian education as central to assimilating Native Americans. While western leaders may have shared some of the larger goals of national reformers, historian Robert Trennert argues, "local political, racial, and economic interests played a much greater role in school affairs than reformers anticipated."[37] Native American schoolchildren in California and the Southwest may have learned English and math, but pressures from local labor markets encouraged school officials to train Indian students to serve the local economy rather than improve reservation life. One Phoenix newspaper, for example, celebrated the opening of the city's Indian school because it promised to provide "cheap and efficient labor" for area cotton farms and fruit growers.[38] Both the Phoenix Indian School and the Sherman Institute in Riverside, California, employed the outing system where educators sent schoolchildren to work on farms or as domestics in local white homes. Not only did these leave Native American students insufficiently prepared to advance in the changing industrial labor market, it also harmed tribal homelands, like northern California's Round Valley Indian Reservation, "where a generation or two of bright

Native students left the reservations."[39] Visitors to San Diego or San Francisco, however, blissfully left these fairs with only positive images of Native American schoolchildren playing instruments or reciting poems in perfect English.

While lectures, exhibits, and staged games and performances encouraged fairgoers to conclude that government efforts to assimilate Native Americans were working, other less orchestrated events reminded visitors that western Indians were not that different from them. Newspapers accounts and photographs taken at the various fairs highlighted, intentionally or not, that Native Americans brought to the expositions to perform native dances or reside in live exhibits were not as primitive as advertised. An *Overland Monthly* article on the San Francisco fair, for example, pictured a couple of traditionally dressed Native Americans standing before a bank teller with the caption: "Indians of the 101 Camp putting their savings in a bank on the grounds."[40] The *Los Angeles Times* noted that while during the day the Indians resided in the PCE Painted Desert exhibit, at night fairgoers could find some "taking in the sights of the Isthmus," the fair's fun zone.[41] Moreover, when given the chance, Native Americans sometimes ventured outside the fairgrounds to explore the host city. A San Diego newspaper recounted the awe and antics of some hundred Native Americans whom fair officials escorted to Ocean Beach. Like many other new visitors to the ocean, the Indians dipped their feet in the water and collected seashells on the shore.[42] In the end, Native Americans riding a Ferris wheel in the fun zone or splashing in the ocean may have given pause to some white fairgoers who thought that Indians were irredeemable heathens.

Visions of Empire

Native Americans were not the only population in which fair officials tried to manipulate or manage popular racial attitudes and mindsets. Like the Portland and Seattle expositions, visions of empire remained an important theme at both California fairs. San Diego and San Francisco leaders urged the American people to look west towards the Pacific Ocean and less towards the Atlantic. But in doing so, California leaders could not ignore that this meant greater contact and interaction with less well-known Asian populations. The *San Diego Union*, for example, announced that its city's fair would further bind the "roaring aggressive Occident and the placid, receptive Orient."[43] Building upon the aggressive advertising campaigns by Pacific Northwest leaders, both California fairs consistently underscored the potential of Asian markets and how their cities were positioned to exploit them. San Francisco, the PPIE's official historian explained, was best suited to build this relationship since it "was accustomed to the finest displays of Oriental art goods, Chinese and Japanese, in the shops of her Oriental and American merchants."[44] San Francisco's status as the nation's official international exposition—despite San Diego's wishes—along with its long commercial ties to China that began during the gold rush and its place as the economic powerhouse of the Far West gave its claim more legitimacy.

Driven by the potential economic windfall of trans-Pacific commerce, San Francisco officials especially focused attention on securing China and Japan's participation in the Panama-Pacific International Exposition. Local businessmen and political leaders rested the city's continuing economic dominance of the Pacific on the fair's efforts to promote and develop American trade with the Far East.[45] The *San Francisco Chronicle*, for example, underscored the vast potential of Asian commerce due to the increased presence of the United States in the region following the Spanish-American War. The paper reminded readers that on the other side of the Pacific "are the 500,000,000 of the Oriental race in Asia, the world's greatest continent. In commercial relations between the United States and this trade area, with its vast population San Francisco already occupies a prominent position." As the "western gateway of the United States," the Golden Gate city could both continue its regional dominance by capturing the lion's share of this commerce and help maintain California's economic vitality that the now-distant gold rush had begun.[46]

San Francisco's size, prestige, and propitious timing of its fair meant that the PPIE would have the most significant Asian presence of the four Pacific Coast celebrations. The preeminence and wealth of the California metropolis not only helped it secure the title as the nation's official international exposition in 1915, but it also helped the city curry support from public officials and business leaders in China and Japan. Timing also proved beneficial to PPIE directors. When Portland hosted the Lewis and Clark Exposition a decade earlier, Japan was at war with Russia, significantly diminishing its participation. Four years later, Seattle leaders expressed hope that they could secure a strong East Asian presence at their city's fair; however, as scholar Shelley S. Lee explained, "without a government's voice to demand respectful treatment, Chinese contributions to the A-Y-P were largely limited to amusements like juggling acts and rickshaw rides."[47] Yet by 1915, China, as a new republic, wished to establish itself among the nations of the world. San Francisco publicity officials seized on this interest and strongly promoted both China and Japan's participation at the Panama-Pacific International Exposition.[48]

San Diego leaders similarly recognized the lucrative potential of the Chinese and Japanese markets. Emphasizing the city's proximity to the soon-to-be-completed Panama Canal, the *San Diego Union* proclaimed in 1910 that ships traveling through the canal were "destined to make San Diego their port of call and destination on the long voyage" between the United States and the emerging Asian economies.[49] However, dreams of capturing this trade and currying Japanese and Chinese participation at the Panama-California Exposition were soon thwarted when San Francisco announced its bid to host a competing fair in 1915. San Diego officials quickly pivoted and, while not completely ignoring China and Japan, refocused their marketing strategy on the community's southwest location. Acknowledging the economic and political power of its northern California neighbor, as well as its place as the nation's official international exposition, San Diego fair directors had little choice but to offer a more muted Asian role at its celebration.

Anti-Asian Feelings

Expectations that the two California expositions would finally demonstrate the great potential of the Asia-Pacific trade were nearly derailed before fair directors turned the first shovel. The same anti-Asian feelings that had plagued the Alaska-Yukon-Pacific Exposition threatened to disrupt California's fairs. Home to the Asiatic Exclusion League, California had a long history of anti-Asian activity stretching back to the early days of the gold rush. Anti-Chinese sentiments spiked in the 1870s as the state confronted the economic and social changes produced by the completion of the first transcontinental railroad. Disgruntled white laborers organized into the Workingmen's Party to press state and local officials to address the supposed Chinese threat, culminating with the passage of the Chinese Exclusion Act in 1882.[50] In addition, renewed tension between workers and employers at the turn of the century prompted labor leaders to form the Asiatic Exclusion League. In the wake of the devastating earthquake that struck the Bay Area in 1906, San Francisco officials responded to inflamed racial tensions by segregating Japanese schoolchildren, an action that quickly ignited an international conflict when the Japanese government complained to American officials, prompting President Theodore Roosevelt to intervene and forge the Gentlemen's Agreement: Japan agreed to curtail emigration of Japanese workers, and San Francisco leaders were pressured to rescind the city's segregation order.[51] While this may have helped put to rest this conflict, racial tension continue to simmer for the next few years, until it erupted once again during the critical planning stage of the Panama-Pacific International Exposition.

Despite the immigration deal between the United States and Japan, anti-Japanese sentiment subsided little in California. Not only was the state home to the Asiatic Exclusion League, but growing numbers of white farmers publicly complained about the competition they faced from Japanese growers. In 1907, 1909, and 1911, the California legislature considered bills that aimed to curtail Japanese land ownership. However, just as in the school controversy, federal officials intervened to urge state leaders to block the bills. As PPIE directors feverishly finalized plans for the fair, they faced an additional obstacle when the state legislature took up another alien land law in early 1913. Governor Hiram Johnson, feeling pressure from the state's farmers, announced his support for the new bill. Such negative publicity threatened to undermine the PPIE's advertising campaign just as it was reaching its zenith. Fearing a backlash from both the Japanese and Chinese governments, San Francisco leaders quickly mobilized to derail this latest bill.[52]

PPIE directors wasted no time lobbying state legislators. President Charles Moore, for example, personally contacted Democratic and Republican party leaders and found allies in Sacramento to educate and pressure the legislature about the danger this Alien Land Law posed to the PPIE. Fair officials argued that San Francisco and California had promised the nation an international exposition, and the proposed bill might encouraged Japan, China, and perhaps other nations to pull their support. The bill, Director in Chief Frederick J. V. Skiff claimed, put at risk the "success of the exposition which the Nation and the people of the United States have entrusted" to California.[53] A *San Francisco Chronicle* editorial put the potential damage of the Alien Land Law in concrete financial terms: The proposed legislation would likely mean fewer countries' participation in the fair, diminished attendance, and lost jobs for San Francisco workers. In short, the law would "endanger and perhaps destroy the enormous investment which this State is investing in the enterprise." The paper, however, did not oppose the law in principle, but simply concluded that little would be lost if the state waited until after the fair to pass it.[54]

The fears of San Francisco leaders were not unfounded. As California legislators debated the proposed bill, Japanese government officials expressed their dismay to both fair directors and to the Woodrow Wilson administration. The Japanese ambassador, for example, told Secretary of State William Jennings Bryan that his nation might pull out of the PPIE if the bill passed. A few weeks later, Japanese officials sent a letter to the exposition directors declaring that if the law was enacted, "Japan will withdraw her support from the Panama-Pacific International Exposition, refusing to exhibit and prohibiting Japanese citizens from having any connection with the Fair."[55] Japanese-American leaders from around California also challenged the racist sentiments behind the bill. Speaking to dignitaries at a banquet on Japan Day at the Panama-California Exposition, the president of the Japanese Association of Southern California declared that "no matter what racial prejudice may exist, . . . no matter what color of hair, skin or eyes, we are just as loyal to this country and just as sincere boosters of Southern California as you gentlemen."[56] Protests aside, the California legislature nevertheless passed the Alien Land Law in May 1913.

Dismayed by the legislature's decision, PPIE officials worked arduously to overcome this setback. Like Seattle leaders' efforts to neutralize labor's anti-Asian feelings, San Francisco fair directors praised Japan and attempted to assuage any hurt feelings. President Moore, for example, assured Japanese officials that their citizens would be welcomed and treated with respect. Moreover, when dignitaries or representatives of the Far East nation visited San Francisco, businessmen and fair directors hosted lavish dinners and celebrations in their honor. No doubt these gestures helped smooth relations with Japan, as did the pragmatism of Japanese businessmen who saw long-term economic benefits from participating in the PPIE and helped convince their government leaders to reject calls to pull out.[57]

Asian Displays and Events

By the time the California expositions' gates swung open in early 1915, the alien land controversy had subsided, though it was not forgotten. Fair directors welcomed Japanese and Chinese participation by holding welcoming ceremonies, celebrating national holidays, and hosting special Japan and China days. In San Francisco, both Asian nations constructed impressive exhibits that combined traditional arts with examples of modernity. The Chinese government, for example, erected a group of buildings "enclosed by a miniature of the Great Chinese Wall," which included a model of a palace and a "portion of the Forbidden City of Peking." Inside the exhibit, fairgoers could look at paintings, hand-carved furniture, and other examples of Chinese art. Chinese displays could also be found in the Palaces of Industry, Transportation, and Mines, and other special exhibit halls.[58] As a new republic, China wished to demonstrate that it belonged among the modern nations of the world. Speaking to a crowd at the dedication of the Forbidden City building, Consul-General S. C. Shu discussed China's recent progress, noting that "visitors to the exposition probably will get an entirely different idea of China from that now held by most people."[59] Proof of the nation's progress could be found at China's educational exhibit, which showed its adoption of a westernized school system by displaying the work of students from grammar school to college.[60]

Like China, Japan's display at the PPIE also wove the traditional with the modern. In addition to a government pavilion, the Far East nation planted four acres of gardens surrounding "tea houses and exhibit buildings containing a reproduction of the Nikko Shrines." As impressive as this might have been, fair publicity officials professed that "they constituted the minor portion of country's participation in the Exposition"[61]—the combined space occupied by Japan in the various palace halls surpassed all foreign nations participating at the PPIE.[62] Fine woodcraft, art, and industrial goods were not the only features of Japan's exhibit that impressed visitors. The *San Francisco Chronicle*, for example, noted that the Japanese "finely illustrated reports of their accomplishments" that accompanied exhibits—something from which American exhibitors could learn.[63] Such praise likely reflected San Francisco's appreciation for Japan's participation, recognition of the Far East nation's place among world powers, and hopes that such attention would help expand American trade with the Orient and further enrich the California metropolis.

Cultural celebrations and observation of special days were an important part of the two California expositions' marketing strategies because they simultaneously enhanced the profile of both China and Japan and deflected the negative publicity of the alien land laws. Fair directors often worked in concert with delegates or exhibitors from the two nations or looked to local Asian residents to help organize and advertise these events. During the Panama-Pacific International Exposition, for example, Japan hosted several traditional events from celebrating the New Year and the Iris Festival to concerts and parades. In contrast, China was more reticent about staging traditional events that might confirm stereotypes that American visitors had of the ancient nation. The opening of the China Building, for example, was marked with little pomp other than some Chinese music and songs sung in both Chinese and English. According to a San Francisco paper, "No Orientalism for Chinese Programme [*sic*]," was the plan Chinese officials had for China Day at the PPIE.[64] Speeches by both Chinese officials and fair directors at the official dedication of the Chinese government pavilion instead emphasized the great strides the Asian nation had recently made.[65]

Unlike the impressive government pavilions and notable visiting Asian dignitaries that marked the PPIE, San Diego's publicity department relied much more on special events and cultural celebrations to highlight the two nations' importance. In early February 1915, for example, some ten thousand visitors to the Panama-California Exposition attended a Chinese New Year celebration replete with drums, firecrackers, and a traditional dragon dance. Along the fair's amusement zone, "The Isthmus," revelers listened to the Toy Kee Orchestra, while others watched the popular Chinese gambling game Fan-Tan.[66] The *San Diego Union*, however, explained that this New Year celebration was different for two reasons. For one, the paper claimed, it was "the first time that Yankee curiosity has been allowed to indulge itself in a Chinese New Year celebration" because previously, most of the event was held behind closed doors. More importantly, since China was now a republic and ruled by a president and not an emperor, the *Union* suggested, the Chinese would "bow beneath the mandate of progress" by celebrating the New Year on the same day as Europeans and Americans did. While the political significance of the fair's Chinese New Year celebration may have escaped most fairgoers, the festivities did not fail to fascinate them. The "California Celestials," the paper concluded, provided ample entertainment for their American audience, who found "the quaint ceremonies of the Orientals" interesting.[67]

The Chinese culture's exotic mien, which the fair's marketing efforts exploited so well, no doubt fascinated the largely American audience, especially those who were first-time visitors to the Far West. Yet without Chinese officials to mediate how their nation was portrayed, as was the case in San Francisco, Fan-Tan gambling games and dragon dances significantly informed San Diego fairgoers' perceptions of China. Local Chinese residents may have done their best to represent their homeland, but they could not fully compensate for the absence of government exhibits needed to offset stereotypical notions of the Chinese. Guests exited the exposition with little more understanding of China other than that its people enjoyed gambling and colorful dances.

While Japan's presence at the PCE paled in comparison to the larger fair to the north, visitors to San Diego saw a more balanced image of the Far East nation than they witnessed of China. Local leaders'

Photograph of Chinese Village buildings at the Panama-Pacific International Exposition. *San Francisco History Center, San Francisco Public Library.*

treatment of Japan encompassed more than simple cultural celebrations or recognition of its colorful history. Exposition directors, for example, displayed examples of both traditional and modern Japanese industries and arts in several exhibit halls.[68] Promotional brochures also praised the tranquil Japanese botanical gardens where fairgoers could stop for a light lunch and tea.[69] Celebrating Japan Day in late July, local Japanese-American residents decorated the grounds with ten thousand lanterns and participated in numerous activities, including a game of tug-of-war and fencing matches.[70] Recognizing Japan's importance to the fair and its place among world powers, fair officials also lavished attention on important dignitaries. When Japanese naval officers visited San Diego, for example, a Marine troop escorted them to the fairgrounds, where local political leaders and fair officials welcomed them with a luncheon at the Cristobal Café.[71] In the end, government support combined with Japan's status in the world to help mitigate unfavorable or biased representations of the Far East power at the Southern California fair.

Contradictory Images of Asian-Americans

San Diego fair directors also did their best to put on a good face and overcome anti-Asian feelings that had not fully subsided in the wake of the passage of the alien land bill two years earlier. Yet, like the conflicting messages about Native Americans, the California fairs presented contradictory images of Asian Americans in the Far West. The spike of anti-Japanese sentiment in California notwithstanding, the Japanese population fared much better. As historian Abigail Markwyn has argued, Japan "did not face the same stereotypes associating its ancient society with decay or decadence that China did." Not only was Japan perceived more as a military and economic threat, the history of Japanese immigration to the United States was shorter.[72] The Chinese population on the West Coast could not say the same. Decades of anti-Chinese feelings and racial prejudice proved more difficult to overcome—the country, and by extension Chinese Americans, were not just exotic and mysterious in eyes of white Americans, but also morally corrupt and culturally inferior. Nowhere was this more evident than at exposition amusement zones.

As they opened the fairground gates in early 1915, PPIE publicity directors likely hoped that visitors to San Francisco might appreciate the birth of a new China. Despite both Chinese officials and exposition officers' efforts to craft a positive image of the new republic, fairgoers nevertheless likely left the fairgrounds wondering if China was truly a changed nation. Industrial and fine arts exhibit halls may have displayed numerous examples of Chinese progress, yet the nearby amusement area "The Zone" presented a more troubling view of Chinese civilization. Amidst the shooting galleries, theaters, and the ever-popular productions of famous natural disasters, stood the Chinese Village. The pagoda-style exhibit offered food in the "Chop Suey House" as well as a chance to witness "awful visual warnings of the fate of the opium smoker and drug fiend" in the Underground Chinatown attraction.[73] Here visitors could explore "the underground warrens of San Francisco's Chinatown where prostitutes and opium addicts conducted their immoral activities."[74] Popular and financially lucrative, PPIE directors initially succumbed to popular stereotypes of Chinese life that dated back nearly fifty years and added the commercial attraction to "The

Zone." Chinese officials and local Chinese residents, however, expressed concern about the image that the Underground Chinatown presented to the public. Angry that his homeland was associated with this spectacle, the Chinese commission-general demanded that the PPIE remove any reference to China. Fair officials agreed, closed the attraction, and then reopened it weeks later under the name Underground Slumming.[75]

The decision to refashion the Underground Chinatown reflected both Chinese officials' influence and the reluctance of fair directors to offend this important economic client. But if visitors to the PPIE wished to reconnoiter the unsavory world of Chinatown opium dens, they only had to journey a few hundred miles south to San Diego's exposition. Since the Chinese government chose to snub San Diego in 1915, PCE directors were free to exploit the public's fascination with these urban enclaves. Just as the Painted Desert exhibit catered to the American public's interest in Native American life, the Chinatown re-creation offered a glimpse into the darker side of Chinese society. Fair publicity officials understood that however seedy the Underground Chinatown was, it would appeal to some who were fascinated by the exotic Far East. The *San Diego Sun*, for example, reported that the PCE's Underground Chinatown attraction located on "The Isthmus" included a "hop joint"—or opium den—with Chinese slave girls and men smoking. Upon entering the exhibit, the paper described, "you feel that you have entered a new and darkly mysterious world."[76] Exposed to this shadowy world, fairgoers could leave the fair confident of the superiority of American culture and suspicious of the morality of the Chinese and, by extension, Chinese Americans.

CHINATOWN

If references to Chinatowns at the Pacific Coast expositions had been limited to the Underground Chinatown or similar commercial attractions found in their respective amusement zones, easterners might have returned home with a very distorted understanding of the Far West's Asian population. Asian Americans, however, were not simply relegated to the fair amusement zones. San Francisco had a large Chinese population residing in the city's famous Chinatown. Rather than

The Panama-Pacific International Exposition's Underground Slumming concession, after the name changed from Underground Chinatown. *Anne T. Kent California Room, Marin County Free Library.*

hide or ignore the local district, PPIE officials made it a central part of their marketing campaign. Despite the early hiccup over the Underground Chinatown exhibit, fair directors and local Chinese leaders wished to prove that the city's Chinese population posed no threat and could no longer be defined by past stereotypes. No place more clearly demonstrated this than San Francisco's Chinatown district. An enclave once associated with vice, filth, and moral depravity was now celebrated alongside notable local points of interest like Golden Gate Park, the Cliff House, and the newly minted Civic Center. Publicity materials, for example, explained that the "New Chinatown"—with its restaurants and temples—was "more characteristic of the Orient than the old one wiped out entirely by the fire."[77] Few PPIE guidebooks or

advertisements failed to feature the city's Chinatown or include depictions of Chinese residents roaming the streets of a neighborhood that exuded "quaint oriental charm."[78] The exotic look of Chinatown, PPIE president Charles C. Moore professed, masked the impact of western ways as evidenced by how visitors "have to hunt today in Chinatown for that disappearing article, the queue."[79] The New Chinatown was no longer a place to fear or avoid, but rather, Abigail Markwyn has suggested, "an attraction to be viewed and again consumed during one's visit to the city."[80]

Like Native Americans, Chinese and Japanese populations were an essential part of the Far West's character. While exposition publicity departments may have aimed for a more nuanced or balanced view of the region's Asian residents, they could not always control the messaging. If visitors to California attended the PCE in San Diego, they saw a much more one-sided perspective of San Francisco's Chinatown. Unlike the PPIE, San Diego fair directors did not close the notorious Underground Chinatown exhibit in 1915. The *San Diego Union* claimed that the exhibit made it easier for a visitor "to imagine he is in on one of the streets in the famous Chinatown in San Francisco" and therefore study "the life of the Chinese and their habits."[81] The local press coverage of San Diego's Chinatown implied that the unsavory milieu of the Underground attraction was not limited to the larger San Francisco ethnic enclave. Newspaper reports, for example, described gambling activities and violent conflicts among local vice operators. In August, the *San Diego Union* featured a front-page headline announcing a San Diego police raid that nabbed "Forty-nine Chinamen."[82] Fairgoers in San Francisco or San Diego who stumbled upon such articles might have wondered if these new Chinatowns, which fair publicity directors and local leaders so praised, were in fact really new.

Imperial Desires

The goal of the expositions to exploit the economic potential of the Pacific Ocean trade, despite it already being home to more than a hundred thousand Asians, only confounded the marketers' representations of Japan and China. For more than a century, Native Americans may have shaped the public's understanding of the West, yet to most local white leaders, Indians seemingly offered little economic value aside from a few isolated tourist attractions in New Mexico or the Grand Canyon. However, most Native Americans lived well outside city limits and had little day-to-day interaction with local residents. Fair officials could not as easily ignore the city's Japanese and Chinese populations. Though segregated, Asian residents worked and lived within blocks of downtown business districts. Local leaders' yearning to expand Pacific Ocean trade with Asia meant that the expositions had to tread carefully in how they presented both the Far East nations and local Asian American residents. Imperial desires and racialist ideology only confounded this effort.

America's Pacific Ocean empire involved more than just the economic windfall that the Far East promised California. San Diego and San Francisco leaders reminded fairgoers that in the previous two decades, the nation had added new island possessions to its empire. Seized by the United States in the wake of the Spanish-American War, the Philippines provided the nation an important place to help it expand its economic and military role in Asia. Held more than fifteen years after the nation seized control of the Philippines, the PPIE hosted the Panama-Pacific Historical Congress, which explored America's place in the Pacific. Discussion topics ranging from "Armament and Military in the Pacific" to "Ownership and Exploitation of Pacific Regions" reminded visitors that American interests in the Pacific had not waned.[83] Connecting American colonial holdings with the Far West helped exposition officials remind the public how central California was to national imperial designs in the Pacific.

The Philippines

Nowhere was the benefit of American rule more evident than with the Philippines. Despite the financial windfall the Igorot Village produced for both the Portland and Seattle expositions, both the PPIE and PCE rejected live exhibits of indigenous peoples and opted instead for a more positive view of the Philippines. In 1911 the *San Francisco Chronicle* reported on a plan by William Pack, governor of the Northern Luzon province in the Philippines, to arrange a "Real Igorote Village" at the upcoming Panama-Pacific International Exposition.[84] It seems clear, though, that fair officials never seriously considered this proposal, as they offered no public response. Moreover, when the gates opened in 1915, the PPIE did not include the popular exhibit.

Unlike the Pacific Northwest expositions, which left the impression that Filipinos were primitive and backward and thus justified American rule, the San Francisco fair presented a more encouraging perspective of the Philippines and Filipinos.[85] Gone from fair advertisements were the references to and images of dog-eaters and headhunters; in their place, exposition directors advertised exhibits highlighting the advances Filipinos made in less than two decades of

American oversight. Fairgoers who toured the Philippine Exhibit, fair officials proclaimed, could witness "the fruits of fifteen years of colonial administration for the benefit of the colony" that all recognized "was the most effective thing of its kind."[86] Despite a few pictures showing Filipinos wearing loincloths and carrying spears, suggesting what one visitor called "primitiveness," in the end Philippine exhibits left most visitors feeling confident that the island possession had made much progress.[87] American rule, the message seemed clear, had produced considerable positive results.

As millions of visitors enjoyed the fair's wonders in 1915, leaders in the nation's capital debated calls for ending American rule in the Philippines. *Sunset Magazine*, for example, reported that Congress was considering the Jones Bill, which promised eventual independence to the Philippines.[88] Leading California progressive leader Chester H. Rowell cautioned that despite signs of progress, Filipinos were not yet ready for self-government.[89] Acknowledging the strides made by the Philippines, the PPIE's official historian claimed that visitors to the exhibit discovered the recent developments in the arts, education, health, and economy that demonstrated the Philippines' "further progress toward self-governing nationalism." Besides examples of exquisite woodwork and fine linens, fairgoers could see photographs of the rare books, literary works, and dictionaries found in the Manila Library.[90] Visitors could also pick up several pamphlets highlighting the territory's economic activity, from sugar and rice yields to timber exports, as well as the numerous items produced by the Philippine Bureau of Printing.[91] The San Francisco exposition, however, never failed to remind guests that the Philippines' success was a direct result of American colonialism. One exhibit, for example, included a display of maps and photographs showing the "public improvements carried to successful conclusion during the American occupancy" by the Bureau of Public Works.[92]

Advances in education and hygiene in the Philippines commanded a great deal of attention at the San Francisco fair. PPIE historian Frank Morton Todd wrote shortly after the exposition that the "United States had something to show the world in colonial education." Besides the Manila Library display, fairgoers could tour the Philippine education exhibit, the largest housed in the Palace of Education, and review charts and displays touting the rapid growth in school attendance, in addition to how the curriculum produced trained craftsmen, professionals, and future leaders.[93] Public health and hygiene offered further evidence of the "large measure of recent improvement" in the Philippines. The Philippine Public Health Service exhibit presented images of modern homes, health education bulletins, and statistics of vaccination efforts.[94] Health officials also published a lengthy pamphlet emphasizing the sanitation and health achievements in the American possession, including strides made against smallpox and leprosy.[95] Upon exiting the fairgrounds, visitors surely would have been impressed by how far the Philippines had progressed since the Spanish-American War, the image of Igorote headhunters having quickly receded into the past following the Alaska-Yukon-Pacific Exposition. So impressed by the San Francisco's Philippines exhibit, San Diego fair directors acquired it from the PPIE to display during the PCE's second year.[96] By 1915 the message was clear: Benign American rule was rapidly transforming the Philippines, and many citizens could now imagine someday granting independence to the island possession.

Indigenous Opinions

Exposition marketing campaigns that advertised live displays of Indians, Filipinos, and other non-European ethnic groups at the four Pacific Coast fairs exploited both the people and prevailing racial attitudes to attract visitors. Throngs of fairgoers peering into the Painted Desert in San Diego or gazing at Igorotes at the Lewis and Clark Exposition not only helped swell gate receipts, but also provided fair directors the opportunity to influence how easterners viewed and understood the West's racial diversity. Indians, visitors learned, were not the dangerous threat to white settlers that they may have read in popular novels. A short tour of the Igorrote Village, in contrast, seemingly demonstrated that the nation's new territory and its people needed more American oversight.

Indigenous peoples put on display, however, were not consulted about what message they wished to convey, and in some cases, whether they wished to participate. Scant evidence makes it difficult to understand fully how Native Americans, Filipinos, or Eskimos felt about the live displays. However, scholars do agree that those inhabiting the exhibits "found ways to operate within this structure, negotiating their relationship with exposition officials, evading visitors' expectations, and use the fair for their own purposes."[97] This process began almost immediately when Native Americans or Filipinos agreed to participate at the Pacific Coast fairs. For some, it meant a few months of good pay that could help families back home. Economic opportunities on most Indian reservations, for example, were quite limited, and so these fairs provided Native Americans the opportunity to improve their lives. For others, a stint at a big-city fair offered excitement and adventure and, in some instances, allowed them to escape "the watch eyes of paternalistic missionaries and government officials."[98] In 1909 one native group from Alaska took advantage of their participation at the AYPE to complain to federal officials about the oppressive behavior of William Duncan, a Christian missionary who ran their settlement.[99]

Native Americans and the other people put on display continued to challenge the narratives of exposition marketing departments in subtle and not so subtle ways. Indians at the Panama-California Exposition's Painted Desert, for example, sometimes mocked white fairgoers or pretended not to understand visitors' comments when, in fact, they had a good command of English. Playing "Indian" when it suited them permitted Native American performers to have the last laugh. Decorating their "primitive" pueblo homes with clocks and steamer trunks likewise challenged the authenticity that exposition directors advertised.[100] At times, more direct action revealed the performers' unwillingness to submit to fair officials' desires. When Pueblo Indians at the San Diego fair discovered that a ritual dance had been surreptitiously filmed at their home village and was publicly presented at the exposition, one or more of them apparently broke into the New Mexico State Building and stole the newsreels.[101] At the AYPE fair, one Inuit tribal leader who resided at the Eskimo Village used her command of English to speak publicly in defense of her people and by doing so challenged misrepresentations of Alaska's indigenous people.[102] Confrontational speeches or simple mockery demonstrated that native performers refused to submit to the fairs' dominant narratives.

Indigenous performers were not the only ones who challenged the popular live exhibits. While exposition officials may have relished the inclusion of these native performers, some missionaries and assimilation advocates bemoaned this decision. In a letter to a Lewis and Clark fair director, Kate C. McBeth, who operated a school for Nez Perce women, wrote: "There is much talk among the Nez Perce about the Portland Fair since some parties have been engaging our wild, long haired ones to go. Of course they will be paid to go through their dances and heathenism. I regret this part of the Fair, it will be demoralizing to all the Western tribes."[103] The Philippine Villages may have produced the most resistance. Some Portland citizens, for example, threatened to boycott the fair if officials did not close the exhibit.[104] In Seattle, visiting sailors from the Philippines echoed the objections of many local Filipinos when they criticized AYPE directors for including the Igorrote Village exhibit on the "Pay Streak."[105] One controversy erupted in early 1909, when a group of twenty-seven angry local Filipino residents urged Washington governor M. E. Hay to force exposition directors to make the Igorots wear pants. In dismissing their request, the governor facetiously responded that he and fair officials should determine if the villagers were "short on dry goods," and if so, "we might take up a collection for them."[106] Despite calls for modesty, the Igorots would complete their stay at the fair sans pants.

Despite their effort, Seattle's Filipino residents failed to alter how exposition directors portrayed the Igorote natives from their homeland. This may have reflected the lack of power of the city's relatively small Filipino population. More likely, it signified the racial attitudes of the region's white leading citizens and the lack of respect they had for people of color. The governor may have thought the pants controversy was humorous, but Filipinos residents understood that the exhibit helped confirm his racist attitudes. The constant references to the Igorots' nakedness, headhunting, and dog-eating would only underscore popular misconceptions of the Philippines backwardness, making it more difficult for Filipinos—including those students and laborers who began to migrate to the West Coast in the first two decades of the twentieth century—to overcome racial stereotypes held by white Americans.

Unlike Native Americans, the AYPE Igorots did have a small group of fellow Filipinos, who, whether out of their own self-interest or legitimate concern for the performers, could intercede on their behalf. Chinese and Japanese residents of the four Pacific Coast exposition cities likewise helped mitigate how Asians and Asian Americans were portrayed at their local fairs. As we have seen, both Chinese and Japanese government officials successfully influenced representations of the two Asian nations at the Seattle and San Francisco fairs. While neither fair included anything like the Painted Desert for the Chinese or Japanese, smaller exhibits and midway concessions threatened to leave visitors with the wrong impression. When the PPIE opened the Underground Chinatown exhibit, Chinese residents mobilized to force exposition directors to close the objectionable concession. Public condemnation of the Underground Chinatown, along with scores of Chinese American students and officials attending fair functions outfitted in Euro-American suits and dresses, defied the racialized perspectives of exposition marketing directors.[107] Similarly, Seattle's Japanese population rarely missed an opportunity to work with fair directors. Local Japanese businessmen, for example, often joined with fair officers to host dignitaries from Japan, while residents constructed parade floats with young Japanese girls dressed "like American girls" for the special Japan Day at the AYPE.[108] Although they operated from a position of limited power, Asian American residents exploited the few opportunities available to moderate expositions' representations of them and their ancestral homelands.

THE CONTRADICTORY IMAGES OF NATIVE AMERICANS and Asians at the four Pacific Coast expositions reflected both the Far West's struggle to confront the region's growing diversity and the nation's conflicted feelings about its imperial aspirations. Sharing similar goals of economic growth and national recognition with the two Pacific Northwest fairs, the 1915 Panama-Pacific International and Panama-California expositions had to respond quickly to changing geopolitical concerns of the United States, China, and Japan. The complicated nature of race, culture, and politics at the dawn of the twentieth century significantly further challenged Pacific Coast fairs' efforts to market the Far West. The completion of the Panama Canal promised an economic windfall, yet rising racial discord in California threatened to derail efforts to secure the profitable but elusive Asian trade. Located at the edge of the nation's empire, California was central to expanding American presence in the Pacific. Sustaining this role rested, however, on maintaining public support for colonialism. Gone were the days of dog-eating Igorote tribes at Pacific Coast fairs, and in their place, visitors saw evidence of the benefits of American rule in the Philippines. Whether it was Portland in 1905 or San Francisco in 1915, issues of race, exposition officials quickly learned, made it challenging to sell the promise of the Far West.

CONCLUSION

JUST A FEW MONTHS AFTER CLOSURE OF THE SAN DIEGO fair, President Wilson asked Congress for a declaration of war, thrusting the nation into World War I. From 1905, when Portland hosted the first Pacific Coast exposition, to 1916, when San Diego ended its two-year fair, the Far West and the Pacific had captured the nation's attention. Western leaders shared with the American public their vision of the nation's future where the Far West occupied the epicenter. If asked to describe the country's upcoming years, many westerners likely would have responded that the twentieth-century would be the American West century. The culmination of four successful expositions over a short ten-year span inspired such confidence. However, the discovery of the Zimmermann Telegram in early 1917, which catapulted the United States into World War I, dashed westerners' dreams and expectations. As American doughboys joined the European conflict, the gaze of the nation would quickly shift from the Pacific to the Atlantic. The momentum of four Pacific Coast fairs soon dissipated, forcing western leaders to wonder what might have been.

While the Great War may have been short in duration, it nevertheless profoundly changed the United States. Hyper-patriotism spawned by the war and the subsequent Red Scare hastened the demise of progressivism and ushered in an era of conservatism. A revived nativism, for example, steered Americans away from nearly all things foreign. Novel national policies erected walls severely curtailing immigration, while a new isolationism discouraged expanding diplomatic ties abroad. By the early 1920s, Americans celebrated a booming industrial economy, which along with the radio and movie industry further engendered a national mass culture. To ensure victory, wartime policies encouraged farmers to expand production, resulting in overproduction and a depressed rural economy. Calls to expand farms and agricultural production at the Pacific Coast expositions a few years earlier now seemed foolhardy at best. The nationalization of American society—resulting from war, a maturing corporate capitalism, and new forms of media—slowly muted the regionalism that Far West exposition directors sought to highlight.

Summing up the impact of their respective expositions a decade after closing the entry gates, most officials looked back fondly on these fairs. Like with any marketing campaign, success is not always realized—however valuable or useful a product might be, the sales pitch might not persuade the consumer to buy what the seller is peddling; it could be the message, the messenger, or other factors that shape consumer behavior. Though some westerners may have viewed them as a success, the fairs came up short in their goal to encourage the nation to reimagine the geographic center of the nation. Whether Portland or San Francisco, local leaders maintained that the expositions left a positive impression of their cities. Some claimed that their ports were busier and business brisker than before they opened their doors to fairgoers.[1] No doubt San Diego or Seattle were better off, yet how much of that could be attributed to hosting an exposition is difficult to gauge. The traffic brought by later fairs likely helped all cities lining the Pacific Ocean. Nevertheless, exposition officials would reluctantly have had to admit that their grand expectations never materialized. However much they hoped, the Far West would not define twentieth-century America.

For the generation who devised and implemented the Pacific Coast expositions, the fairs would not be soon forgotten. The energy and excitement they produced for their communities did not quickly subside. As Carl Abbott has suggested, the Lewis and Clark Exposition—and for that matter, the other three fairs—"confirmed a new generation of civic leaders."[2] While proud of their accomplishments, these leaders looked forward, not backward. The fate of each city's fairgrounds reflected this. Just short of a year after it opened, demolition crews had leveled nearly all the buildings that comprised the Lewis and Clark Exposition; even Guild's Lake succumbed to silt by the early 1910s. While a few buildings were saved and moved to other locations, fairgoers who returned to Portland years after the fair ended would have not recognized the site.[3] Similar fate awaited those who visited San Francisco. Most of the magnificent buildings that adorned the Panama-Pacific International Exposition grounds were demolished, including the Tower of Jewels and the Arch of the Rising Sun. The Ohio Building was moved to nearby San Mateo, where it survived into the 1950s. City leaders, however, saved the Palace of Fine Arts, which is the only remaining building still inhabiting the old fairgrounds.[4]

Although they removed some exposition buildings, Seattle and San Diego leaders saw more value in salvaging what remained behind. Alaska-Yukon-Pacific Exposition directors turned over several buildings to the University of Washington, which served as lecture halls and laboratories for several decades. Today, only the former AYPE Women's Building, now Cunningham Hall, and Architecture Hall still stand on the Lake Washington campus.[5] San Diego leaders debated the future of the Spanish Colonial fairgrounds, but eventually chose to keep many of the buildings as museums. In fact, Balboa Park would house museums, the Spreckels Organ Pavilion, and the iconic California Tower, and in 1916 Dr. Harry Wegeforth would collect a number of animals that resided at the fair and create the San Diego Zoo just north of the exposition's main plaza. In 1935–36, the old fairgrounds would again be put to use when city leaders, in an effort to promote economic recovery during the Great Depression, invited the world to the California-Pacific International Exposition.[6]

When the Lewis and Clark Exposition closed its gates in late 1905, Portland officials brimmed with confidence that their city would dominate the Pacific Northwest for decades to come. Yet by the time the Seattle fair ended five years later, the Puget Sound city's population had surged past that of its Oregon neighbor to the south. The good feelings that the Alaska-Yukon-Pacific Exposition engendered soon gave way to violent labor strife by the start of World War I as radical labor groups like the Industrial Workers of the World challenged the region's business elites.[7] The two California expositions likewise failed to produce the results that local leaders expected. San Diego, for example, never became the entrepôt for the greater Southwest. City residents would soon find themselves battling over the future of their seaside community. The mayoral election in 1917 pitted candidates with different visions for the city in what would become known as the "Smokestacks" versus "Geraniums" debate.[8] In the end, San Diego residents chose industry over tourism, yet fair directors' dreams of a bustling port dominating Pacific Ocean trade were soon forgotten. Even the golden jewel of California, San Francisco, lost its shine in the decades following the PPIE, and by the 1920s, the booming metropolis of Los Angeles had eclipsed the Bay Area city in both population and economic significance.[9]

While the Pacific Coast expositions may not have lived up to the grand expectations of city leaders, they did offer a glimpse into how westerners saw themselves and their region. Above all, these expositions were community events created to market the city and region where they took place. Each may have crafted a theme or message that connected it to a historical memory or important event, whether that was an exploratory expedition or the opening of a major waterway, but in the end these locales hosted fairs to boost their cities. Marketing, in short, requires the seller—in this case, host cities—to define and package their product in order to fulfill the needs or desires of the customer. Success depended as much on having something to sell and fashioning an effective message as it did knowing one's customer. Exposition directors aptly tapped into the fears and anxieties of early-twentieth-century America and presented the Far West as the answer to them. Perhaps in the end, these anxieties were insufficient to dislodge easterners from their neighborhoods or villages during a time of uncertainty.

The conquest of the West, imperial expansion into the Pacific, and the industrialization of American society produced a unique moment in the Far West. From Seattle to San Diego, local leaders seized on the renewed interest in the West during the early twentieth century to define their homeland to those outside the region. This process, however, also encouraged westerners to engage in a level of self-analysis about themselves, their region, and their region's place in American society. Hosting an exposition compelled them to consider, or perhaps in some cases imagine, what made the Far West unique or special. Whether it was beautiful landscapes, untapped economic opportunities, agreeable climates, exotic but unthreatening populations, or some combination of these, fair officials and local elites believed that western living was distinctive. Selling that to others proved more difficult.

While Far West identity may have changed with time, remnants of the values, beliefs, and viewpoints that defined this region in the early twentieth century would not fully disappear. The surrounding scenic landscapes and westerners' relationship with nature and the environment continues to strongly characterize western identity. Whether it is the dense forests or majestic peaks dotting the Pacific Northwest or the balmy climate and beautiful beaches of Southern California, geography remains central to how western inhabitants understand their region. One only has to glance at tourism websites and ads to see how the Pacific Coast states continue to tout their stunning landscapes and natural beauty.[10] Likewise, racial diversity continues to influence their sense of place. For many, Indian reservations no longer invoke images of poverty, but rather, whether right or wrong, centers of new wealth and amusement marked by glitzy casinos. Similarly, Asian-Americans and Latinos continue to increasingly redefine the culture, economy, and politics of the Far West, though not without moments of tension and conflict.

While World War I may have dashed the economic hopes of exposition directors and western politicians, ironically it was another world war that may have finally allowed the Far West to realize these dreams. Any existing feelings of colonialism in the Far West disappeared with the profound economic transformation spawned by World War II. The "Westward Tilt" of the nation to the Far West, as former San Diego journalist Neil Morgan coined this phenomenon, achieved what Pacific Coast exposition directors only dreamed of a century ago.[11] However one measures success, be it economic, political, cultural, or technological, few could argue that the Pacific Slope has not succeeded. While today Portland, Seattle, San Francisco, and San Diego leaders might still court tourists, few now seek the permanent settlers that their predecessors so feverishly wished to attract. Locals who once thirsted for new colonists now complain about congestion and a degrading quality of life. Nevertheless, the region continues to attract newcomers and attention. Perhaps the message does not matter much, because the selling of the Far West may never be complete.

NOTES

Introduction

1 For a comprehensive study of late-nineteenth- and early-twentieth-century American expositions, see Robert W. Rydell, *All the World's a Fair: Visions of Empire at American International Expositions, 1876–1916* (Chicago: University of Chicago Press, 1984); Robert W. Rydell, John E. Findling, and Kimberly D. Pelle, *Fair America: World's Fairs in the United States* (Washington, DC: Smithsonian Institution Press, 2000).

2 Rydell, *All the World's a Fair*; James Gilbert, *Perfect Cities: Chicago's Utopias of 1893* (Chicago: University of Chicago Press, 1991); Curtis Hinsley and David Wilcox, ed., *Coming of Age in Chicago: The 1893 World's Fair and the Coalescence of American Anthropology* (Lincoln: University of Nebraska Press, 2016); Neil Harris, Wim De Wit, James Gilbert, and Robert W. Rydell, *Grand Illusions: Chicago's World's Fair of 1893* (Chicago: Chicago Historical Society, 1993).

3 Rydell, *All the World's a Fair.*

4 David M. Wrobel, *Promised Lands: Promotion, Memory, and the Creation of the American West* (Lawrence: University Press of Kansas, 2002), 2.

5 Rydell, *All the World's a Fair*, 4.

6 Sandwiched between the Portland and Seattle fairs, the Jamestown Exposition of 1907 marked the three hundredth anniversary of the settlement's founding.

7 Lisa Blee, "Completing Lewis and Clark's Westward March: Exhibiting a History of Empire at the 1905 Portland World's Fair," *Oregon Historical Quarterly* 106.2 (Summer 2005).

8 Sarah J. Moore, *Empire on Display: San Francisco's Panama-Pacific International Exposition of 1915* (Norman: University of Oklahoma Press, 2013).

9 Matthew F. Bokovoy, *The San Diego World's Fairs and Southwestern Memory, 1880–1940* (Albuquerque: University of New Mexico Press, 2005). See also Phoebe S. Kropp, *California Vieja: Culture and Memory in a Modern American Place* (Berkeley: University of California Press, 2006), chapter 3.

10 Abigail M. Markwyn, *Empress San Francisco: The Pacific Rim, the Great West, and California at the Panama-Pacific International Exposition* (Lincoln: University of Nebraska Press, 2014).

11 Carl Abbott, *The Great Extravaganza: Portland and the Lewis and Clark Exposition* (Portland: Oregon Historical Society, 1981).

12 The New Western History literature is immense. For a sample of the discussion comparing it to the earlier historiography of the region, see Clyde A. Milner II, ed., *A New Significance: Re-envisioning the History of the American West* (New York: Oxford University Press, 1996); Patricia N. Limerick, Clyde A. Milner II, and Charles E. Rankin, eds., *Trails: Toward a New Western History* (Lawrence: University Press of Kansas, 1991); William Cronon, George Miles, and Jay Gitlin, eds., *Under an Open Sky*; John Wunder, "What's Old about the New Western History? Race and Gender, Part 1," *Pacific Northwest Quarterly* 85.2 (April 1994), 50–58; "What's Old about the New Western History? Part II: Environment and Economy," *Pacific Northwest Quarterly* 88.2 (Spring 1998), 84–94.

13 David Wrobel has argued that by the early twentieth century, residents recognized the end of the frontier stage, and "for them, when the frontier process ended, regional consciousness could begin to develop." See David M. Wrobel, "Beyond the Frontier-Region Dichotomy," *Pacific Historical Review* 65.3 (August 1996), 414.

14 David M. Emmons, "Constructed Province: History and the Making of the Last American West," *Western Historical Quarterly* 25.4 (Winter 1994), 458–59. See also the responses from other scholars that followed this article. For more on regionalism, see William G. Robbins, Robert J. Frank, and Richard E. Ross, eds., *Regionalism and the Pacific Northwest* (Corvallis: Oregon State University Press, 1983).

15 Western tourism has attracted a lot of attention. See Earl Pomeroy, *In Search of the Golden West: The Tourist in Western America*, 2nd ed. (Lincoln: University of Nebraska Press, 1957); Hal Rothman, *Devil's Bargain: Tourism in the Twentieth-Century American West* (Lawrence: University Press of Kansas, 2000); Marguerite S. Shaffer, *See America First: Tourism and National Identity, 1880–1940* (Washington, DC: Smithsonian Institution Scholarly Press, 2001); David M. Wrobel and Patrick T. Long, eds., *Seeing and Being Seen: Tourism in the American West* (Lawrence: University Press of Kansas, 2001); "Tourism and the American West" special issue, *Pacific Historical Review* 65.4 (November 1996).

16 Wrobel, *Promised Lands*, 11.

17 Carl Abbott, *Boosters and Businessmen: Popular Economic Thought and Urban Growth in the Antebellum Middle West* (Westport, CT: Greenwood Press, 1981), 11.

18 Wrobel, *Promised Lands*, chapter 1; Pomeroy, *In Search of the Golden West*, 122; Paul J. P. Sandul, *California Dreaming: Boosterism, Memory, and Rural Suburbs in the Golden State* (Morgantown: West Virginia University Press, 2014), 10–12; Carlos A. Schwantes, "Landscapes of Opportunity: Phases of Railroad Promotion of the Pacific Northwest," *Montana: The Magazine of Western History* 43.2 (Spring 1993), 39–41; Kevin Starr, *Inventing the Dream: California through the Progressive Era* (New York: Oxford University Press, 1985), chapters 2–3.

19 Hal Rothman, "Selling the Meaning of Place: Entrepreneurship, Tourism, and Community Transformation in the Twentieth-Century American West," *Pacific Historical Review* 65.4 (November 1996), 557; Marguerite S. Shaffer, "'See America

First': Re-Envisioning Nation and Region through Western Tourism," *Pacific Historical Review* 65.4 (November 1996), 559–581.

20 G. J. Ashworth and H. Voogd, *Selling the City: Marketing Approaches in Public Sector Urban Planning* (London: Belhaven Press, 1990), 18.

21 Steven V. Ward and John R. Gold, "Introduction," in *Place Promotion: The Use of Publicity and Marketing to Sell Towns and Regions*, eds. Steven V. Ward and John R. Gold (Chichester, GB: John Wiley & Sons, 1994), 9.

22 Daniel Pope, *The Making of Modern Advertising* (New York: Basic Books Inc., 1983); Pamela Walker Laird, *Advertising Progress: American Business and the Rise of Consumer Marketing* (Baltimore: Johns Hopkins University Press, 1998); Roland Marchand, *Advertising the American Dream: Making Way for Modernity, 1920–1940* (Berkeley: University of California Press, 1985); Jackson Lears, *Fable of Abundance: A Cultural History of Advertising in America* (New York: Basic Books, 1994); James D. Norris, *Advertising and the Transformation of American Society, 1865–1920* (New York: Greenwood Press, 1990).

23 John M. Findlay, "A Fishy Proposition: Regional Identity in the Pacific Northwest," in David M. Wrobel and Michael C. Steiner, eds., *Many Wests: Place, Culture, and Regional Identity* (Lawrence: University Press of Kansas, 1997), 54; Wrobel, *Promised Lands*, 193.

24 Wrobel, *Promised Lands*, 2.

Chapter 1

1 Wrobel, *Promised Lands*, chapter 2.

2 For a comprehensive study of late-nineteenth- and early-twentieth-century American exposition, see Rydell, *All the World's a Fair*; and Rydell, Findling, and Pelle, *Fair America*.

3 "Dan McAllen's Account of the Origins of the Lewis and Clark Fair," Lewis and Clark Centennial Exposition—Official Records, Volume 4, File 15, Portland Public Library, Wilson Room (hereafter Wilson Room); *Evening Telegram*, February 20, 1905.

4 Quote from H. W. Corbett, "The Exposition: Extract from the Annual Report of President Corbett to the Board of Commissioners," in *The Centennial: Bulletin of Scope and Progress* 1.1 (1903), 5, Wilson Room. See also Abbott, *The Great Extravaganza*, xii, 13–21.

5 Carl Abbott, *Portland in Three Centuries: The Place and the People* (Corvallis: Oregon State University Press, 2011), 27–33.

6 Abbott, *Portland in Three Centuries*, 52–60; Carl Abbott, *How Cities Won the West: Four Centuries of Urban Change in Western North America* (Albuquerque: University of New Mexico Press, 2008), 62.

7 E. Kimbark MacColl, *The Shaping of a City: Business and Politics in Portland, Oregon, 1885–1915* (Portland: The Georgian Press Company, 1967), 224–26.

8 Abbott, *Portland in Three Centuries*, 42, 64–65.

9 *Lewis and Clark Journal* 1.2 (February 1904), 6.

10 "To Advertise the Fair," newspaper clipping, June 2, 1901, Scrapbook 27, Oregon Historical Society Research Library (hereafter OHS).

11 *Evening Telegram*, September 27, 1904.

12 *Lewis and Clark Journal* 2.2 (August 1904), 8–9; Henry Reed, *Portland and Columbia Watershed* (1901), in Lewis and Clark Centennial Exposition, Manuscript 1609, Box 27, File 50, OHS; Henry E. Reed, *Oregon: A Story of Progress and Development Together with an Account of the Lewis and Clark Centennial Exposition* (Portland, 1905) in OHS.

13 "To Bring 200,000 People Here in Exposition Year," newspaper clipping, November 13, 1901, Scrapbook 27, OHS.

14 Corbett, "The Exposition," 5; "Centennial of 1905," newspaper clipping, June 16, 1901, Scrapbook 27, OHS.

15 *Evening Telegram*, May 31, 1905; Joseph Gaston, *Portland Oregon: Its History and Builders*, vol. 1 (Chicago-Portland: S. J. Clarke Publishers, 1911), 584

16 "Portland Day" pin, in Lewis and Clark Centennial Exposition, MSS 1609, Box 1, envelope.

17 "Press and the 1905 Fair," newspaper clipping, September 25, 1901, Scrapbook 27, OHS; *Evening Telegram*, September 27, 1904.

18 "Oregon's Big Fair," *Eugene Register*, newspaper clipping, ca. 1901, Scrapbook 27.

19 Corbett, "The Exposition," 5.

20 Richard White, *"It's Your Misfortune and None of My Own": A New History of the American West* (Norman: University of Oklahoma Press, 1991), 363–65.

21 "For a Fair in 1902," newspaper clipping, December 29, 1900, Scrapbook 27, OHS.

22 "Exposition Confers Lasting Benefits," *Lewis and Clark Journal* 4.4 (October 1905); "Slump After Fair? Oh No!" *Los Angeles Times*, August 9, 1906; "Portland's Successful Exposition," *Literary Digest* 31 (October 28, 1905); Abbott, *The Great Extravaganza*, 18.

23 Secretary Reed to Mr. Arthur Gutteridge, December 20, 1905, in Lewis and Clark Centennial Exposition, MSS 1609, Box 20, Correspondence with Secretary of Exploitation; *Report of the Lewis and Clark Centennial Exposition Commission for the State of Oregon* (1906), in Lewis and Clark Centennial Exposition, MSS 1609, Box 27, File 36; *Oregonian*, October 14, 1906; *Evening Telegram*, November 2, 1921.

24 *Oregonian*, November 14, 1906.

25 *Evening Telegram*, October 14, 1905; *Oregon Journal*, May 30, 1915, Sect. 3, 1; *Lewis and Clark Journal* 4.6 (December 1905).

26 Alan Stein and Paula Becker, *Alaska-Yukon-Pacific Exposition: Washington's First World Fair, A Timeline History* (Seattle: History Ink/History Link and the University of Washington Press, 2009), 14–15; *Seattle Daily Times*, February 14, 1909; *Hearing before the Committee on Industrial Arts and Exposition of the House of Representatives. Alaska-Yukon-Pacific Exposition.* January 27, 1908 (Washington, DC: Government Printing Office, 1908), 16; Erik Smith, "Selling Seattle's First World's Fair," *Columbia: The Magazine of Northwest History* 23.3 (Fall 2009).

27 Robert E. Ficken, *Washington Territory* (Pullman: Washington State Press, 2002), 12–13.

28 White, *"It's Your Misfortune and None of My Own,"* 246–55; Robert C. Nesbit, *"He Built Seattle": A Biography of Judge Thomas Burke* (Seattle: University of Washington Press, 1961), chapter 4.

29 Murray Morgan, *Skid Road: An Informal Portrait of Seattle* (New York: Viking Press, 1951), 160–62; Robert Ficken, *The Forested Land: A History of Lumbering in Western Washington* (Seattle: University of Washington Press, 1987), 88.

30 Clarence B. Bagley, *The History of Seattle From the Earliest Settlement to the Present*, vol. 2 (Chicago: S. J. Clarke Publishing Co., 1916), 481–82, 540–41; Calvin Schmid, *Social Trends in Seattle* (Seattle: University of Washington Press, 1944), 31–32.

31 Bagley, *The History of Seattle*, 534.

32 John C. Putman, *Class and Gender Politics in Progressive-Era Seattle* (Reno: University of Nevada Press, 2008), 37–40; *Thirteenth Census of the United States: Manufactures, Vol. IX* (Washington, DC: Government Printing Office, 1912), 1301–1302; Alexander Norbert MacDonald, "Seattle's Economic Development, 1880–1910," Ph.D. dissertation (University of Washington, 1959), 102, 163, 186–87, 196, 201; Eugene P. Moehring, *Urbanism and Empire in the Far West, 1840–1890* (Reno: University of Nevada Press, 2004), 233–38; Earl Pomeroy, *The Pacific Slope: A History of California, Oregon, Washington, Idaho, Utah, and Nevada* (Seattle: University of Washington Press, 1973, originally Knopf, 1965), 119 (quote).

33 Putman, *Class and Gender Politics in Progressive-Era Seattle*, 32–37; Janice L. Reiff, "Urbanization and Social Structure: Seattle, Washington, 1852–1910," Ph.D. dissertation (University of Washington, 1981), 5, 8, 110, 128, 231.

34 John E. Chilberg, "The Organization and Management of the Business of the Alaska Yukon Pacific Exposition of 1909" (typescript, 1953), in John Edward Chilberg Papers, Manuscript and Archives, Suzzallo and Allen Library, University of Washington, VF 0248.

35 *Seattle Daily Times*, June 1, 1906.

36 *The Alaska-Yukon-Pacific Exposition: Seattle, June 1–October 16, 1909* (St. Paul, MN: Northern Pacific Railway, 1909), 6, in Alaska-Yukon-Pacific Exposition Digital Collection, Seattle Public Library (accessed April 4, 2013).

37 Stein and Becker, *Alaska-Yukon-Pacific Exposition*, 16.

38 "Report," *Committee on Industrial Arts and Exposition of the House of Representatives. Alaska-Yukon-Pacific Exposition*, March 18, 1908 (Washington, DC: Government Printing Office, 1908), 4.

39 James A. Wood, "The Alaska-Yukon-Pacific Exposition: World View," in *Souvenir Information Guide: Seattle and A. Y. P. Exposition Diary and Official Calendar* (Seattle, 1909), 7, in Alaska-Yukon-Pacific Exposition Digital Collection, Seattle Public Library (accessed April 1, 2013).

40 *The Alaska-Yukon-Pacific Exposition*, 5.

41 J. S. Foster, "The Alaska-Yukon-Pacific Exposition: How it Differs From Other World's Fairs and What it Means to the Great Northwest 57 Exposition Number," *The 57* 9.8 (Pittsburgh: H. J. Heinz Company, 1909), 4, in Alaska-Yukon-Pacific Exposition Digital Collection, Seattle Public Library (accessed April 1, 2013).

42 *Seattle A. Y. P. Exposition Scrapbook*, vol. 1 (June 1906–December 1906), Pacific Northwest Collection, University of Washington (first quote); "An Address by Henry Alberts McClean, President of Washington State Commission for the Alaska-Yukon-Pacific Exposition at Seattle in 1909" (delivered June 1, 1907), in *Alaska-Yukon-Pacific—Pamphlets*, Folder 2 in Special Collections, University of Washington.

43 *Seattle Daily Times*, February 14, 1909.

44 Letter from Will Parry, AYP Exposition Chairman of Ways and Means committee, to F. G. Whitaker, September 22, 1906, in F. G. Whitaker Papers, box 1, folder 4, Manuscripts and Archives, University of Washington Library.

45 Frank Merrick, "Alaska-Yukon-Pacific Exposition," in *Seattle: The Exposition City* (Seattle, 1909), 4, in Alaska-Yukon-Pacific Exposition Digital Collection, Seattle Public Library, http://cdm16786.contentdm.oclc.org/cdm/ref/collection/ptec/id/2420 (accessed April 1, 2013).

46 Stein and Becker, *Alaska-Yukon-Pacific Exposition,* 48, 135–36.

47 *Seattle Daily Times*, September 15, 1909; *Report of the Alaska-Yukon-Exposition Commission of the State of Washington* (Seattle: Pacific Press, Inc., 1910), in Special Collections, University of Washington.

48 Richard W. Amero, "The Making of the Panama-California Exposition, 1909–1915," *Journal of San Diego History* 36.1 (Winter 1990).

49 Iris Engstrand, *San Diego: California's Cornerstone* (San Diego: Sunbelt Publications, 2005), chapter 6.

50 Phoebe S. Kropp, "'All Our Yesterdays': The Spanish Fantasy Past and the Politics of Public Memory in Southern California, 1884–1939," Ph.D. dissertation (University of California, San Diego, 1999), 183–86.

51 Grace L. Miller, "The I.W.W. Free Speech Fight: San Diego, 1912," *Southern California Quarterly* 54.3 (Fall 1972), 211–38.

52 Kropp, "'All Our Yesterdays,'" 204–209 (quote, 208); *San Diego Sun*, May 7, 1910, in Richard Amero Collection (hereafter Amero Collection), MS 76, Balboa Park Notes 1910, Binder 63, San Diego History Center Research Library; Amero, "The Making of the Panama-California Exposition," n.p.

53 *WPA Prospectus of the 1915 Exposition,* MS 51 (San Diego History Center Research Library), 728; Mark S. Watson, "The Panama-California Exposition" *California's Magazine* 1.1 (July 1915), 350, Archive.org, https://archive.org/details/californias magazoosanf.

54 *WPA Prospectus*, 566.

55 Walter V. Woehlke, "Staging the Big Show: An Inside Story of What Is Going on Behind the Scenes at the Panama-California Exposition at San Diego," *Sunset Magazine* 33.2 (August 1914), 337.

56 *San Francisco Chronicle*, December 8, 1914.

57 *San Diego Union*, January 2, 1911; *Exposition News* 1.1 (December 1911), 8, in San Diego History Center Research Library.

58 *San Diego Sun*, January 8, 1910. Fair officials also used financial gains that Seattle's AYPE produced when rallying support for bond measures needed to improve City Park (*San Diego Union*, August 8, 1910).

59 *Exposition News* 1.1 (December, 1911), 17; Kropp, "*'All Our Yesterdays,'*" 208–10.

60 Woehlke, "Staging the Big Show," 338. On the San Diego and Arizona Railway, see John A. Wilson, "Formidable Places: Building a Railroad in Carriso Gorge," *Journal of San Diego History* 40.4 (Fall 1994).

61 *San Diego Panama-California Exposition, 1915: San Diego All the Year* in Expositions—Panama-California Brochures, F3–4, San Diego History Center Research Library. Another article noted that the curvature of the state of California put San Diego closer to the East and claimed that San Diego was "heralding of something to come, the Canal's operation, a heralding of the opening of the West." See *WPA Prospectus*, 799.

62 *San Diego Panama-California Exposition, 1915: San Diego All the Year.*

63 *WPA Prospectus*, 149, 206, 730; Watson, "The Panama-California Exposition," 350–51*; Panama-California International Exposition, 1915* (n.p) in Expositions—Panama-California Brochures, F3–4, San Diego History Center Research Library.

64 Woehlke, "Staging the Big Show," 339.

65 Amero, "The Making of the Panama-California Exposition," n.p.

66 *Panama-California International Exposition: Unique, Entrancing, Educational, San Diego, 1915*, Archive.org, archive.org/details/PanamaCaliforniaInternational ExpositionUniqueEntrancingEducationalSan (accessed June 13, 2015).

67 Rufus Choate, "San Diego to Control the Canal Commerce of the Southwest," *Exposition News* 1.1 (December 1911), 12.

68 *San Diego Union*, January 10, 1915.

69 Walter V. Woehlke, "Nueva España by the Silver Gate," *Sunset, the Pacific Monthly* 33.6 (December 1914), 1128.

70 *San Diego Union*, October 21, 1915; *Los Angeles Times*, October 21, 1915.

71 Richard W. Amero, *Panama-California Exposition San Diego, 1915–1916*, chapters 5–6 (San Diego History Center), http://www.sandiegohistory.org/archives/amero/1915expo (accessed April 2, 2017).

72 *San Diego Union*, January 1, 1917.

73 William Lipsky, *San Francisco's Panama-Pacific International Exposition* (Charleston, SC: Arcadia Publishing, 2005), 21.

74 Frank Morton Todd, *The Story of the Exposition: Being the Official History of the International Celebration Held at San Francisco in 1915 to Commemorate the Discovery of the Pacific Ocean and the Construction of the Panama Canal*, vol. 1 (New York: G.P. Putnam's Sons, 1921), 34–36; James Henry MacLafferty, "San Francisco and the Panama-Pacific International Exposition" (n.p., 1915), www.books-about-california.com/Pages/San_Francisco_PPIE/San_Francisco_PPIE_text.html (accessed May 11, 2012); Burton Benedict, *The Anthropology of World's Fairs: San Francisco's Panama Pacific International Exposition of 1915* (Berkeley: Scholar Press, 1983), 66–79; Donna Ewald and Peter Clute, *San Francisco Invites the World: The Panama-Pacific International Exposition of 1915* (San Francisco: Chronicle Books, 1991), 5–6.

75 William Deverell, *Railroad Crossing: Californians and the Railroad, 1850–1910* (Berkeley: University of California Press, 1994), 38–60.

76 Jules Tygiel, "Where Unionism Holds Undisputed Sway: A Reappraisal of San Francisco's Union Labor Party," *California History* 62.3 (Fall 1983), 196–215; Deverell, *Railroad Crossing*, 154–69.

77 *San Francisco Chronicle*, January 16, 18 (quotes), 1910; Todd, *Story of the Exposition*, 1:63–64.

78 *San Francisco Chronicle*, March 22, 23 (quotes), August 13, 1910; Todd, *Story of the Exposition*, 1:63; Benedict, *The Anthropology of World's Fairs*, 79–80.

79 Lipsky, *San Francisco's Panama-Pacific International Exposition*, 26; *San Francisco Chronicle*, July 13, 1910 (quote).

80 *San Francisco Chronicle*, June 5, 1910 (second quote); May 21, 1910; MacLafferty, "San Francisco and the Panama-Pacific International Exposition" (first quote); Benedict, *The Anthropology of World's Fairs*, 80–81.

81 *San Francisco Chronicle*, August 17, 1910.

82 *San Francisco Chronicle*, December 22, 1910.

83 *San Francisco Chronicle*, September 14, 1910 (quote); June 5, 1910; August 17, 1910.

84 *San Francisco Chronicle*, May 21, 1910; Benedict, *The Anthropology of World's Fairs*, 81.

85 Todd, *Story of the Exposition*, 1:36–37, 53.

86 *San Francisco Chronicle*, Februrary 4, 1911 (quote), October 11, 1913; *Washington Post* reprint in *San Francisco Chronicle*, August 27, 1913; Charles C. Moore, "San Francisco and the Exposition: The Relation of the City to the Nation as Regards the World's Fair," *Sunset Magazine* 28.4 (April 1912), 196–98.

87 Todd, *Story of the Exposition*, 2:133–34; *New York Times*, August 5, 1914.

88 "Panama-Pacific International Exposition," *Bulletin of the Pan American Union* 40.3 (March 1915), 298 (quote); *San Francisco Chronicle*, September 20, 1914.

89 "The European War and the Panama-Pacific Exposition—A Monumental Contrast," *Current Opinion* 58.5 (May 1915), 319.

90 *San Francisco Chronicle*, August 6, 1914.

91 Shaffer, "Seeing America First: The Search for Identity in the Tourist Landscape" in Wrobel and Long, eds., *Seeing and Being Seen: Tourism in the American West*, 165–66.

92 James D. Phelan, "California's Invitation to the Country," *American Review of Reviews* 51.2 (February 1915), 161; "The European War and the Panama-Pacific Exposition," 315.

93 *San Francisco Chronicle*, February 24, 25; December 6, 1915; Todd, *Story of the Exposition*, 2:10, 269–70.

94 *San Francisco Chronicle*, December 5, 1915.

95 *San Francisco Chronicle*, November 28, 1915.

96 *San Francisco Chronicle*, December 5, 1915.

Chapter 2

1 Carl Abbott, *Portland: Planning, Politics, and Growth in a Twentieth-Century City* (Lincoln: University of Nebraska Press, 1983), 43.

2 Minute Book of the Executive Committee of the Board of Directors of the Panama-California Exposition, January 27, 1910, p. 24, San Diego History Center Research Library, MS 263, Box 1.

3 Todd, *The Story of the Exposition*, 1:99–100.

4 A. L. Hall, "How the Exposition was Advertised," in *Seattle and the Pacific Northwest: Washington, Oregon, California, Alaska, British Columbia, Yukon* (Seattle: Seattle Publishing Company, 1909), 59, in Special Collections, University of Washington.

5 Pope, *The Making of Modern Advertising*, 31; Laird, *Advertising Progress*, 50–51.

6 Quoted in Pope, *The Making of Modern Advertising*, 135–40.

7 Laird, *Advertising Progress,* chapters 6–7; Rob Schorman, Claude Hopkins, Earnest Calkins, "Bissell Carpet Sweepers and the Birth of Modern Advertising," *The Journal of the Gilded Age and Progressive Era* 7.2 (April 2008), 191–92; Lears, *Fable of Abundance*, 198–201.

8 *Report of the Alaska-Yukon-Pacific Exposition Commission of the State of Washington*, 117.

9 *San Francisco Chronicle*, February 27, 1913.

10 See George Hough Perry, "Fundamentals of Introductory Advertising," Seventh Annual Convention of the Associated Advertising Clubs of America, 1911 (Boston: Pilgrim Publicity Association, 1912), Google Books, https://books.google.com (accessed May 15, 2018); George Hough Perry, "How Country Editors Can Get National Advertising," *University of Kansas News-Bulletin* 15.4 (October 1914), https://babel.hathitrust.org/cgi/pt?id=osu.32435014436927;view=1up;seq=5 (accessed May 15, 2018).

11 "Municipal and State Publicity," Seventh Annual Convention of the Associated Advertising Clubs of America (1911), 356, 362, 375.

12 "Contents," Seventh Annual Convention of the Associated Advertising Clubs of America 1911, n.p.

13 Ward and Gold, "Introduction," 2.

14 Ward and Gold, "Introduction," 9. See also Gregory J. Ashworth and Henk Voogd, "Marketing and Place Promotion," in Ward and Gold, eds., *Place Promotion*, 43–45.

15 Weir, "The Awakening of the Cities," *Putnam's Magazine* (1910), 674–75.

16 Pope, *The Making of Modern Advertising*, 237–43; Susan Strasser, "Customer to Consumer: The New Consumption in the Progressive Era," *OAH Magazine of History* 13.3 (Spring 1999), 101–14.

17 Michael McMahon, "An American Courtship: Psychologists and Advertising Theory in the Progressive Era," *American Studies* 13.2 (Fall 1972), 5–18 (quote, 13).

18 J. Walter Thompson quoted in Laird, *Advertising Progress*, 356. For more on new advertising techniques, see Marchand, *Advertising the American Dream*, 9–16; John R. Gold, "Locating the Message: Place Promotion as Image Communication," in Ward and Gold, eds., *Place Promotion*, 30–31.

19 McMahon, "An American Courtship," 11.
20 John R. Gold and Margaret M. Gold, "'Home at Last!': Building Societies, Home Ownership and the Imagery of English Suburban Promotion in the Interwar Years," in Ward and Gold, eds., *Place Promotion*, 77; Marchand, *Advertising the American Dream*, xix.
21 Marchand, *Advertising the American Dream*, xxi, 166; Laird, *Advertising Progress*, 39; Lears, *Fable of Abundance*, chapter 6.
22 *San Diego Union*, May 12, 1914.
23 *Report of the Manager of the General Press Bureau* (1905), 6, in Lewis and Clark Centennial Exposition, MSS 1609, Box 12, File—Report of the Manager of the General Press.
24 Todd, *The Story of the Exposition*, 1:252.
25 *San Francisco Chronicle*, September 15, 1914.
26 *San Diego Union*, August 11, 1914.
27 Smith, "Selling Seattle's First World's Fair."
28 Letter from Director of Exploitation (Henry Reed) to I.A. Nadeau, Director General, November 11, 1907, Edmond S. Meany Papers (Acc# 106-001), Box 103, F-8, University of Washington, Manuscripts and Archives.
29 Secretary (Henry Reed) to Hon. W. B. Heyburn, United States Senator, May 6, 1905, in Lewis and Clark Centennial Exposition, MSS 1609, Box 19, File 1; *San Francisco Chronicle*, July 13, 1910.
30 Todd, *The Story of the Exposition*, 1:248; Laird, *Advertising Progress*, 73, 170; Holly J. Myers-Jones and Susan R. Brooker-Gross, "Newspapers as Promotional Strategists for Regional Definition," in Ward and Gold, eds., *Place Promotion*, 196–97; Michael E. Zega, "Advertising the Southwest," *Journal of the Southwest* 43.3 (Autumn 2001), 281.
31 *Report of the Manager of the General Press Bureau*, 8; *San Diego Union*, March 25, 1914 (quote); *Seattle Daily Times,* February 6, 14, April 21, 1909.
32 Todd, *The Story of the Exposition*, 1:247.
33 Todd, *The Story of the Exposition*, 1:247–50; *San Diego Union*, June 15, 1911.
34 Hall, "How the Exposition was Advertised," 59; Todd, *The Story of the Exposition*, 1:255.
35 *San Diego Union*, May 12, 1914.
36 *San Francisco Chronicle*, April 9, 1913; December 13, 1913.
37 *Report of the Manager of the General Press Bureau*, 5.
38 Secretary Reed to Mr. C.M. Idleman, September 27, 1904, in Lewis and Clark Centennial Exposition, MSS 1609, Box 19, File 1.
39 Todd, *The Story of the Exposition*, 1:253.
40 Ashworth and Voogd, "Marketing and Place Promotion," 50.
41 Norris, *Advertising and the Transformation of American Society*, 34–41.
42 *San Diego Evening Tribune*, June 30, 1914.
43 *Report of the Manager of the General Press Bureau*, 7.
44 *Report of the Manager of the General Press Bureau*, 7.

45 Laird, *Advertising Progress*, 170; Norris, *Advertising and the Transformation of American Society*, chapter 2.

46 *Seattle Daily Times*, April 6, 1909.

47 *San Diego Union*, February 28, 1915.

48 *San Diego Union*, January 7, 1915. For a brief history of *Sunset Magazine*, see L. W. "Bill" Lane Jr., "*Sunset Magazine*: A Century of Western Living," http://sunset-magazine.stanford.edu/html/magazine.html (accessed July 27, 2012).

49 Minute Book of the Executive Committee of the Board of Directors of the Panama-California Exposition, December 13, 1909, p. 17.

50 Schwantes, "Landscapes of Opportunity," 47–50. *Sunset* absorbed *Pacific Monthly* in 1911.

51 Olin D. Wheeler, *The Lewis and Clark Exposition: Portland, Oregon June 1 to October 15, 1905* (St. Paul, MN: Northern Pacific Railway Company, 1905). Wheeler was the primary author of *Wonderland*.

52 *Lewis and Clark Review and Gazetteer* 1.1 (July 1901), OHS; *The Exposition: A Magazine Devoted to the Lewis and Clark Centennial, American Pacific Exposition and Oriental Fair*, 1.1 (November 1902), in Wilson Room, Portland Public Library; *Lewis and Clark Journal* 1.1 (January 1904); Abbott, *The Great Extravaganza*, 38.

53 *San Diego Union*, December 22, 1911.

54 *Report of the Alaska-Yukon-Pacific Exposition Commission of the State of Washington*, 134.

55 *The Alaska-Yukon-Pacific Exposition and Seattle: The Beautiful Exposition City* (Seattle: Robert A. Reid Publisher, 1909), in Special Collections, University of Washington; *The Red Book of Views of the Panama-Pacific International Exposition* (San Francisco: The Panama-Pacific International Exposition Company, 1915), http://books.google.com (accessed July 30, 2012); T. Brown Elton, *The 1916 Exposition in Black and White: Bering a series of pencil drawings of the Panama California International Exposition, 1916* (Coronado, CA: The Coronado Strand, 1916), http://archive.org/details/1916expositionin01brow (accessed July 30, 2012). See also *Guide to San Francisco and the Panama Pacific Exposition*; *Information for Visitors to the Panama-Pacific International Exposition* (San Francisco: The Panama-Pacific International Exposition Company, 1915), http://www.books-about-california.com/Pages/Info_for_Visitors_PPIE/Info_for_Visitor_PPIE_text.html (accessed July 30, 2012); *Alaska Yukon Pacific Exposition Seattle U.S.A., June 1st to October 15th, 1909* (Seattle: Issued by Department of Publicity, 1907), in Seattle Public Library AYPE Digital Collection, http://cdm16118.contentdm.oclc.org/cdm/compoundobject/collection/p200301coll1/id/2018/rec/13 (accessed July 30, 2012).

56 Marchand, *Advertising the American Dream*, 149–53; Lears, *Fable of Abundance*, 287–88, 324. For examples of the use of imagery in western promotional efforts, see Alfred Runte, "Promoting the Golden West: Advertising and the Railroad," *California History* 70.1 (Spring 1991), 62–75; Zega, "Advertising the Southwest," 299–309.

57 *Report of the Alaska-Yukon-Pacific Exposition Commission of the State of Washington*, 134.

58 Pomeroy, *In Search of the Golden West*, 122; quote in Schwantes, "Landscapes of Opportunity," 40. For discussion of how the experience of traveling on railroads changed in the late nineteenth century, see Catherine Cocks, *Doing the Town: The Rise of Urban Tourism in the United States, 1850–1915* (Berkeley: University of California Press, 2001), chapter 2.

59 Ervin H. Zube and Janet Galante, "Marketing Landscapes of the Four Corner States," in Ward and Gold, eds., *Place Promotion*, 215–20; Pomeroy, *In Search of the Golden West*, 131–35.

60 Quote in Zega, "Advertising the Southwest," 297; Elliott West, "Selling the Myth: Western Images in Advertising," *Montana: The Magazine of Western History* 46.2 (Summer 1996), 41.

61 *Seattle Sunday Times*, January 10, 1909; February 14, 1909.

62 Letter from Director General to Mr. H. Dickson, n.d., in Lewis and Clark Centennial Exposition, MSS 1609, Box 1, F-President's Correspondence Great Northern Railway.

63 *San Diego Union*, January 24, 1915.

64 *Seattle Daily Times*, November 9, 1908.

65 Zube and Galante, "Marketing Landscapes of the Four Corner States," 220.

66 *Oregonian*, July 22, 1906.

67 *Official Guidebook to the Lewis and Clark Exposition* (Lewis and Clark Centennial and American Pacific Exposition and Oriental Fair, 1905), 58, Wilson Room, Portland Public Library; Hall, *Oregon, Washington, Idaho and Their Resources*, n.p.; Olin D. Wheeler, *The Lewis and Clark Exposition*, 30–31.

68 *New York Times*, January 22, 1915. Similar side trips to western cities and sites were included in railroad pamphlets. See "Union Pacific: Low Rates to Lewis and Clark Exposition, Portland, Oregon," in Lewis and Clark Centennial Exposition, MSS 1609, Box 19.

69 *Lewis and Clark Journal* 3.1 (January 1905), 9. See also "The Railways and the California Expositions," *Railway Age Gazette* 59.11 (September 10, 1915), 461, https://babel.hathitrust.org (accessed October 21, 2014).

70 *San Francisco Chronicle*, January 30, 1910 (quote); August 25, 1912.

71 *San Diego Union*, January 1, 1912; "The Railways and the California Expositions," 461; Zega, "Advertising the Southwest," 282–83.

72 *Seattle Daily Times*, January 5, 1909. Railroads also began advertising two years before the Lewis and Clark Exposition. See *Oregonian*, July 22, 1906.

73 *San Francisco Chronicle*, August 17, 1910.

74 Director General to Mr. H. Dickson, General Agent, Great Northern Railway Company, in Lewis and Clark Centennial Exposition, MSS 1609, Box 1, President Correspondence. See also William G. Robbins, *Landscapes of Promise: The Oregon Story, 1800–1940* (Seattle: University of Washington Press, 2008), 197–98.

75 Letter from Secretary Henry Reed to Mr. G.W. Westerdahl, Union Pacific Passenger Office, October 6, 1904, in Lewis and Clark Centennial Exposition, MSS 1609, Box 19; *San Diego Union*, August 13, 1914. For examples of other activities taken by passenger agents, see Schwantes, "Landscapes of Opportunity," 40.

76 Letter from Secretary Henry Reed to Mr. G. W. Westerdahl, Union Pacific Passenger Office, October 6, 1904, in Lewis and Clark Centennial Exposition, MSS 1609, Box 19.
77 *New York Times*, June 20, 1909.
78 *Seattle Daily Times*, July 14, 1907.
79 *Lewis and Clark Journal* 3.6 (June 1905), 5; *Seattle Daily Times*, April 16, 1908.
80 *San Francisco Chronicle*, February 25, 1915.
81 "The Railways and the California Expositions," 462–63.
82 *Oregonian*, July 22, 1906.
83 *Seattle Daily Times*, January 5 and 24, 1909. For the marketing efforts of the Santa Fe Railroad, see Victoria E. Dye, *All Aboard the Santa Fe: Railway Promotion of the Southwest, 1890s to 1930s* (Albuquerque: University of New Mexico Press, 2005), chapter 2.
84 *San Diego Union*, January 1, 1915.
85 Robbins, *Landscapes of Promise*, 229.
86 *San Francisco Chronicle*, March 21, 1911.
87 Henry E. Dosch, *Official Catalogue of the Alaska-Yukon-Pacific Exposition, Seattle, Washington*, 86, in Special Collections, University of Washington; *San Diego Union*, January 1, 1912.
88 *Seattle Daily Times*, March 14, 1909.
89 *San Diego Union*, December 12, 1914.
90 *San Francisco Chronicle*, November 27, 1912.
91 *San Diego Union*, December 12, 1914.
92 *Seattle Daily Times*, March 14, 1909; *San Francisco Chronicle*, November 27, 1912.
93 Miller, "The Trans-Mississippi and International Exposition Commemorative Stamp Issue," 63; Dye, *All Aboard the Santa Fe*, 24–25.
94 *Report of the Manager of the General Press Bureau*, 15–16.
95 *New York Times*, February 19, 1905.
96 *Seattle Daily Times*, March 3, 1909.
97 Isaac W. Baird and Calvin Heilig to Henry Reed, Director of Exploitation, October 11, 1904, in Lewis and Clark Centennial Exposition, MSS 1609, Box 19, F-1.
98 *San Francisco Chronicle*, May 23, 1912.
99 Clara Colby to Henry Reeed, Director of Exploitation, June 28, 1904 and Richard C. Hill to Director General, Exposition, August 22, 1904, in Lewis and Clark Centennial Exposition, MSS 1609, Box 15, F-1.
100 *San Francisco Chronicle*, June 9, 1913.
101 *San Diego Union*, September 10, 1910.
102 R. W. Hall to H. W. Goode, Director, Lewis and Clark Exposition, March 31, 1904, in Lewis and Clark Centennial Exposition, MSS 1609, Box 19, F-1.
103 W. F. Williamson to Henry E. Reed, December 8, 1904, in Lewis and Clark Centennial Exposition, MSS 1609, Box 19, File 1.
104 Henry K. Slauter to H. W. Goode, October 13, 1904, and J. W. Brunbaugh to Manager of the Exposition of Portland, February 25, 1905, in Lewis and Clark Centennial Exposition, MSS 1609, Box 19, File 1.

105 Minute Book of the Executive Committee of the Board of Directors of the Panama-California Exposition, November 23, 1909, 7.
106 *San Diego Union*, June 26, 1913.
107 Delos Snynder, General Advertising Manager, Imperial Curtain Co., to Lewis and Clark Fair Company, April 14, 1905, in MSS 1609, Box 19, File 1.
108 Todd, *The Story of the Exposition*, 1:253.

Chapter 3

1 *New York Times*, July 18, 1909.
2 Richard Slotkin, *Gunfighter Nation: The Myth of the Frontier in Twentieth-Century America* (New York: Atheneum, 1992), 61.
3 *Report of the Legislative Committee from the State of New York to the AYP Exposition* (1910), 165, in Special Collections, University of Washington.
4 *Seattle Times*, July 7, 1906; Pomeroy, *In Search of the Golden West*, 71–72.
5 Robert G. Athearn, *The Mythic West in Twentieth-Century America* (Lawrence: University Press of Kansas, 1986), 17.
6 Walter H. Page, "The Land and the People," *World's Work* 10.4 (1905), 6459 (quote), 6464.
7 Athearn, *The Mythic West in Twentieth-Century America*, 160.
8 Christine Bold, "Malaeska's Revenge; or, The Dime Novel Tradition in Popular Fiction," in Richard Aquila, ed., *Wanted Dead or Alive: The American West in Popular Culture* (Urbana: University of Illinois Press, 1996), 21–24 (quote, 22).
9 Bold, "Malaeska's Revenge," 24–27. For more on dime-novel portrayals of Buffalo Bill Cody, see Joy S. Kasson, *Buffalo Bill's Wild West: Celebrity, Memory, and Popular History* (New York: Hill and Wang, 2000), 20–27. For more on Cody as a problematic western figure, see Richard White, "Frederick Jackson Turner and Buffalo Bill," in Richard White, Patricia Nelson Limerick, and James R. Grossman, *The Frontier in American Culture* (Berkeley: University of California Press, 1994), 18–52.
10 Athearn, *The Mythic West in Twentieth-Century America,* 166–75 (quote, 167); William Bloodworth, "Writers of the Purple Sage: Novelists and the American West," in Richard Aquila, ed., *Wanted Dead or Alive: The American West in Popular Culture* (Urbana: University of Illinois Press, 1996), 45–49.
11 Slotkin, *Gunfighter Nation*, 87.
12 Kasson, *Buffalo Bill's Wild West*, 15.
13 Kasson, *Buffalo Bill's Wild West*, 55–56.
14 Kasson, *Buffalo Bill's Wild West*, 34–40, 221 (quote); Thomas Altherr, "Let 'er Rip: Popular Cultural Images of the American West in Wild West Shows, Rodeos, and Rendezvous," in Aquila, ed., *Wanted Dead or Alive*, 83, 87, 101; Slotkin, *Gunfighter Nation*, 66–79.
15 Joseph Blethen, "What the Northwest Is: The Size and Qualities of the Country and the Characteristics of the People," *World's Work* 10.4 (1905), 6474.
16 Walter H. Page, "The Larger Coast Cities," *World's Work* 10.4 (1905), 6502.

17 *Report of the Legislative Committee from the State of New York to the AYP Exposition*, 165.

18 Page, "The Larger Coast Cities," 6502.

19 *Seattle Post-Intelligencer*, June 6, 1909. Seattle mayor John F. Miller likewise noted the East's lack of knowledge of the region; see *AYP Daily News*, June 1, 1909, 5, in Seattle Public Library.

20 "The Next World's Fair," *Coast* 16.1 (July 1908), 18. The exact same statement also found in "Seattle: The Alaska-Yukon-Pacific Exposition and the Scenic Pacific Route," *Chicago Illustrated Review* 1.27 (1909), in Special Collections, University of Washington.

21 "The Next World's Fair," 18.

22 Altherr, "Let 'er Rip," 81–82. According to one scholar, between 1883 and 1957 no less than 116 different Wild West shows entertained the American public. See Don Russell, *The Wild West or, A History of the Wild West Shows, Being an Account of the Prestigious, Peregrinatory Pageants Pretentiously Presented before the Citizens of the Republic, the Crowned Heads of Europe, and Multitudes of Awe-Struck Men, Women, and Children around the Globe, Which Created a Wonderfully Imaginative and Unrealistic Image of the American West* (Fort Worth: Amon Carter Museum of Western Art, 1970), 121–27.

23 West, "Selling the Myth: Western Images in Advertising," 41.

24 *Lewis and Clark Journal* 1.2 (February 1904), 13.

25 *Washington Post*, August 8, 1905; *Morning Oregonian*, January 2, 1905. Similar ethnographic exhibits or displays were common not only in American expositions, but also European fairs. See Raymond Corbey, "Ethnographic Showcases, 1870–1930," *Cultural Anthropology* 8.3 (August 1993), 338–69.

26 *Alaska-Yukon-Pacific Weekly News*, July 17, 1909, in Special Collections, University of Washington.

27 *Seattle Post-Intelligencer*, May 23, 1909.

28 *Seattle Daily Times*, July 15, 1909.

29 *Seattle Daily Times*, July 16, 1909.

30 Wrobel, *Promised Lands*, 14.

31 Henry E. Reed, "The Great West and the Two Easts," *North American Review* 178 (April 1904), 526.

32 Keith L. Bryant Jr., "Entering the Global Economy," in Clyde A. Milner II, Carol A. O'Connor, and Martha A. Sandweiss, *The Oxford History of the American West* (New York City: Oxford University Press, 1994), 195–236; William G. Robbins, *Colony and Empire: The Capitalist Transformation of the American West* (Lawrence: University Press of Kansas, 1994), chapter 1.

33 John Commons, Selig Perlman, and Philip Taft, *History of Labor in the United States*, vol. 4 (New York: Macmillan, 1921–35).

34 Melvin Dubofsky, *We Shall Be All: A History of the Industrial Workers of the World* (Urbana: University of Illinois Press, 1988); Fred Glass, *From Mission to Microchip: A History of the California Labor Movement* (Berkeley: University of California Press, 2016), chapters 11, 12, 14, and 15.

35 Carlos Schwantes, "The Concept of the Wageworkers' Frontier: A Framework for Future Research," *Western Historical Quarterly* 18.1 (January 1987), 39–55; and *Radical Heritage: Labor, Socialism, and Reform in Washington and British Columbia, 1885–1917* (Seattle: University of Washington Press, 1979).

36 *Seattle Post-Intelligencer*, June 2, 1909.

37 Page, "The Larger Coast Cities," 6494; Abbott, *The Great Extravaganza*, xv, 33; Pomeroy, *In Search of the Golden West*, 135.

38 Page, "The Larger Coast Cities," 6494.

39 Blethen, "What the Northwest Is," 6474.

40 "Address delivered by Mr. James J. Hill at the Opening of the Alaska-Yukon-Pacific Exposition, Seattle, WA, June 1, 1909," Minnesota Historical Society, www.mnhs.org/library/findaids/00698/pdf/00698-000034.pdf (accessed January 13, 2014), 12.

41 Page, "The Land and the People," 6463.

42 John M. Findlay, "A Fishy Proposition: Regional Identity in the Pacific Northwest," in David M. Wrobel and Michael C. Steiner, eds., *Many Wests: Place, Culture, and Regional Identity* (Lawrence: University Press of Kansas, 1997), 54; Wrobel, *Promised Lands*, 193.

43 Arthur I. Street, "Another 'Go West' Period," *Sunset Magazine* 14.3 (January 1905), 205.

44 Page, "The Larger Coast Cities," 6491, 6502 (quote). For much of the second half of the twentieth century, scholarship on the American West has suggested that westerners possessed a kind of inferiority complex in relation to the East because of that region's political, economic, and cultural power. The colonial or dependency thesis, as it is often called, posits that the West was little more than a colonial possession of the East. For an excellent review of this debate, see William G. Robbins, "The 'Plundered Province' Thesis and the Recent Historiography of the American West," *Pacific Historical Review* 55.4 (November 1986), 577–97.

45 Wrobel, *Promised Lands*, 8.

46 *Seattle Post-Intelligencer*, June 2, 1909.

47 White, *"It's Your Misfortune and None of My Own,"* 363–65.

48 Corbett, "The Exposition," 5.

49 "Statement: The Lewis and Clarke [*sic*] Exposition" (1901), "Lewis and Clark Fair," November 14, 1901, Scrapbook 27, OHS; H.W. Goode Speech to Oregon Development League, *Evening Telegram*, April 26, 1905, 5. For the place of China in the American imagination, see Matthew Frye Jacobson, *Barbarian Virtues: The United States Encounters Foreign Peoples at Home and Abroad, 1876–1917* (New York: Hill and Wang, 2000), 26–38.

50 Blethen, "What the Northwest Is," 6479.

51 *Seattle Post-Intelligencer*, June 1, 1909.

52 "Address delivered by Mr. James J. Hill."

53 Reed, *Portland and Columbia Watershed*, 6. Lewis and Clark Centennial Exposition, OHS.

54 *Seattle Post-Intelligencer*, June 2, 1909. For similar views on how the canal would transform San Diego and Los Angeles, see article on G.A. Davidson's speech to Los

Angeles visitors in *San Diego Union*, January 10, 1915, in Amero Collection, Balboa Park Notes 191, Binder 71.

55 Reed, *Portland and Columbia Watershed*, 22.

56 Reed, *Oregon: A Story of Progress and Development*, 44. This publication also included similar detail for dairying, mines and minerals, and lumber.

57 "Address delivered by Mr. James J. Hill." Seattle officials also noted Alaska's economic activity, including royalties from sealskins and furs, as well as $125 million of gold the territory had produced. See *United States House Hearings, Industrial Art and Exposition Committee* (1908), in University of Washington Special Collections; General History Alaska-Yukon-Pacific Exposition: Meet Me in Seattle 1909, 82–83, in Seattle Public Library Digital Collection (accessed October 30, 2014), https://cdm16118.contentdm.oclc.org/digital/collection/p20030coll1/id/2423.

58 *Seattle Daily Times*, August 9, 1908 (quote); February 14, 1909.

59 Reed, *Portland and Columbia Watershed*, 7.

60 "For a Fair in 1902," *Lewis and Clark Review and Gazetteer* 1.1 (July 1901), 6–7.

61 "Address delivered by Mr. James J. Hill." A special commemorative diploma given to King County exhibitors included a collage of images of ships, factories, and railroads and included the words: "SEATTLE THE GATEWAY TO THE ORIENT—WHERE SHIP AND RAIL MEET." See *Seattle Post-Intelligencer*, May 23, 1909.

62 *The Alaska-Yukon-Pacific Exposition: Seattle, June 1–October 16, 1909*, 12.

63 "Address delivered by Mr. James J. Hill."

64 Reed, *Oregon: A Story of Progress and Development*, 14.

65 *Seattle Post-Intelligencer*, May 27, 1909.

66 *San Francisco Chronicle*, March 21, 1912.

67 *Los Angeles Times*, August 6, 1905.

68 Reed, *Oregon: A Story of Progress and Development*, 22.

69 *Seattle Post-Intelligencer*, June 1, 1909 (quote); *Town Crier*, May 27, 1911; "Address delivered by Mr. James J. Hill."

70 *Town Crier*, May 27, 1911.

71 For example, see Reed, *Oregon: A Story of Progress and Development*; *The Cities of Puget Sound, Your Hosts for 1909*, in Special Collections, University of Washington; Jones Jr., "What the Visitor Sees at the Seattle Fair," 65–68.

72 *Town Crier*, May 27, 1911.

73 *General History Alaska-Yukon-Pacific Exposition: Meet Me in Seattle 1909*, 100; *Alaska-Yukon-Pacific Exposition Souvenir Cookbook, 1909*, 12, in Special Collections, University of Washington. One AYPE guidebook predicted that western Washington alone would double in population from 1.5 million to more than 3 million within a decade. See *Seattle and the Pacific Northwest*, 96.

74 Reed, *Portland and Columbia Watershed*, 8; *Morning Oregonian*, January 1, 1904.

75 *Evening Telegram*, May 31, 1905, 18; September 27, 1904, 3.

76 *General History Alaska-Yukon-Pacific Exposition*, 100.

77 Quoted in *Los Angeles Times*, August 6, 1905.

78 *Oregon: Land of Opportunity* (Portland: Portland Chamber of Commerce, 1911), 5, https://babel.hathitrust.org/cgi/pt?id=mdp.39015027928319;view=1up;seq=5 (accessed September 24, 2014).

79 *General History Alaska-Yukon-Pacific Exposition,* 105.
80 Reed, "The Great West and the Two Easts," 518–19.
81 *San Francisco Chronicle*, January 1, 1914.
82 "Speech of Hon. Samuel H. Piles of Washington in the Senate of the United States," February 3, 1908 (Washington, DC), 11, in in Seattle Public Library Alaska-Yukon-Pacific Exposition Digital Collection, https://cdm16118.contentdm.oclc.org/digital/collection/p200301coll1/id/2608 (accessed August 15, 2012).
83 *Lewis and Clark Review and Gazetteer* 1.1 (July 1901), 17–18.
84 Page, "The Land and the People," 6461
85 *Morning Oregonian*, January 2, 1905.
86 Piper, "Portland and the Lewis and Clark Centennial Exposition," 421–22.
87 Henry Reed, "Material Development of the Oregon Country," *Lewis and Clark Journal* 1.1 (January 1904), 22.
88 *General History Alaska-Yukon-Pacific Exposition,* 105.
89 "Yakima Land Company" ad in *Seattle and the Pacific Northwest*, n.p.

Chapter 4

1 *Report of the Country Life Commission: Special Message from the President of the United States Transmitting the Report of the Country Life Commission* (Washington, DC: Government Printing Office, 1909), 5–6.
2 Letter from President Theodore Roosevelt to Professor L. H. Bailey, August 10, 1908, in *Report of the Country Life Commission*, 24.
3 Scott J. Peters and Paul A. Morgan, "The Country Life Commission: Reconsidering a Milestone in American Agricultural History," *Agricultural History* 78.3 (Summer 2004), 289–316.
4 Peters and Morgan, "The Country Life Commission," 300. For more on how the Country Life Commission reflected larger progressive impulses, see William L. Bowers, "Country-Life Reform, 1900–1920: A Neglected Aspect of Progressive Era History," *Agricultural History* 45.3 (July 1971), 211–21.
5 Peters and Morgan, "The Country Life Commission," 294.
6 Richard White, "Poor Men on Poor Lands: The Back-to-the-Land Movement of the Early Twentieth Century: A Case Study," *Pacific Historical Review* 49.1 (February 1980), 106.
7 White, "Poor Men on Poor Lands," 106; Shaffer, " 'See America First,' " 175.
8 *Seattle Sunday Times*, September 19, 1909.
9 White, "Poor Men on Poor Lands," 110–11.
10 *Seattle Sunday Times*, April 17, 1904.
11 *Seattle Sunday Times*, January 6, 1908.
12 *Seattle Times*, April 20, 21, 1911.
13 Street, "Another 'Go West' Period," 206, 217; Wrobel, *Promised Lands*, 60.
14 Wrobel, *Promised Lands*, 40–45, 52 (quote).
15 Samuel P. Hays, *Conservation and the Gospel of Efficiency: The Progressive Conservation Movement, 1890–1920* (Pittsburgh: University of Pittsburgh Press, 1999;

originally published Harvard University Press, 1959), 9–14; Mark Fiege, *Irrigated Eden: The Making of an Agricultural Landscape in the American West* (Seattle: University of Washington Press, 2000).

16 William E. Smythe, *The Conquest of Arid America* (New York: Harper & Brothers Publishers, 1900), xiii.

17 Smythe, *The Conquest of Arid America*, xiv; Wrobel, *Promised Lands*, 54–55; Elizabeth Raymond, "When the Desert Won't Bloom: Environmental Limitation and the Great Basin," in Wrobel and Steiner, eds., *Many Wests*, 77–81.

18 *Seattle Sunday Times*, February 14, 1909.

19 *Lewis and Clark Journal* 1.1 (January 1904), 11.

20 Reed, *Portland and Columbia Watershed*, 15.

21 Advertisement by Oregon Land & Water Company, *Lewis and Clark Journal* 1.1 (January 1904), 16–17.

22 E. T. Perkins, "Redeeming the West: Present Status of Government Irrigation Projects Involving the Expenditure of $33,000,000, and Making Fertile Over 18,000,000 Acres of Land," *Sunset Magazine* 16.1 (November 1905), 3–25.

23 James B. Meikle, "American Mastery of the Pacific," *World's Work* 10.4 (1905), 6473; Blethen, "What the Northwest Is," 6483.

24 Hays, *Conservation and the Gospel of Efficiency*, 15.

25 *The Alaska-Yukon-Pacific Exposition: Seattle, June 1–October 16, 1909*, 43.

26 *Seattle Sunday Times*, February 14, 1909.

27 *Seattle Daily Times*, June 7, 1909.

28 Wrobel, *Promised Lands*, 65–70.

29 Blethen, "What the Northwest Is," 6475. A *Morning Oregonian* special piece entitled "Irrigation Makes Desert Bear Fruit" likewise described reclamation efforts in Oregon, including a before-and-after picture of its impact. See *Morning Oregonian*, January 1, 1904.

30 *Morning Oregonian*, January 1, 1904.

31 *New York Times*, August 24, 1905.

32 *Seattle Daily Times*, June 7, 1909.

33 Love, "The Lewis and Clark Fair," 6447–48.

34 *The Alaska-Yukon-Pacific Exposition: Seattle, June 1–October 16, 1909*, 24; *Seattle Sunday Times*, September 13, 1908.

35 *Morning Oregonian*, January 1, 1904; Page, "The Land and the People," 6461.

36 Page, "The Land and the People," 6461. For a history of early irrigation efforts in the Yakima Valley, see Dorothy Zeisler-Vralsted, "Reclaiming the Arid West: The Role of the Northern Pacific Railway in Irrigating Kennewick, Washington," in James E. Sherow, ed., *A Sense of the American West: An Anthology of Environmental History* (Albuquerque: University of New Mexico Press, 1998).

37 *Seattle Sunday Times*, February 14, 1909. Irrigation companies often preferred smaller farms because it meant farmers, not speculators, would settle and use the land and thus also purchase water. Speculators would leave land empty, and irrigation companies could struggle without the income that came from users. See Zeisler-Vralsted, "Reclaiming the Arid West," 134.

38 *San Diego Union*, January 1, 1915.
39 *Morning Oregonian*, January 1, 1904; Page, "The Land and the People," 6461.
40 *Seattle Sunday Times*, February 14, 1909.
41 *Seattle Sunday Times*, February 14, 1909; *1915 All the Year, Panama-California Exposition*, n.d., n.p; *San Diego Union*, January 1, 1915.
42 Walter Nugent, "The People of the West Since 1890," in Gerald D. Nash and Richard W. Etulain, eds., *The Twentieth-Century West: Historical Interpretations* (Albuquerque: University of New Mexico Press, 1989), 40.
43 Page, "The Land and the People," 6462.
44 Blee, "Completing Lewis and Clark's Westward March," 248.
45 *Seattle Sunday Times*, February 14, 1909.
46 Wheeler, *The Lewis and Clark Exposition*, 19; Abbott, *The Great Extravaganza*, xiii–xiv.
47 *Seattle Sunday Times*, February 14, 1909.
48 *The Alaska-Yukon-Pacific Exposition, 1909*, 9–10; Wheeler, *The Lewis and Clark Exposition*, 29–30.
49 *Seattle Sunday Times*, February 14, 1909
50 Shaffer, "'See America First,'" 165–66.
51 Reed, *Oregon: A Story of Progress and Development*, 12.
52 *Seattle Sunday Times*, February 14, 1909; Page, "The Land and the People," 6462.
53 Jones, "What the Visitor Sees at the Seattle Fair," 67; Anne Farrar Hyde, *An American Vision: Far Western Landscape and National Culture, 1820–1920* (New York: New York University Press, 1990), 144.
54 "Statement of John H. McGraw, Vice-President of the Exposition Company of Seattle, Wash., and President of the Seattle Chamber of Commerce," *United States House Hearings, Industrial Art and Exposition Committee* (1908), in University of Washington Special Collections.
55 "The Exposition Grounds and the Environment," *Lewis and Clark Journal* 1.1 (January 1904), 13; Piper, "Portland and the Lewis and Clark Centennial Exposition," 427.
56 Hyde, *An American Vision*, 259. See also Marta Weigle and Barbara A. Babcock, *The Great Southwest of the Fred Harvey Company and the Santa Fe Railway* (Phoenix, AZ: Heard Museum, 1996); West, "Selling the Myth," 41.
57 Wheeler, *The Lewis and Clark Exposition*, 43–47 (quote, 43).
58 *The Alaska-Yukon-Pacific Exposition, 1909*, 37–38 (quote, 37); Chicago and North Western Railway Alaska-Yukon-Pacific Exposition pamphlet in *Alaska-Yukon-Pacific—Pamphlets*, Folder 2, in University of Washington Special Collections.
59 *New York Times*, June 6, 15, 1905; May 14, 19, 1909.
60 Wheeler, *The Lewis and Clark Exposition*, 30–31.
61 *Glimpses of the Lewis and Clark Exposition and the Golden West* (Chicago, 1905), n.p., in https://archive.org/details/glimpsesoflewiscoolairrich (accessed September 24, 2013). n.p.
62 *The Alaska-Yukon-Pacific Exposition, 1909*, 15–16.

63 *Seattle Sunday Times*, February 14, 1909.

64 *Glimpses of the Lewis and Clark Exposition and the Golden West*, n.p.; Abbott, *How Cities Won the West*, 116.

65 *Lewis and Clark Journal* 2.4 (November 1904), 24.

66 Page, "The Larger Coast Cities," 6491.

67 Wrobel, *Promised Lands*, 42–49 (quote, 42).

68 Wrobel, *Promised Lands*, 63–65.

69 *Lewis and Clark Review and Gazetteer* 1.1 (July 1901), 14.

70 Reed, *Portland and Columbia Watershed*, preface.

71 Reed, *Oregon: A Story of Progress and Development*, 57.

72 "Statement of Congressman W. E. Humphrey," 7, *United States House Hearings, Industrial Art and Exposition Committee* (1908), in University of Washington Special Collections (first quote); *Seattle Post-Intelligencer*, January 2, 1909.

73 *General History Alaska-Yukon-Pacific Exposition: Meet Me in Seattle 1909*, 106; *Alaska-Yukon-Pacific Exposition, Seattle, U.S.A., June 1st to October 15th, 1909*, 19.

74 Reed, *Oregon: A Story of Progress and Development*, 56.

75 Piper, "Portland and the Lewis and Clark Centennial Exposition," 423. A *Morning Oregonian* article not only compared Portland to other U.S. cities, but also provided a map showing the major cities that shared the same latitude. See *Morning Oregonian*, January 2, 1905.

76 "Where Rolls the Oregon," 14.

77 *Alaska-Yukon-Pacific Exposition, Seattle, U.S.A., June 1st to October 15th, 1909*, 19.

78 Reed, *Portland and Columbia Watershed*, 17; *Morning Oregonian*, January 2, 1905.

79 "Oregon as a Health Resort," *Lewis and Clark Journal* 2.1 (July 1904), 8–9.

80 "Where Rolls the Oregon," 14; *Lewis and Clark Journal* 1.1 (January 1904), 11.

81 *Sights and Scenes at the Lewis and Clark Centennial Exposition, Portland, Oregon*, n.d., n.p., https://archive.org/details/sightsscenesatleoolewi (accessed December 12, 2017).

82 Reed, *Portland and Columbia Watershed*, 15. At the AYPE four years later, a guidebook pictured a Portland home surrounded by blooming roses. See *The Alaska-Yukon-Pacific Exposition: Seattle, June 1–October 16, 1909*, 18.

83 *The Alaska-Yukon-Pacific Exposition: Seattle, June 1–October 16, 1909*, 17.

84 West, "Selling the Myth," 41; Abbott, *How Cities Won the West*, 116, 120–22.

85 "Oregon as a Health Resort," 8–9.

86 *General History Alaska-Yukon-Pacific Exposition: Meet Me in Seattle 1909*, 106; "Where Rolls the Oregon," 14.

87 Henry S. Curtis, *The Play Movement and Its Significance* (New York: Macmillan, 1917), preface, https://archive.org/details/playmovementitssoocurt (accessed July 10, 2014), 191.

88 Theodore Roosevelt, *The Strenuous Life: Essays and Addresses* (New York: Century, 1900), chapter 10; John R. Haddad, "The Wild West Turns East: Audience, Ritual, and Regeneration in Buffalo Bill's Boxer Uprising," *American Studies* 49.3/4 (Winter 2008), 5–38.

89 Page, "The Land and the People," 6459; *Los Angeles Times*, August 6, 1905.

90 Wheeler, *The Lewis and Clark Exposition*, 30.

91 "The Exposition Grounds and the Environment," 13.
92 J. E. Chilberg, President of the Alaska-Yukon-Pacific Exposition to the Honorable Theodore Roosevelt, November 11, 1906, in Meany Papers, Box 103, F-7. See also Carlos A. Schwantes, "No Aid and No Comfort: Early Transportation and the Origins of Tourism in the Northern West," in Wrobel and Long, eds., *Seeing and Being Seen*, 137.
93 *Argus*, February 20, 1909.
94 *Morning Oregonian*, January 1, 1904.
95 *The Alaska-Yukon-Pacific Exposition: Seattle, June 1–October 16, 1909*, 13.
96 Reed, *Portland and Columbia Watershed*, 13.
97 Reed, *Oregon: A Story of Progress and Development*, 52.
98 *The Alaska-Yukon-Pacific Exposition: Seattle, June 1–October 16, 1909*, 13 (quote); Henry B. Dewey, *History of Education in Washington: Preliminary Edition Issued for Distribution at the A-Y-P Exposition* (Olympia, Washington, 1909), in Alaska-Yukon-Pacific Exposition—Pamphlets, University of Washington Special Collections.
99 *Argus*, February 20, 1909.
100 *The Alaska-Yukon-Pacific Exposition and Seattle the Beautiful Exposition City*, n.p.; "Seattle: The Alaska-Yukon-Pacific Exposition and the Scenic Union Pacific Route," 5; *Alaska-Yukon-Pacific Exposition, Seattle, U.S.A., June 1st to October 15th, 1909*, 24.
101 *Morning Oregonian*, January 2, 1905; *Souvenir Information Guide: Seattle and A.Y.P. Exposition Diary and Official Calendar* (Seattle, 1909), 7, in Alaska-Yukon-Pacific Exposition Digital Collection, Seattle Public Library, 59–69.
102 Reed, *Portland and Columbia Watershed*, 13; Reed, *Oregon: A Story of Progress and Development*, 10.
103 *Argus*, February 20, 1909 (first quote); Page, "The Larger Coast Cities," 6499.
104 Page, "The Land and the People," 6460.
105 Reed, *Portland and the Columbia Watershed*, cover page, 50–64; Page, "The Larger Coast Cities," 6497.
106 *Portland's Scenic Beauties: Souvenir of the Convention of the National Livestock Association* (1904), in Lewis and Clark Centennial Exposition, MSS 1609, Box 27, File 57; *Lewis and Clark Journal* 3.6 (June 1905), 15–22; Reed, *Portland and the Columbia Watershed*, 59–61.
107 *Glimpses of the Lewis and Clark Exposition and the Golden West*, n.p.
108 *Chicago Illustrated Review* 1.27 (1909), 5–6.
109 *Argus*, February 20, 1909.
110 *Chicago Illustrated Review* 1.27 (1909), 14–15.

Chapter 5

1 Rydell, *All the World's a Fair*, 27. See also Jacobson, *Barbarian Virtues*, 226–28.
2 L. G. Moses, *Wild West Shows and the Images of American Indians, 1883–1933* (Albuquerque: University of New Mexico Press, 1996), 1, 5; Christina Welch, "Savagery on Show: The Popular Visual Representation of Native American Peoples and

Their Lifeways at the World's Fairs (1851–1904) and in Buffalo Bill's Wild West (1884–1904)," *Early Popular Visual Culture* 9.4 (November 2011), 337–52.

3 Kasson, *Buffalo Bill's Wild West*; Richard White, "When Frederick Jackson Turner and Buffalo Bill Cody Played Chicago in 1893," in Richard W. Etulain, ed., *Does the Frontier Experience Make America Exceptional?* (Boston: Bedford/St. Martin's, 1999), 46–57.

4 *Evening Telegram*, February 21, 1905.

5 *New York Times*, April 21, 1901.

6 *Lewis and Clark Journal* 1.5 (May 1904), 5.

7 *Washington Post*, September 3, 1905; Wrobel, *Promised Lands*, 179.

8 *Seattle Post-Intelligencer*, November 15, 1908, in Alaska-Yukon-Pacific Exposition—Finance to Miscellaneous mounted clippings, Special Collections, University of Washington; Bonnie M. Miller, "The Incoherencies of Empire: The 'Imperial' Image of the Indian at the Omaha World's Fairs of 1898–99," *American Studies* 49.3/4 (Fall/Winter 2008), 45.

9 Nancy Shoemaker, *American Indian Population Recovery in the Twentieth Century* (Albuquerque: University of New Mexico Press, 1999), 36.

10 *Seattle Sunday Times*, May 9, 1909. For brief analysis of the Curtis volumes, see David R. M. Beck, "The Myth of the Vanishing Race," https://davidrmbeck.files.wordpress.com/2017/09/myth-of-the-vanishing-race-web-grab.pdf (accessed March 25, 2020); and Alan Trachtenberg, *Shades of Hiawatha: Staging Indians, Making Americans, 1880–1930* (New York: Hill and Wang, 2004), 171–203.

11 Josh Reid, "Professor Igloo Jimmie and Dr. Boombang Meet the Heathens: Indigenous Representations and the Geography of Empire at the Alaska-Yukon-Pacific Exposition," *The Pacific Northwest Quarterly* 101.3/4 (Summer/Fall 2010), 121.

12 *Evening Telegram*, June 1, 1905, 3.

13 *Seattle Post-Intelligencer*, November 15, 1908, in Alaska-Yukon-Pacific Exposition—Finance to Miscellaneous mounted clippings, Special Collections, University of Washington.

14 *Official Daily Program, Lewis and Clark Centennial Exposition* (Sunday 1905), in Lewis and Clark Centennial Exposition, MSS 1609, Box 27, File 14; *Union Pacific: Lewis and Clark Centennial Exposition, Portland, Oregon U.S.A.* (1905), in Lewis and Clark Centennial Exposition, MSS 1609, Box 27, File 25.

15 Stein and Becker, *Alaska-Yukon-Pacific Exposition*, 116; "Hello Bill! Meet Me on the Pay Streak at the Alaska Yukon Pacific Exposition, Seattle USA, 1909," Museum of History & Industry, http://digitalcollections.lib.washington.edu/cdm/ref/collection/imlsmohai/id/3501 (accessed August 10, 2015). One AYPE guidebook also included two totem poles on the front cover. See *Alaska-Yukon-Pacific Exposition: Seattle, June 1–October 16, 1909*.

16 John A. Buchanan, *Indian Legends and Other Poems: Souvenir Edition of the Lewis and Clark Fair* (San Francisco: Whitaker & Ray, 1905).

17 Kenneth Greg Watson, "Chief Seattle" *Historylink.org: The Free Online Encylcopedia of Washington State History*, http://www.historylink.org/index.cfm?DisplayPage=output.cfm&file_id=5071 (accessed September 8, 2014); Helen

Chase Keliehor, *Memories: The Alaska-Yukon-Pacific Exposition, Seattle Washington, June 1 to October 15, 1909* (Seattle: Washington, 1984), 11, in Special Collections, University of Washington.

18 Zega, "Advertising the Southwest," 288–91; Leah Dilworth, "Tourists and Indians in Fred Harvey's Southwest," in Wrobel and Long, eds., *Seeing and Being Seen*, 145–46; Shelby J. Tisdale, "Railroads, Tourism, and Native Americans in the Greater Southwest," *Journal of the Southwest* 38.4 (Winter 1996), 438–39.

19 *Seattle Post-Intelligencer*, November 15, 1908, in Newspaper clips without name and date, Alaska-Yukon-Pacific Exposition—Finance to Miscellaneous mounted clippings; *Seattle Sunday Times*, August 29, 1909.

20 *Seattle Post-Intelligencer*, November 15, 1908, in Newspaper clips without name and date, Alaska-Yukon-Pacific Exposition—Finance to Miscellaneous mounted clippings. Three years before the city hosted its fair, the *Seattle Sunday Times*, June 17, 1906, noted that Indian and Eskimo exhibits will "have a strong attraction for the Eastern tourist."

21 *Lewis and Clark Journal* 1.1 (January 1904), 10.

22 *Participation in the Alaska-Yukon-Pacific Exposition: Message from the President of the United States, transmitting the report of the United States Government Board of Managers of the Government participation in the Alaska-Yukon-Pacific Exposition* (Washington, DC: Government Printing Office, 1911), 43, http://catalog.hathitrust.org/Record/011209847 (accessed January 6, 2015).

23 *Evening Telegram*, March 19, 1905, 4.

24 "Indian Village at the Fair," General Press Bureau, Lewis and Clark Exposition (August 1905), in Lewis and Clark Centennial Exposition, MSS 1609, Box 22, File—Press Releases. For the presentation of Southwestern Indians at the 1915 San Diego fair, see Bokovoy, *The San Diego World's Fairs and Southwestern Memory*, chapter 4.

25 *Seattle Daily Times*, July 23, 1909.

26 *Seattle Post-Intelligencer,* May 23, 1909.

27 *Evening Telegram*, January 14, 1905, 6; "Pick of Indian Belles: Piquant and Refined as Their Caucasian Sisters," *Washington Post*, September 3, 1905.

28 *Seattle Post-Intelligencer* clippings, Folder 3 of 4, mount #79, in Alaska-Yukon-Pacific Exposition—National and Foreign Participation to P.I. Clippings, Special Collections, University of Washington.

29 *Seattle Daily Times*, August 15, 1909, quoted in Paula Becker, "Miss Columbia Is Declared Queen of the Carnival at the Alaska-Yukon-Pacific Exposition in Seattle on August 19, 1909" *Historylink.org: The Free Online Enclyclopedia of Washington State History,* http://www.historylink.org/index.cfm?DisplayPage=output.cfm&file_id=8881 (accessed February 17, 2015).

30 Becker, "Miss Columbia"; Jennifer Ott, "Siberian Yupik Arrive in Olympia en Route to the Alaska-Yukon-Pacific Exposition on September 27, 1908," *Historylink.org: The Free Online Enclyclopedia of Washington State History,* http://www.historylink.org/index.cfm?DisplayPage=output.cfm&file_id=8913 (accessed February 17, 2015).

31 *Seattle Post-Intelligencer*, February 16, 1908.

32 *Official Catalogue of the Lewis and Clark Centennial and American Pacific Exposition and Oriental Fair* (Portland: A. Hess & Co., 1905), 37, Archive.org, https://archive.org/details/officialcataloguoolewi (accessed December 28, 2015); Linda Peavy and Ursula Smith, "World Champions: The 1904 Girls' Basketball Team from Fort Shaw Indian Boarding School," *Montana: The Magazine of Western History* 51.4 (Winter 2001), 2–25.

33 *Evening Telegram*, January 14, 1905, 6; "Pick of Indian Belles," *Washington Post*, September 3, 1905.

34 *Evening Telegram*, January 14, 1905, 6.

35 "Pick of Indian Belles," *Washington Post*, September 3, 1905; *Evening Telegram*, February 21, 1905.

36 Abbott, *The Great Extravaganza*, xiv–xv.

37 Paige Raibmon, *Authentic Indians: Episodes of Encounter from the Late-Nineteenth-Century Northwest Coast* (Durham, NC: Duke University Press, 2005), 198.

38 *Participation in the Alaska-Yukon-Pacific Exposition. Message from the President of the United States*, 43.

39 *Seattle Post-Intelligencer*, May 19, 1909.

40 For more on Indian education and the Carlisle school, see Jacqueline Fear-Segal, "Nineteenth-Century Indian Education: Universalism versus Evolutionism," *Journal of American Studies*, 33.2 (August 1999), 323–41. See also Welch, "Savagery on show," 341–43.

41 *Report of the Commissioner of Indian Affairs* (1905), 57, https://digitalcollections.lib.washington.edu/digital/collection/lctext/id/5857/rec/26 (accessed October 31, 2012).

42 *Washington Post*, September 3, 1905.

43 Kat Cleland, "Disruptions in the Dream City: Unsettled Ideologies at the 1905 World's Fair in Portland, Oregon," Master's thesis (Portland State University, 2013), 38.

44 David Wallace Adams, *Education for Extinction: American Indians and the Boarding School Experience, 1875–1928* (Lawrence: University Press of Kansas, 1995), 53–59.

45 Frederick E. Hoxie, *A Final Promise: The Campaign to Assimilate the Indians, 1880–1920* (Lincoln: University of Nebraska Press, 1984), 191–93. See also Brian Klopotek, "Indian Education under Jim Crow" in Brenda J. Child and Brian Klopotek, *Indian Subjects: Hemispheric Perspectives on the History of Indigenous Education* (Santa Fe, NM: School for Advanced Research Press, 2014).

46 K. Tsianina Lomawaima, "Estelle Reel, Superintendent of Indian Schools, 1898–1910: Politics, Curriculum, and Land," *Journal of American Indian Education*, 35.3 (Spring 1996), 9–14 (quote, 13); Hoxie, *A Final Promise*, 193–97.

47 William J. Bauer, Jr., "The Economy of Indian Education in California, 1902–1945," in Child and Klopotek, *Indian Subjects*, 96; Lomawaima, "Estelle Reel, Superintendent of Indian Schools, 1898–1910," 13–17, 22 (quote); Frederick E. Hoxie, "Redefining Indian Education: Thomas J. Morgan's Program in Disarray," *Arizona and the West* 24.1 (Spring 1982), 9 (quote).

48 Hoxie, *A Final Promise*, 92, 120, 126, 129 (quote); Sherry L. Smith, *Reimaging Indians: Native Americans through the Anglo Eyes, 1880–1940* (Oxford: Oxford University Press, 2000), 7.

49 Hoxie, "Redefining Indian Education," 14. See also K. Tsianina Lomawaima, "Domesticity in the Federal Indian Schools: The Power of Authority over Mind and Body," *American Ethnologist* 20.2 (May 1993), 227–40.

50 Adams, *Education for Extinction*, chapters 7–8; Michael C. Coleman, *American Indians, the Irish, and Government Schooling* (Lincoln: University of Nebraska Press, 2007), chapter 8.

51 Lomawaima, "Domesticity in the Federal Indian Schools," 236.

52 Bauer, "The Economy of Indian Education in California," 108.

53 Adams, *Education for Extinction*, 336.

54 *Seattle Sunday Times*, August 22, 1909.

55 *Seattle Post-Intelligencer*, August 24, 1909. McGee served in several federal departments during his career and in 1904 served as anthropological director for the 1904 Louisiana Purchase Exposition. For more on McGee's views of anthropology and race, see Nancy J. Parezo and Don D. Fowler, *Anthropology Goes to the Fair: The 1904 Lousisana Purchase Exposition* (Lincoln: University of Nebraska Press, 2007).

56 *Seattle Sunday Times*, May 23, 1909 (quote); *Seattle Daily Times*, May 25, 1909.

57 *Seattle Post-Intelligencer*, August 22, August 24 (quote), 1909.

58 *Seattle Post-Intelligencer*, August 24, 1909.

59 *Lewis and Clark Journal* 2.6 (December 1904), 15.

60 *Washington Post*, September 3, 1905.

61 *Seattle Post-Intelligencer*, August 24, 1909.

62 *Seattle Daily Times*, August 24, 1909.

63 *Seattle Post-Intelligencer*, August 25, 1909.

64 Keliehor, *Memories: The Alaska-Yukon-Pacific Exposition;* Stein and Becker, *Alaska-Yukon-Pacific Exposition*, 105.

65 *Seattle Post-Intelligencer*, August 26, 1909.

66 Rydell, *All the World's a Fair*, 4.

67 "Speech of Charles W. Fulton of Oregon in the Senate of the United States, December 18, 1903" (Washington, DC: 1904), Oregon Historical Society.

68 *Leslie's Weekly* (June 1905), 578.

69 "Address delivered by Mr. James J. Hill," 12.

70 Day Allen Willey, "The Course of Empire: As Exemplified by the Lewis and Clark Exposition," n.d., 310, Wilson Room, Portland Public Library.

71 Love, "The Lewis and Clark Fair," 6457.

72 *Lewis and Clark Journal* 1.1 (January 1904). On the ties between western expansion and American imperialism, also see *Lewis and Clark Review and Gazetteer* 1.1 (July 1901), 4, and "Oregon Points the Way," August 6, 1901, Scrapbook 27, Oregon Historial Society; *Morning Oregonian*, June 2, 1905.

73 Secretary (Henry Reed) to R.M. LaFollette, March 3, 1904, in Lewis and Clark Centennial Exposition, MSS 1609, Box 20, President's correspondence.

74 *The World's Most Beautiful Exposition, Alaska-Yukon-Pacific Exposition*, issued by Department of Publicity, in Alaska-Yukon-Pacific Exposition—Pamphlets, University of Washington Special Collections.
75 *Salt Lake Tribune*, quoted in *Lewis and Clark Review* 1.3 (September 1901), 112. See also *Lewis and Clark Review and Gazetteer* 1.1 (July 1901), 5–6; Secretary Henry E. Reed to Manufacturers' Club of Ohio, August 23, 1904, in Lewis and Clark Centennial Exposition, MSS 1609, Box 20, President's correspondence.
76 Reed, "The Great West and the Two Easts," 512.
77 Wrobel, *Promised Lands*, 175.
78 Jacobson, *Barbarian Virtues*, 4–5.
79 *Souvenir View Book of the Lewis and Clark Centennial Exposition and Oriental Fair*, n.p.
80 *Leslie's Weekly* (June 1905), 578.
81 *Lewis and Clark Review and Gazetteer* 1.1 (July 1901), 6.
82 "'Where Rolls the Oregon': Lewis and Clark Centennial, American Pacific Exposition and Oriental Fair," *The Exposition: A Magazine Devoted to the Lewis and Clark American Pacific Exposition and Oriental Fair* 1.1 (November 1902), 5.
83 "Speech of Charles W. Fulton of Oregon in the Senate of the United States," 7–8; *Lewis and Clark Review and Gazetteer* 1.1 (July 1901), 3–8.
84 Shelley S. Lee, "The Contradictions of Cosmopolitanism: Consuming the Orient at the Alaska-Yukon-Pacific Exposition and the International Potlatch Festival, 1909–1934," *Western Historical Quarterly* 38.3 (Autumn 2007), 280, 283.
85 Lee, "The Contradictions of Cosmopolitanism," 282.
86 "Address delivered by Mr. James J. Hill," 13–14.
87 Frank Merrick, "Alaska-Yukon-Pacific Exposition," n.d, in Alaska-Yukon-Pacific Exposition—Publicity, Folder 1, Alaska-Yukon-Pacific Exposition—Programs to Publicity, Special Collections, University of Washington.
88 For more on intellectuals' fascination with Asia and Orientalism, see T. J. Jackson Lears, *No Place of Grace: Antimodernism and the Transformation of American Culture, 1880–1920* (New York: Pantheon Books, 1981), 142–43, 225–41.
89 *Lewis and Clark Journal* 1.3 (March 1904), 7.
90 Director of Exhibits Report to President and Commissioner of Exhibits and Transportation, January, 1906, 2, in Lewis and Clark Centennial Exposition, Official Records, Part 5, Vol. 1, F-6, in Wilson Room, Portland Public Library.
91 Rydell, *All the World's a Fair*, 202–203.
92 *Official Guide to the Lewis and Clark Exposition*, compiled by Lewis G. Bradley (Portland, 1905), 16, Archive.org, https://archive.org/details/officialguidetoloolewi (accessed December 28, 2015); *Official Catalogue of the Lewis & Clark Centennial and American Pacific Exposition and Oriental Fair*, 121–22.
93 *Official Guide to the Lewis and Clark Exposition*, 50; *Official Catalogue of the Lewis and Clark Centennial and American Pacific Exposition and Oriental Fair* (map), n.p.
94 *Evening Telegram*, May 31, 1905.

95 John M. Findlay, "Fair City: Seattle as Host of the 1909 Alaska-Yukon-Pacific Exposition," *Pacific Northwest Quarterly* 100.1 (Winter 2008/2009), 8; Lee, "The Contradictions of Cosmopolitanism," 285.

96 *Seattle Post-Intelligencer*, June 2, 1909.

97 *Seattle Post-Intelligencer*, May 27, 1909.

98 "Seattle Opens Doors of Country to Japanese Commissioners," *Pacific Northwest Commerce* 1.4 (October 1909), 11.

99 *Seattle Post-Intelligencer*, June 4, 1909.

100 *General History Alaska Yukon Pacific Exposition: Meet Me in Seattle 1909*, 90.

101 "Seattle Opens Doors of Country to Japanese Commissioners," 17; *Seattle Post-Intelligencer*, August 26, 1909; Lee, "The Contradictions of Cosmopolitanism," 286–87.

102 *The Exposition Beautiful* (Seattle: Seattle Publishing Company, ca. 1909), 5, in Alaska-Yukon-Pacific Exposition Digital Collection, Seattle Public Library, http://cdm16118.contentdm.oclc.org/cdm/compoundobject/collection/p200301coll1/id/2055/rec/10 (accessed December 29, 2015).

103 *The Exposition Beautiful*, 11.

104 *New York Times*, October 24, 1909.

105 *The Exposition Beautiful*, 13.

106 *The Exposition Beautiful*, 13.

107 Phil Dougherty, "Alaska-Yukon-Pacific Exposition (1909): Chinese Village," HistoryLink.org, http://www.historylink.org/index.cfm?DisplayPage=output.cfm&file_id=8964 (accessed January 15, 2010).

108 *The Exposition Beautiful*, 13.

109 Phil Dougherty, "Alaska-Yukon-Pacific Exposition in Seattle Celebrates China Day and Montesano Day on September 13, 1909," HistoryLink.org, http://www.historylink.org/index.cfm?DisplayPage=output.cfm&file_id=8962 (accessed January 15, 2010); Stein and Becker, *Alaska-Yukon-Pacific Exposition*, 119.

110 Jones, "What the Visitor Sees at the Seattle Fair," 66.

111 Quoted in Rydell, *All the World's a Fair*, 205.

112 John Putman, "Racism and Temperance: The Politics of Class and Gender in Late 19th-Century Seattle," *Pacific Northwest Quarterly* 95.2 (Spring 2004), 70–81.

113 Roger Daniels, *Asian America: Chinese and Japanese in the United States since 1850* (Seattle: University of Washington Press, 1988), 125–28; Abbott, *How Cities Won the West*, 68.

114 *Los Angeles Times*, February 6, 1908; Rydell, *All the World's a Fair*, 205.

115 *New York Times*, February 7, 1908.

116 Rydell, *All the World's a Fair*, 205.

117 *Seattle Post-Intelligencer* clippings, Folder 4 of 4, mount #149 in Alaska-Yukon-Pacific Exposition—National and Foreign Participation to P.I. clippings.

118 *Seattle Post-Intelligencer*, May 27, 1909.

119 *Evening Telegram*, May 31, 1905, 3; Marie Rose Wong, *Sweet Cakes, Long Journey: The Chinatowns of Portland, Oregon* (Seattle: University of Washington Press, 2004), 165–69. Matthew Frye Jacobson argues that William Seward envisioned

China as both a market for American producers and an unrestricted source of Chinese labor to build the infrastructure of the developing American West. See his *Barbarian Virtues*, 28–29.

120 Seid Back Jr., *A Trip Through Chinatown: Chinese Souvenir of the Lewis and Clark Exposition* (Portland: R. W. Steele, 1905), n.p., Oregon Historical Society; Cleland, "Disruptions in the Dream City," 74–75.

121 Robert Rydell, "Visions of Empire: International Expositions in Portland and Seattle, 1905–09," *Pacific Historical Review* 52.1 (February 1983), 37.

122 Alaska-Yukon-Pacific Exposition, "Report," Committee on Industrial Arts and Expositions; House of Representatives (60th Congress, 1st session: 1907–1908) in Archive.org, https://archive.org/details/alaskayukonpacif01unit.

123 *Seattle Daily Times*, February 14, 1909.

124 *The Exposition Beautiful*, 13

125 Cleland, "Disruptions in the Dream City," 36.

126 Rydell, "Visions of Empire," 58.

127 Jacobson, *Barbarian Virtues*, 31.

128 Director of Exhibits (Henry Dosch) to President and Committee of Exhibits and Transportation, 2; Paul Kramer, "Making Concessions: Race and Empire Revisted at the Philippine Exposition, St. Louis, 1901–1905," *Radical History Review* 73 (Winter 1991), 75–114; Reid, "Professor Igloo Jimmie and Dr. Boombang Meet the Heathens," 110–11.

129 Parezo and Fowler, *Anthropology Goes to the Fair*, 165–66.

130 Director of Exhibits (Henry Dosch) to H. W. Goode, President, October 7, 1904; Rydell, *All the World's a Fair*, 120. The *Seattle Daily Times* of April 29, 1905, noted that the Igorrote exhibit at the St. Louis exposition made more than $200,000, while exhibits of other Filipino tribes made little. For an excellent discussion of the St. Louis exhibit, see Parezo and Fowler, *Anthropology Goes to the Fair*, chapter 7.

131 "Portland Dogs Doomed," August 1905, and "Lewis and Clark Notes," Summer 1905, General Press Bureau, in Lewis and Clark Centennial Exposition, MSS 1609, Box 22, Press Releases; Emily Trafford, "Hitting the Trail: Live Displays of Native American, Filipino, and Japanese People at the Portland World's Fair," *Oregon Historical Quarterly* 116.2 (Summer 2015), 174. The proper spelling of the Filipino tribe was Igorot, yet the more common spelling in the early twentieth century was Igorrotes.

132 *Washington Post*, September 17, 1905.

133 *Evening Telegram*, April 22, 24 (quote), 1905, 6; "Portland Dogs Doomed."

134 Rydell, *All the World's a Fair*, 5; Moore, *Empire on Display*, 36–37.

135 *Lewis and Clark Journal* 4.4 (October 1905), 4; Abbott, *The Great Extravaganza*, xv.

136 Comparisons between Native Americans and Filipinos were common: one contemporary study compared the different Filipino tribes to the various tribes that occupied the United States. See reference to this in Trafford, "Hitting the Trail," 173; Jon Olivera, "Colonial Ethnology and the Igorrote Village at the AYP," *Pacific Northwest Quarterly* 101.3/4 (Summer/Fall 2010), 143.

137 Abbott, *The Great Extravaganza*, xv.

138 Some American scientists claimed that Filipinos could reach a high state of development. See Trafford, "Hitting the Trail," 179; and Paul Sabin, "Home and Abroad: The Two 'Wests' of Twentieth-Century United States History," *Pacific Historical Review* 66.3 (August 1997), 305–35. On how Oregon soldiers equated Filipinos with Indians, see Sean McEnroe, "Painting the Philippines with an American Brush: Visions of Race and National Mission among the Oregon Volunteers in the Philippine Wars of 1898 and 1899," *Oregon Historical Quarterly* 104.1 (Spring 2003), 24–61.
139 Quoted in Rydell, *All the World's a Fair*, 196.
140 Olivera, "Colonial Ethnology and the Igorrote Village at the AYP," 145.
141 *The Exposition Beautiful*, 3; *Seattle Sunday Times*, February 14, 1909; Reid, "Professor Igloo Jimmie and Dr. Boombang Meet the Heathens," 110.
142 *Seattle Sunday Times*, June 13, 1909.
143 *Seattle Post-Intelligencer*, n.d., P.I. Clippings, Folder 1 of 4, mount #7 in Alaska-Yukon-Pacific Exposition—National and Foreign Participation to P.I. Clippings, Special Collections, University of Washington Library.
144 *Seattle Post-Intelligencer*, n.d., P.I. Clippings, Folder 4 of 4, mount #147 in Alaska-Yukon-Pacific Exposition—National and Foreign Participation to P.I. Clippings, Special Collections, University of Washington Library; Reid, "Professor Igloo Jimmie and Dr. Boombang Meet the Heathens," 116.
145 *Seattle Sunday Times*, May 30, 1909; "The Philippine Exhibit," 33; *Seattle Post-Intelligencer*, August 22, 1909.
146 "Smithsonian and National Museum Exhibit," *Coast* 18.1 (July 1909), 28–29.
147 Official Catalogue of the Lewis and Clark Centennial and Amerian Pacific Expositiion and Oriental Fair, 29–30.
148 *Official Guide to the Alaska-Yukon-Pacific Exposition* (Seattle: Alaska-Yukon-Pacific Exposition Publishing Company, 1909), 44, in Alaska-Yukon-Pacific Exposition Digital Collection, Seattle Public Library.
149 *Seattle Post-Intelligencer*, May 30, 1909; June 2, July 18, 1909; *Argus*, February 20, 1909, 48.
150 *Seattle Post-Intelligencer*, July 7, 8, 13, 1909.
151 *Seattle Post-Intelligencer*, July 12, 1909.
152 *Seattle Post-Intelligencer*, July 7, 1909.

Chapter 6

1 *San Diego Union*, January 1, 1913, in Amero Collection, Balboa Park Notes 191, Binder 67.
2 Woehlke, "Nueva Espana by the Silver Gate," 1129; *WPA Prospectus*, 206.
3 For a brief overview of the Lopez case, see *Salt Lake Tribune*, September 13, 2009, https://archive.sltrib.com/article.php?id=13329636&itype=NGPSID (accessed March 25, 2020).
4 Walter Woehlke, "Real Wild-West Shows," *Sunset, the Pacific Monthly* 32.2 (February 1913), 412.
5 *San Diego Union*, September 4, December 12, 1914.

6 *Official Guide Book of the Panama-California Exposition* (San Diego, 1915), 39, https://archive.org/stream/TheOfficialGuideBookOfThePanama-california ExpositionSanDiego1915/c100_2012_007#page/n0/mode/2up.
7 "News Notes From San Diego," *Santa Fe Magazine* 9.6 (April 1914/15), 39.
8 *San Francisco Chronicle*, April 23, 25, 1915.
9 Lipsky, *San Francisco's Panama-Pacific International Exposition*, 94.
10 Todd, *The Story of the Exposition*, 2:363; *San Francisco Chronicle*, May 10, 11, 1915. For more on the 101 Ranch show, see Michael Wallis, *The Real Wild West: The 101 Ranch and the Creation of the American West* (New York: St. Martin's Press, 1999).
11 *San Francisco Chronicle*, January 16, 1915.
12 Barbara Berglund, " 'The Days of Old, the Days of Gold, the Days of '49': Identity, History, and Memory at the California Midwinter International Exposition, 1894," *Public Historian* 25.4 (Fall 2003), 27–28 (quote, 27).
13 *San Diego Evening Tribune*, March 12, April 3, 1915.
14 Bascom Johnson, "Moral Conditions in San Francisco and at the Panama-California Exposition," *Social Hygiene* 1.4 (September 1915), 598–99.
15 Todd, *The Story of the Exposition*, 2:362.
16 *San Diego Union*, March 28, 1915.
17 "News Notes From San Diego," *Santa Fe Magazine* 9.6 (April 1914/15), 39.
18 *San Diego Union*, July 18, 19, 20, September 9, 1915; Amero, *Panama-California Exposition—San Diego, 1915–1916*, chapter 5, http://www.sandiegohistory.org/archives/amero/1915expo/ch5.
19 *San Francisco Chronicle*, March 9, 1913.
20 *WPA Prospectus*, 260.
21 *WPA Prospectus*, 904–905. For similar views, see also " 'Opportunity Exposition' in 1915 Will Exploit the New Pacific Southwest," Expositions—Panama-California/Brochures, Box 5, F 3–4, San Diego History Research Center.
22 Ben Macomber, *The Jewel City: Its Planning and Achievements; Its Architecture, Sculpture, Symbolism, and Music; Its Gardens, Palaces, and Exhibits* (San Francisco: John H. Williams Publisher, 1915), 11–12.
23 Gavin McNab, "California's Promise to Posterity," *California Magazine* 1.1 (July 1915), 62.
24 *San Diego Union*, January 2, 1911.
25 Winfield Hogaboom, "Looking Into The Future: The Purpose of the Panama-California Exposition, at San Diego, in 1915, 'To Show What Will Be By What Has Been,' " *Sunset Magazine* 32.2 (February 1913), 339.
26 Lewis H. Falk, "Panama-California Exposition at San Diego," *Overland Monthly* 66.3 (November 1915), 451.
27 *1915 All the Year, Panama-California Exposition*, n.d., n.p., Archive.org, https://archive.org/details/C1002013084 (accessed June 15, 2014).
28 Falk, "Panama-California Exposition at San Diego," 451.
29 *San Diego Union*, January 10, 1915, in Amero Collection, Balboa Park Notes 191, Binder 71.

30 E. J. Wickson, "The High Quality of California Rural Life," *California Magazine* 1.1 (July 1915), 78.

31 McNab, "California's Promise to Posterity," 63.

32 Quoted in *California's Magazine* 1.1 (July 1915), 192.

33 William Deverell and Tom Sitton, eds., *California Progressivism Revisited* (Berkeley: University of California Press, 1994).

34 *San Diego Union*, January 1, 1914, in Amero Collection, Balboa Park Notes 191, Binder 69.

35 R. L. Bernier, "To the Public," *California Magazine* 1.1 (July 1915), 4.

36 Letter from David Starr Jordan to Editor of *Current Opinion*, *Current Opinion* 58.5 (May 1915), 318.

37 Benjamin Ide Wheeler, "The Meaning of the Canal," *American Review of Reviews* 51.2 (February 1915), 163. A 1913 article *in Scribner's Magazine* likewise claimed that the canal would "promote the political unity as well as the economic solidarity of the country." See Emory R. Johnson, "What The Canal Will Accomplish," *Scribner's Magazine* 54.1 (July 1913), 43.

38 McNab, "California's Promise to Posterity," 62–63.

39 McNab, "California's Promise to Posterity," 62. See also *Fore-Glance at Panama-California Exposition, San Diego, 1915: Unique International Year 'Round Jan. 1–Dec. 31*, n.p., Archive.org, https://archive.org/details/Fore-glanceAtPanamaCaliforniaExpositionSanDiego1915Unique (accessed June 28, 2014). This brochure also included a word map with trade routes and explained how San Diego's geographic advantages primed the city for commercial success.

40 *San Diego Union*, November 20, 1912.

41 Abbott, *How Cities Won the West*, 8.

42 Homer S. King, "California's Exposition Ambitions," *Sunset Magazine* 25.4 (December 1910), 623–24.

43 Robert E. Connolly, "California's Opportunity," *Sunset Magazine* 25.4 (December 1910), 610.

44 "San Diego Is a City of Peace, Happiness and Plenty"; *California and the Expositions—Union Pacific System,* http://www.books-about-california.com/Pages/California_and_the_Expositions/California_and_Expos_text.html (accessed February 25, 2014), n.p.

45 Hogaboom, "Looking Into The Future," 338; *Fore-Glance at Panama-California Exposition, San Diego, 1915*, n.p.

46 *1915 All the Year, Panama-California Exposition*, n.d., n.p.; *California and the Expositions—Union Pacific System,* n.p.

47 *Fore-Glance at Panama-California Exposition, San Diego, 1915*, n.p; *1915 All the Year, Panama-California Exposition*, n.d., n.p.

48 Street, "Another 'Go West' Period," 207.

49 Forbes, "California Coming Into Its Own," 192.

50 *San Diego Union*, January 10, 1915, in Amero Collection, Balboa Park Notes 191, Binder 71.

51 Governor James N. Gillett, "What California Offers," *Sunset Magazine* 25.6 (December 1910), 621.
52 *Fore-Glance at Panama-California Exposition,* n.p.
53 *Southern California: Comprising the Counties of Imperial, Los Angeles, Orange, Riverside, San Bernardino, San Diego, Ventura* (Southern California Panama Expositions Commission, 1914), 27, 39–40, 233.
54 *Panama Pacific International Exposition, San Francisco 1915* [Hercules cover], n.p.
55 *Panama Pacific International Exposition, San Francisco 1915* [Hercules cover], n.p.
56 Lynch, "Looking East From the West," 292.
57 Choate, "San Diego to Control the Canal Commerce of the Southwest," 12.
58 *San Diego Union*, January 4, 1915.
59 *1915 All the Year, Panama-California Exposition*, n.d., n.p.; *San Francisco Chronicle*, January 2, 1915.
60 McNab, "California's Promise to Posterity," 63
61 *San Francisco Chronicle*, January 8, 1911.
62 *Official Address of G. A. Davidson, President Panama-Californa Exposition San Diego Union*, January 1, 1915 in "Balboa Park History, 1915" in Richard Amero Collection, http://www.sandiegohistory.org/archives/amero/balboapark/bp1915/ (accessed November 10, 2015); Street, "Another 'Go West' Period," 206, 217; *San Diego Union*, January 1, 1916.
63 *Fore-Glance at Panama-California Exposition, San Diego, 1915*, n.p.
64 *San Francisco Chronicle*, January 8, 1911; January 5, 1913.
65 Hogaboom, "Looking Into The Future," 339; *San Diego Union*, January 1, 1914, in Amero Collection, Balboa Park Notes 191, Binder 69. Hogaboom staked his growth claims on the estimate of seven persons per farm as well as the number of people who would service these new farms.
66 Street, "Another 'Go West' Period," 207.
67 Wrobel, *The End of American Exceptionalism*, 47–52.
68 Robert Newton Lynch, "Welcoming the Immigrant," *Sunset Magazine* 32.3 (March 1913), 593.
69 Lynch, "Welcoming the Immigrant," 593, 596–98.
70 Wrobel, *Promised Lands*, 59.
71 *Hearing before the Committee on Industrial Arts and Exposition of the House of Representatives. Proposed Panama Canal Exposition*, January 10, 1911 (Washington, DC: Government Printing Office, 1911).
72 *San Francisco Chronicle*, January 5, 1913.
73 " 'Opportunity Exposition' in 1915 Will Exploit the New Pacific Southwest," Expositions—Panama-California/Brochures, Box 5, F 3–4.
74 Woehlke, "Nueva Espana by the Silver Gate," 1129.
75 *The Official Guide Book of the Panama California Exposition*; *The Official Guide and Descriptive Book: Panama California International Exposition* (San Diego, 1916), n.p., Archive.org, https://archive.org/details/TheOfficialGuideAndDescriptiveBookPanama-californiaInternational (accessed June 19, 2014); Kropp, " 'All Our Yesterdays,' " 258; *San Francisco Chronicle*, January 5, 1913.

76 *San Francisco Chronicle*, January 5, 1913.

77 *San Diego Union*, January 1, 1915. San Francisco leaders likewise compared the region's agricultural potential to that of the gold rush. See *San Francisco Chronicle*, January 5, 1913.

78 *WPA Prospectus*, 405.

79 Woehlke, "Staging the Big Show: An Inside Story of What Is Going on Behind the Scenes at the Panama-California Exposition at San Diego." *Sunset Magazine* 33.2 (August 1914), 338–39; *San Diego Union*, January 1, 1914, in Amero Collection, Balboa Park Notes 191, Binder 69; Jerre C. Murphy, "San Diego's Evolutionary Exposition," *Collier's: The National Weekly* (December 5, 1914), 22.

80 *San Francisco Chronicle*, January 5, 1913.

81 *San Francisco Chronicle*, January 5, 1913. Horne's calculation of start-up costs included buildings, tools, and initial payment for land.

82 *Southern California: Comprising the Counties of Imperial, Los Angeles, Orange, Riverside, San Bernardino, San Diego, Ventura.*

83 Forbes, "California Coming Into Its Own," 192.

84 *San Francisco Chronicle*, January 5, 1913.

85 *San Diego Union*, January 1, 1915.

Chapter 7

1 *San Francisco Chronicle*, April 18, 1914.

2 See Steven Stoll, *The Fruits of Natural Advantage: Making the Industrial Countryside in California* (Berkeley: University of California Press, 1998); David Vaught, *Cultivating California: Growers, Specialty Crops, and Labor, 1875–1920* (Baltimore: Johns Hopkins, 2002).

3 *Seattle Sunday Times*, May 12, 1912.

4 *San Diego Union*, January 1, 1916; *WPA Prospectus*, 204.

5 *Los Angeles Examiner*, December 22, 1914.

6 *WPA Prospectus*, 260; *San Diego Union*, January 1, 1916.

7 Woehlke, "Staging the Big Show," 338.

8 McNab, "California's Promise to Posterity," 63.

9 Wheeler, "A Forecast for California and the True Significance of the Panama Canal," 277.

10 Woehlke, "Nueva Espana by the Silver Gate," 1130.

11 Julius Kahn, "The Immigration Problem in California," *California's Magazine* 1.1 (July 1915), 185. See also *The Official Guide Book of the Panama California Exposition*, 11.

12 *San Diego Panama-California Exposition, 1915*, in Expositions—Panama-California/Brochures, Box 5, File 4, San Diego History Research Center.

13 *San Francisco Chronicle*, January 6, 1914.

14 See Donald Worster, *Rivers of Empire: Water, Aridity, and the Growth of the American West* (New York: Pantheon Books, 1985); Marc Reisner, *Cadillac Desert: The American West and Its Disappearing Water* (New York: Viking Penguin, 1986).

15 *1915 All the Year, Panama-California Exposition*, n.d., n.p.
16 *WPA Prospectus*, 315.
17 *San Diego California: The Harbor City of the Southwest*, issued by Board of Supervisors, San Diego County (1911), n.p. https://archive.org/details/C1002013095 (accessed June 4, 2014); Choate, "San Diego to Control the Canal Commerce of the Southwest," 12; Walter V. Woehlke, "The Land of Before-and-After: The Miracle-Story of Imperial Valley, California," *Sunset, The Pacific Monthly* 28.4 (April 1912), 391–400.
18 *San Francisco Chronicle*, January 8, 1911; January 5, 1913; *San Diego California: The Harbor City of the Southwest*, n.p.; *Exposition News* 1.1 (December 1911), 12.
19 *Southern California: Comprising the Counties of Imperial, Los Angeles, Orange, Riverside, San Bernardino, San Diego, Ventura*, 19–23. For railroads promotion of irrigation, see Schwantes, "Landscapes of Opportunity," 41–42.
20 *New York Times*, August 24, 1905; Todd, *The Story of the Exposition*, 2:69; 3:147.
21 Todd, *The Story of the Exposition*, 3:107.
22 *Panama Canal, Panama-Pacific International and Panama-California Expositions*, souvenir issued by International Harvester Companies (1915), 32, in https://archive.org/details/Panama-pacificPanama-californiaSouvenir1915 (accessed June 6, 2014).
23 "The Little Landers' Colony," *Exposition News* 1.1 (December 1911), 16; "Horticulture," *Exposition News*, 1.1 (December 1911), 14.
24 *Panama Canal, Panama-Pacific International and Panama-California Expositions*, 32; "The Little Landers' Colony," *Exposition News* 1.1, 16.
25 *WPA Prospectus*, 134–35, 516–24, 556 (quote); *San Diego Union*, January 1, 27, 1915.
26 *Seattle Daily Times*, October 21, 1914.
27 *San Francisco Chronicle*, January 8, 1911; January 5, 1913.
28 *San Diego Union*, January 1, 1914, in Amero Collection, Balboa Park Notes 191, Binder 69.
29 *Panama Canal, Panama-Pacific International and Panama-California Exposition*, 16.
30 Smythe, *The Conquest of Arid America*, 124–25, 149, 248, 253–54.
31 Smythe, *The Conquest of Arid America*, 309.
32 Lawrence B. Lee, "The Little Landers Colony of San Ysidro," *Journal of San Diego History* 21.1 (Winter 1975); Matthew F. Bokovoy, "Inventing Agriculture in Southern California," *Journal of San Diego History* 45.3 (Summer 1999).
33 "The Little Landers' Colony," *Exposition News* 1.1,16; *WPA Prospectus*, 135.
34 *San Diego Union*, January 1, 1914, in Amero Collection, Balboa Park Notes 191, Binder 69; "The Little Landers' Colony," *Exposition News* 1.1, 17.
35 Bokovoy, "Inventing Agriculture in Southern California," n.p.
36 *San Francisco Chronicle*, January 6, 1914.
37 *San Diego Panama-California Exposition, 1915*. Seattle leaders also noted the availability of mail and electricity. See *Seattle Sunday Times*, February 14, 1909.
38 *Standard Guide to Los Angeles, San Diego, and the Panama-California Exposition* (Los Angeles, 1916), 13, https://archive.org/details/standardguidetolooooffi (accessed January 15, 2013).

39 *San Diego Union*, January 1, 1916; January 31, 1915. Pacific Northwest promoters also used pictures and descriptions of nice homes when discussing farm life. See Blethen, "What the Northwest Is," 6478; Page, "The Land and the People," 6461.
40 *Panama Canal, Panama-Pacific International and Panama-California Expositions*, 34–46; *The Official Guide Book of the Panama California Exposition*, 11–14.
41 *San Diego Union*, January 1, 1916; January 1, 1917.
42 Watson, "The Panama-California Exposition," 352.
43 Wickson, "The High Quality of California Rural Life," 79.
44 Falk, "Panama-California Exposition at San Diego," 452.
45 *San Diego Panama-California Exposition, 1915.*
46 *The Official Guide Book of the Panama California Exposition*, 12, 30; Falk, "Panama-California Exposition at San Diego," 452.
47 *The Official Guide Book of the Panama California Exposition*, 12, 30; *San Diego Panama-California Exposition, 1915.*
48 Falk, "Panama-California Exposition at San Diego," 453.
49 Bokovoy, "Inventing Agriculture in Southern California," n.p.
50 Perkins, "Redeeming the West," 4; *San Francisco Chronicle*, February 25, 1915. For similar view in which Nevada was compared to the Arabian Desert, see Clarence J. Blanchard, "An Object-Lesson in Irrigation: The Great Truckee-Carson System," *American Monthly Review of Reviews* 31.6 (June 1905), 702.
51 Perkins, "Redeeming the West," 4.
52 *San Diego Panama-California Exposition, 1915.*
53 *San Diego Union*, January 1, 1915.
54 Wheeler, "A Forecast for California and the True Significance of the Panama Canal," 276.
55 *San Diego Union*, January 1, 1915.
56 Susan Rhoades Neel, "A Place of Extremes: Nature, History, and the American West," *Western Historical Quarterly* 25.4 (Winter 1994), 490.
57 King, "California's Exposition Ambitions," 624.
58 *The Official Guide Book of the Panama California Exposition*, 33; *San Francisco Chronicle*, December 22, 1910.
59 *WPA Prospectus*, 904–905.
60 Charles Dudley Warner, *Our Italy* (New York: Harper & Brothers, 1891); Hyde, *An American Vision*, 162–63, 184–85, 190.
61 *WPA Prospectus*, 230.
62 *WPA Prospectus*, 611; Hyde, *An American Vision*, 215.
63 *San Francisco Chronicle*, September 14, 1910.
64 "The Celebration," *Panama Pacific International Exposition, San Francisco, 1915* [Hercules cover] (San Francisco: Panama-Pacific International Exposition Company, 1914), n.p., https://archive.org/details/cu31924101862732 (accessed September 23, 2013).
65 *Los Angeles Standard Guide San Diego, Including the Panama-California Exposition at San Diego* (Published by North American Press Association, 1915), n.p.,

https://archive.org/details/LosAngelesStandardGuideSanDiegoIncludingThePanamaCaliforniaExposition (accessed July 27, 2016).

66 *California and the Expositions—Union Pacific System,* 42; *Panama-California Exposition Entire Year 1915,* n.p., http://www.books-about-california.com/Pages/San_Diego_Brochure/San_Diego_Brochure_text.html (accessed June 24, 2014).

67 *Panama-Pacific International Exposition, San Francisco, 1915,* Virtual Museum of the City of San Francisco, http://www.sfmuseum.net/hist9/ppietxt1.html (accessed June 23, 2014).

68 *California and the Expositions—Union Pacific System,* 27–42; F. Burnham McLeary, "Following the Sunset to the Golden Gate," *World's Work* 29.6 (April 1915), advertising section.

69 Moore, "San Francisco and the Exposition," 198; Rufus Steele, "A Matter of Millions: How the Experts Are Hearing in Advance the Click of the Expositions Gates," *Sunset Magazine* 34.1 (January 1915); Moore, *Empire on Display,* 142.

70 *California and the Expositions—Union Pacific System,* 54–59 (quote, 54); *Panama Pacific International Exposition: Popular Information* (1915), n.p., https://babel.hathitrust.org/cgi/pt?id=mdp.39015058345524 (accessed July 9, 2015). Railway advertisements similarly highlighted the scenic western landscapes that the Grand Canyon, Yellowstone, and Glacier National Parks offered fairgoers. See *New York Times,* August 9, December 6, 1914; April 4, June 21, 1915.

71 Arthur Henry Chamberlain, "Our Western Wonderlands," *National Education Association and International Congress of Education, 1915, Complimentary Souvenir Program,* 103, http://books.google.com (accessed June 24, 2014); Menard Gilbert, "California: Playground of the World" *California's Magazine* 1.1 (July 1915), 83–92; C.A. Higgins, *To California Over the Santa Fe Trail* (Chicago: Passenger Department, Santa Fe Railway Company, 1915), 211–16, https://archive.org/details/tocaliforniaoveroohigg (accessed June 25, 2014).

72 *California and the Expositions—Union Pacific System,* 15.

73 Hyde, *An American Vision,* 278.

74 *California and the Expositions—Union Pacific System,* 16–20 (quote, 16); Moore, *Empire on Display,* 153.

75 Moore, *Empire on Display,* 151.

76 *California and the Expositions—Union Pacific System,* 44–45.

77 "California the Hostess," *Panama Pacific International Exposition, San Francisco, 1915* [Hercules cover], n.p.; *San Francisco Chronicle,* December 13, 1910; McLeary, "Following the Sunset to the Golden Gate," n.p.

78 *California and the Expositions—Union Pacific System,* 41; Gilbert, "California: Playground of the World," 83–92. A Panama-Pacific guidebook included full-page pictures of California's big trees, photos of Yosemite Park, and another page called "Scenic California." See "California the Hostess," *Panama Pacific International Exposition, San Francisco 1915* [Hercules cover], n.p.

79 *Sunset: The Pacific Monthly* 28.6 (June 1912), n.p.

80 Charles Nordhoff, *California: For Health, Pleasure, and Residence. A Book for Travellers and Settlers* (New York: Harper & Brothers Publishers, 1873), chapter 8.

81 Charles C. Moore, "'San Francisco Knows How!' An Answer to the World's Questions: 'Can This Exposition Be Different?'" *Sunset Magazine* 28.1 (January 1912), 14 (first quote); Wheeler, "A Forecast for California and the True Significance of the Panama Canal," 279; *California and the Expositions—Union Pacific System,* 4.

82 *Guide to San Francisco and the Panama Pacific Exposition, 1915* (San Francisco: Baldwin Piano Company, 1915), n.p., http://www.books-about-california.com/Pages/Guide_to_SF_and_Expo/Guide_to_SF_and_Expo_main.html (accessed January 26, 2012); *California and the Expositions—Union Pacific System,* 5.

83 *San Diego Panama-California Exposition, 1915*, n.p.

84 *San Diego Union*, January 27, 1915.

85 *San Diego Panama-California Exposition, 1915*, n.p. One brochure included on the front cover a thermometer that depicted the city's temperature range, to show visually that a year-round fair was possible in San Diego. See *Fore-Glance at Panama-California Exposition, San Diego, 1915*, n.p.

86 *San Diego Union*, December 15, 1914

87 Rufus Steele, "San Francisco the Exposition City," *Sunset Magazine* 25.4 (December 1910), 614 (first and third quote); *San Diego Union*, March 28, 1915 (second quote).

88 William G. Reed, "The Climate of California," *California Magazine* 1.1 (July 1915), 148–49.

89 Wheeler, "A Forecast for California and the True Significance of the Panama Canal," 279.

90 "Horticulture," *Panama California Exposition News* 1.1 (December 1911), 14.

91 *Panama Pacific International Exposition: Popular Information* (1915), n.p.

92 Woehlke, "Nueva Espana by the Silver Gate," 1125.

93 "The Celebration: Panama-Pacific International Exposition," *Panama Pacific International Exposition, San Francisco 1915* [Hercules cover], n.p.; *Panama Pacific International Exposition: Popular Information* (1915), n.p.

94 Murphy, "San Diego's Evolutionary Exposition," 22.

95 Falk, "Panama-California Exposition at San Diego," 451 (first quote); *The Official Guidebook of the Panama California Exposition: San Diego, 1915*, 36 (second quote); *Panama-California Exposition Entire Year 1915*, n.p.

96 Wrobel, *Promised Lands*, 44–45; Nordhoff, *California: For Health, Pleasure, and Residence.*

97 *San Diego California: The Harbor City of the Southwest*, n.p.

98 Wheeler, "A Forecast for California and the True Significance of the Panama Canal," 279.

99 *Panama-California Exposition Entire Year 1915*, n.p.

100 "California the Hostess," *Panama Pacific International Exposition, San Francisco 1915* [Hercules cover], n.p.; *California for the Tourist: The Charm of the Land of Sunshine by Summit Sea and Shore* (San Francisco: Southern Pacific, 1910), 5–7, https://archive.org/details/californiafortou00sout (accessed September 14, 2013).

101 Timothy A. Reardon, "Modern City Building," *California's Magazine* 1.1 (July 1915), 198.

102 "California the Hostess," *Panama Pacific International Exposition, San Francisco 1915* [Hercules cover], n.p. (first quote); *Panama-California Exposition Entire Year 1915*, n.p. (second quote); *WPA Prospectus*, 688; *San Francisco Chronicle*, January 6, 1914. For more on how western cities exploited nearby national parks in selling their communities, see Peter Blodgett, "Selling the Scenery: Advertising and the National Parks, 1916–1933," in Wrobel and Long, eds., *Seeing and Being Seen*, 281–82.

103 *San Diego Union*, January 1, 1913, in Amero Collection, Balboa Park Notes 191, Binder 67.

104 *East San Diego Press*, October 17, 1913, in Amero Collection, Balboa Park Notes 191, Binder 67.

105 Wheeler, "A Forecast for California and the True Significance of the Panama Canal," 279.

106 "California: Playground of the World," 83–92.

107 *Panama-California Exposition Entire Year 1915*, n.p.; *San Diego California: The Harbor City of the Southwest*, n.p.

108 *Official Guide Panama-Pacific International Exposition San Francisco 1915* (San Francisco: Wahlgreen, 1915), 119; A. C. Barker, *"Educational Opportunities of Oakland," National Education Association and International Congress of Education, 1915, Complimentary Souvenir Program*, 119–22.

109 W. D. Egilbert, "California's Education Exhibit—The Panama-Pacific International Exposition," *National Education Association and International Congress of Education, 1915, Complimentary Souvenir Program*, 8, 77–79.

110 *San Francisco Chronicle*, January 6, 1914; William MacDonald, "The California Expositions," *The Nation* (October 21, 1915), reprinted in *Fifty Years of American Idealism: The New York Nation, 1865–1915* (Boston: Houghton Mifflin, 1915), 443.

111 *San Diego California: The Harbor City of the Southwest*, n.p.

112 *San Diego California: The Harbor City of the Southwest*, n.p.

113 *Los Angeles Times*, January 17, 1915, in Amero Collection, Balboa Park Notes 191, Binder 71; *San Diego Union*, January 1, 1917.

114 *Guide to San Francisco and the Panama Pacific Exposition, 1915*, n.p.

115 MacDonald, "The California Expositions," 443.

116 *San Francisco Chronicle*, January 6, 1914.

117 MacDonald, "The California Expositions," 453.

118 *San Diego Union*, January 1, 1916.

119 *Panama-California Exposition Entire Year 1915*, n.p. (quote); *San Diego California: The Harbor City of the Southwest*, n.p. For article on California's roads, see George B. Harrison, "Roads and Highways of California," *California's Magazine* 1.1 (July 1915), 227–34.

120 *Panama Pacific International Exposition: Popular Information* (1915), n.p.

121 *San Francisco Chronicle*, January 6, 1914; Steele, "San Francisco the Exposition City," 610.

122 *Guide to San Francisco and the Panama Pacific Exposition, 1915*, n.p.

123 Street, "Another 'Go West,' " 212.

124 *San Diego California: The Harbor City of the Southwest*, n.p.

125 *San Diego International Panama-California Exposition* (published by Santa Fe Railroad), in Expositions—Panama-California/Brochures, Box 5, File 12 in San Diego History Center; Mark Daniels, "California as a Place of Homes," *California's Magazine* 1.1 (July 1915), 201–208; Arthur R. Kelly, "Homes of California," *California's Magazine* 1.1 (July 1915), 209–17.

126 *Panama-California Exposition Entire Year 1915*, n.p.

127 *San Diego California: The Harbor City of the Southwest*, n.p. For similar pictures of other Southern California cities, see *Southern California: Comprising the Counties of Imperial, Los Angeles, Orange, Riverside, San Bernardino, San Diego, Ventura*, 51–57.

128 *San Francisco and Vicinity—When the Golden State . . . Is Golden* (San Francisco: Cardinell-Vincent, 1915), 1–13, in http://www.books-about-california.com/Pages/SF_and_Vicinity/SF_and_Vicinity_main.html (accessed March 17, 2013); Cocks, *Doing the Town*, 156–63.

129 *Panama Pacific International Exposition, San Francisco, 1915* [Hercules cover], n.p.; *San Francisco and Vicinity—When the Golden State . . . Is Golden*, 14–16; *Panama Pacific International Exposition: Popular Information* (1915), n.p.; *California and the Expositions—Union Pacific System*, 32–42.

Chapter 8

1 Macomber, *The Jewel City*, 82; Abigail Markwyn, "Beyond *The End of the Trail*: Indians at San Francisco's 1915 World's Fair," *Ethnohistory* 63.2 (April 2016).

2 Lipsky, *San Francisco's Panama-Pacific International Exposition*, 99; Moore, *Empire on Display*, 163–64.

3 *San Diego Union*, February 7, 1915; *Official Guide Book of the Panama-California Exposition*, 23.

4 Richard Amero, *Panama-California Exposition San Diego, 1915–1916*, chapter 3; Kevin Armitage, "Commercial Indians: Authenticity, Nature, and Industrial Capitalism in Advertising at the Turn of the Twentieth Century," *Michigan Historical Review* 29.2 (Fall 2003), 70–95.

5 One Southern California advertising piece began its 250-page book with a dozen or more pages devoted to pictures of several missions accompanied by a history of Spanish missionaries activities in the region. See *Southern California: Comprising the Counties of Imperial, Los Angeles, Orange, Riverside, San Bernardino, San Diego, Ventura*, 3–18.

6 *Fore-Glance at Panama-California Exposition, San Diego 1915*, n.p.

7 Berglund, " 'The Days of Old, the Days of Gold, the Days of '49,' " 37–38.

8 *Los Angeles Times*, March 28, 1915, in Amero Collection, Balboa Park Notes 191, Binder 72.

9 Leah Dilworth, "Discovering Indians in Fred Harvey's Southwest," in Weigle and Babcock, ed., *The Great Southwest of the Fred Harvey Company and the Santa Fe Railway*, 161.

10 Ewald and Clute, *San Franciso Invites the World*, 58–59.

11 Lipsky, *San Francisco's Panama-Pacific International Exposition*, 99; Rydell, *All the World's a Fair*, 227–28; Todd, *The Story of the Exposition*, 2:355–56.

12 Todd, *The Story of the Exposition*, 2:362; Moore, *Empire on Display*, 158–61.

13 *San Diego Union*, December 14, 1914; January 13, 1915.

14 *WPA Prospectus*, 641.

15 *San Diego Union*, January 13, 1915.

16 Amero, *Panama-California Exposition San Diego, 1915–1916*, chapter 3; Bokovoy, *The San Diego World's Fairs and Southwestern Memory*, 68–72; Phoebe S. Kropp, "'There is a little sermon in that': Constructing the Native Southwest at the San Diego Panama-California Exposition of 1915," in *The Great Southwest of the Fred Harvey Company and the Santa Fe Railway*, edited by Marta Weigle and Barbara A. Babcock, 36–46. The Harvey Company provided dining and hotel services as well as curio and promotion for the Santa Fe Railway Company.

17 *WPA Prospectus*, 838.

18 Amero, *Panama-California Exposition San Diego, 1915–1916*, chapter 3; Bokovoy, *The San Diego World's Fairs and Southwestern Memory*, 60–62, 64.

19 Quoted in Kropp, "'There is a little sermon in that,'" 36.

20 Amero, *Panama-California Exposition San Diego, 1915–1916*, chapter 3; *Painted Desert Exhibit—San Diego Exposition*, (1915), https://archive.org/details/C100 2013086_201308 (accessed June 22, 2014).The Painted Desert was also a popular image for exposition postcards. For a sample, see San Diego History Center Exposition Postcards, http://sandiegohistory.org/collection/photographs/list390 (accessed June 19, 2015).

21 *San Diego Union*, March 14, 1915; December 14, 1914.

22 *San Diego Union*, January 13, 1915 (quote); January 1, 1916.

23 *Los Angeles Times*, March 7, 1915. For discussion of the Painted Desert's authenticity, see Kropp, "'There is a little sermon in that,'" 40–42.

24 *San Diego Sun*, January 18, 1915, Amero Collection, Balboa Park Notes 191, Binder 71; Bokovoy, *The San Diego World's Fairs and Southwestern Memory*, 70.

25 A. E. Bishop, ed., "San Diego Exposition," *Journal of Education* 81.4 (January 28, 1915), 88.

26 *San Diego Union*, September 5, 1914. For more on the Pueblo Indian dances, see Bokovoy, *The San Diego World's Fairs and Southwestern* Memory, 132–34.

27 *San Diego Union*, December 14, 1914.

28 Leah Dilworth, *Imaging Indians in the Southwest: Persistent Visions of a Primitive Past* (Washington, DC: Smithsonian Institution Press, 1996), 90.

29 Moore, *Empire on Display*, 166.

30 Raibmon, *Authentic Indians*, 202.

31 Markwyn, "Beyond *The End of the Trail*," 279. The Wanamaker Indian exhibit located in the Palace of Education offered three lectures a day on "Indian Life and Customs." See Todd, *The Story of the Exposition*, 3:8, 4:34, 5:64. For more on the Congress on Indian Progress meeting, see *The Carlisle Arrow: A Weekly Letter to Our People*, vol. 11 (May 28, 1915), n.p.; vol. 12 (October 22, 1915), n.p.

32 *Fore-Glance at Panama-California Exposition, San Diego, 1915*.

33 *The Official Guide and Descriptive Book, Panama California International Exposition, San Diego 1916*, 13. On Hewett's concerns, see Amero, *Panama-California Exposition San Diego, 1915–1916*, chapter 3.
34 *San Diego Union*, February 28, 1915.
35 *San Diego Union*, July 14, 1915. Another newspaper article suggested that visitors to the federal government's Indian school exhibits at the San Diego fair could "see the progress of the Indian race by comparing this exhibit with the archaeological exhibit already installed at our Exposition." See *San Diego Union*, January 1, 1916.
36 *Official Daily Program, Panama-California Exposition, San Diego, 1915* (July 16, 1915) in Expositions—Panama-California/Programs, San Diego History Center; Markwyn, "Beyond *The End of the Trail*," 280.
37 Robert A. Trenner, *The Phoenix Indian School: Forced Assimilation in Arizona, 1891–1935* (Norman: University of Oklahoma Press, 1988), 12.
38 Robert A. Trennert, "From Carlisle to Phoenix: The Rise and Fall of the Indian Outing System, 1878–1930," *Pacific Historical Review* 52.3 (August 1983), 278; Hoxie, *A Final Promise*, 99–101.
39 Bauer, "The Economy of Indian Education in California," 96.
40 Edward H. Hurlbut, "Features of the Panama-Pacific Exposition," *Overland Monthly* 66.5 (November 1915), 382–83
41 *Los Angeles Times*, March 7, 1915, Amero Collection, Balboa Park Notes 191, Binder 73.
42 *San Diego Union*, February 28, 1915.
43 *San Diego Union*, March 13, 1910, Amero Collection, Balboa Park Notes 191, Binder 63.
44 Todd, *The Story of the Exposition*, 4:127.
45 Markwyn, *Empress San Francisco*, 139.
46 W. B. Thompson, "Opportunities for Commercial Development," *San Francisco Chronicle*, December 31, 1911.
47 Lee, "The Contradictions of Cosmopolitanism," 288; Rydell, *All the World's a Fair*, 228. The president of the Lewis and Clark Exposition, Henry E. Reed, likewise complained of the impact of travel restrictions and "regulations for the admission of Chinese subjects who wish to attend the Exposition in the capacity of exhibitors or visitors." See Henry E. Reed to Henry E. Dosch, May 12, 1904, in Lewis and Clark Centennial Exposition, MSS 1609, Box 20, Box 1, Folder 2, OHS.
48 Abigail Markwyn, "Economic Partner and Exotic Other: China and Japan at San Francisco's Panama-Pacific International Exposition" *Western Historical Quarterly* 39.4 (Winter 2008), 441; Abbott, *How Cities Won the West*, 73.
49 *San Diego Union*, March 13, 1910, Amero Collection, Balboa Park Notes 191, Binder 63.
50 Deverell, *Railroad Crossing*, chapter 2.
51 Markwyn, *Empress San Francisco*, 142; Frank W. Van Nuys, "A Progressive Confronts the Race Question: Chester Rowell, the California Alien Land Act of 1913, and the Contradictions of Early Twentieth-Century Racial Thought," *California History* 73.1 (Spring 1994), 2.

52 Markwyn, *Empress San Francisco*, 146–47; Van Nuys, "A Progressive Confronts the Race Question," 3–4.
53 *San Francisco Chronicle*, April 3, 1913; Markwyn, *Empress San Francisco*, 146–49.
54 *San Francisco Chronicle*, April 4, 25, 1913.
55 Markwyn, *Empress San Francisco*, 150–51 (quote, 150).
56 Amero, *Panama-California Exposition San Diego, 1915–1916*, chapter 5.
57 Markwyn, *Empress San Francisco*, 151–53.
58 *Official Guide Panama-Pacific International Exposition San Francisco 1915*, 82; Markwyn, *Empress San Francisco*, 158–59.
59 *San Francisco Chronicle*, March 10, 1915.
60 Markwyn, *Empress San Francisco*, 158.
61 *Official Guide Panama-Pacific International Expsition San Francisco 1915*, 85.
62 Markwyn, *Empress San Francisco*, 159.
63 *San Francisco Chronicle*, July 10, 1915; February 25, 1915.
64 Markwyn, *Empress San Francisco*, 161.
65 *San Francisco Chronicle*, March 10, 1915.
66 *San Diego Union*, February 14, 1915.
67 *San Diego Union*, February 8, 13, 14, 1915.
68 *Panama California Exposition Entire Year 1915*.
69 *The Official Guide Book of the Panama California Exposition*, 13.
70 Amero, *Panama-California Exposition San Diego, 1915–1916*, chapter 5; *San Diego Union*, February 7, 1915.
71 Amero, *Panama-California Exposition San Diego, 1915–1916*, chapter 5; *San Diego Union*, March 9, 1915.
72 Markwyn, *Empress San Francisco*, 163–64; Rydell, *All the World's a Fair*, 228.
73 Todd, *The Story of the Exposition*, 2:358 (quote); Markwyn, "Economic Partner and Exotic Other," 461.
74 Markwyn, "Economic Partner and Exotic Other," 460.
75 Todd, *The Story of the Exposition*, 2:358; Markwyn, "Economic Partner and Exotic Other," 461–62; Lipsky, *San Francisco's Panama-Pacific International Exposition*, 96.
76 *San Diego Sun*, January 21, 1915, Amero Collection, Balboa Park Notes 191, Binder 71.
77 *Guide to San Francisco and the Panama Pacific Exposition*; *Information for Visitors*, n.p.
78 *San Francisco and Vicinity: When the Golden Gate is Golden*, 23; *Panama-Pacific International Exposition, San Francisco 1915*, n.p.
79 Charles C. Moore, "'San Francisco Knows How!' An Answer to the World's Questions: 'Can This Exposition Be Different?'" *Sunset Magazine* 28.1 (January 1912), 6; Steele, "San Francisco the Exposition City," 618.
80 Markwyn, *Empress San Francisco*, 165.
81 *San Diego Union*, April 25, 1915. Carl Abbott describes how local San Francisco companies exploited the unsavory image of Chinatown in tours they organized for visitors. See Abbott, *How Cities Won the West*, 65–66.
82 *San Diego Union*, July 13, August 16, September 6, 1915. San Diego's Chinatown was much smaller and less well-known than San Francisco's. For more on San Diego's Chinese community, see Elizabeth MacPhall, "San Diego's Chinese Mission," *Journal of San Diego History* 23.2 (Spring 1977).

83 Todd, *The Story of the Exposition*, 5:55.
84 *San Francisco Chronicle*, September 23, 1911.
85 The Filipino population in the United States began to increase significantly between 1910 and 1930, with the lion's share in California. See Yen Le Espiritu, *Filipino American Lives* (Philadelphia: Temple University Press, 1995), 9.
86 Todd, *The Story of the Exposition*, 3:376.
87 Markwyn, *Empress San Francisco*, 53–54.
88 Daniel R. Williams, "Watchful Waiting for the Philippines," *Sunset Magazine* 35 (December 1915), 1086.
89 Chester H. Rowell, "Philippine Independence," *California Outlook* 18.2 (January 9, 1915), 7; Williams, "Watchful Waiting for the Philippines," 1086.
90 Todd, *The Story of the Exposition*, 3:376 (quote), 378–79.
91 *The Philippine Islands: Their Industrial and Commercial Possibilities* (1914), https://archive.org/details/philippineislandoopanarich (accessed November 13, 2016). This volume includes series of special pamphlets produced by the the Manila Bureau of Printing for the Panama-Pacific International Exposition.
92 Todd, *The Story of the Exposition*, 3:379.
93 Todd, *The Story of the Exposition*, 4:48 (quote), 49–50.
94 Todd, *The Story of the Exposition*, 4:59.
95 "The Philippine Islands: Public Health, Panama-Pacific International Exposition," in *The Philippine Islands: Their Industrial and Commercial Possibilities.*
96 *San Diego Union*, December 2, 1915; April 6, 1916 (quote).
97 Kropp, *California Vieja*, 104.
98 Reid, "Professor Igloo Jimmie and Dr. Boombang Meet the Heathens," 113 (quote); Coll Thrush, *Native Seattle: Histories for the Crossing-Over Place* (Seattle: University of Washington Press, 2007), 119–20; Bokovoy, *The San Diego World's Fairs and Southwestern Memory*, 115; Lisa Blee, " 'I came voluntarily to work, sing and dance': Stories from the Eskimo Village at the 1909 Alaska-Yukon-Pacific Exposition," *Pacific Northwest Quarterly* 101.3/4 (Summer/Fall 2010), 127–29.
99 Thrush, *Native Seattle*, 120–21.
100 Kropp, *California Vieja*, 150–51.
101 Bokovoy, *The San Diego World's Fairs and Southwestern Memory*, 132.
102 Blee, " 'I came voluntarily to work, sing and dance,' " 135.
103 Cleland, "Disruptions in the Dream City," 42.
104 Cleland, "Disruptions in the Dream City," 62.
105 Olivera, "Colonial Ethnology and the Igorrote Village at the AYP," 142, 146–47.
106 *Seattle Post-Intelligencer*, July 18, 1909; Manish Chalana, "The Pay Streak Spectacle: Representations of Race and Gender in the Amusement Quarters of the Alaska-Yukon-Pacific Exposition," *Pacific Northwest Quarterly* 100.1, Part 1 (Winter 2008/2009), 31.
107 Markwyn, *Empress San Francisco*, 106, 112, 129.
108 Lee, "The Contradictions of Cosmopolitanism," 285–88 (quote, 287), 292.

⊧ Conclusion

1 Markwyn, *Empress San Francisco*, 255–56; *Oregonian*, October 14, 1906; *Evening Telegram*, November 2, 1921; *Report of the Alaska-Yukon-Exposition Commission of the State of Washington.*

2 Abbott, *The Great Extravaganza*, 65.

3 Abbott, *The Great Extravaganza*, 61–63.

4 Lipsky, *San Francisco's Panama-Pacific International Exposition*, 123.

5 *Report of the Alaska-Yukon-Exposition Commission of the State of Washington*; Alaska-Yukon-Pacific Exposition, Special Collections, University of Washington, http://www.lib.washington.edu/specialcollections/collections/exhibits/ayp.

6 Bokovoy, *The San Diego World's Fairs and Southwestern Memory*, chapter 5; Amero, *Panama-California Exposition San Diego, 1915–1916*, chapter 7, http://www.sandiegohistory.org/archives/amero/1915expo/ch7; "Balboa Park History," https://www.balboapark.org/about/history.

7 Putman, *Class and Gender Politics in Progressive-Era Seattle*, 183–86, 203–10.

8 Bokovoy, *The San Diego World's Fairs and Southwestern Memory*, 144–45; Uldis Ports, "Geraniums vs. Smokestacks: San Diego's Mayoralty Campaign of 1917," *Journal of San Diego History* 21.3 (Summer 1975).

9 Markwyn, *Empress San Francisco*, 260.

10 The Washington State tourism website, http://experiencewa.com (accessed August 5, 2018), featured a picture of a snow-capped mountain, while the Visit California website, http://visitcalifornia.com (accessed August 5, 2018), showcased the Pacific Ocean hugging the coastline. Oregon's state tourism webiste, https://traveloregon.com (accessed August 5, 2018), highlighted Crater Lake, the Oregon coast, and hiking in nearby mountains.

11 Neil Morgan, *Westward Tilt: The American West Today* (New York: Random House, 1963).

BIBLIOGRAPHY

Archival Sources

Oregon Historical Society

Lewis and Clark Centennial Exposition. Manuscript 1609.
Lewis and Clark Scrapbooks.

Portland Public Library

Lewis and Clark Centennial Exposition—Official Records.

San Diego History Research Center

Amero, Richard Collection. MS 76.
Expositions—Panama-California/Brochures.
Expositions—Panama-California/Programs.
Minute Book of the Executive Committee of the Board of Directors of the Panama-California Exposition. MS 263.
WPA Prospectus of the 1915 Exposition. MS 51.

Seattle Public Library

Alaska-Yukon-Pacific Exposition Digital Collection.

University of Washington

Alaska-Yukon-Pacific Exposition—Pamphlets.
Alaska-Yukon-Pacific Exposition—Programs to Publicity.
Alaska-Yukon-Pacific Exposition—Finance to Miscellaneous mounted clippings.
Alaska-Yukon-Pacific Exposition—National and Foreign Participation to P.I. Clippings.
Chilberg, John Edward. Papers.
Meany, Edmond S. Papers.
Seattle A.Y.P. Exposition Scrapbook.
Whitaker, F.G. Papers.

Newspapers and Periodicals

Alaska-Yukon-Pacific Weekly News.
American Review of Reviews.
Argus (Seattle).
AYP Daily News.
Bulletin of the Pan American Union.
California's Magazine.
California Outlook.
Century.
Chicago Illustrated Review.
Coast.
Collier's: The National Weekly.
Current Opinion.
Evening Telegram (Portland, OR).
Exposition News (San Diego).
Leslie's Weekly.
Lewis and Clark Journal.
Lewis and Clark Review and Gazetteer.
Literary Digest.
Los Angeles Examiner.
Los Angeles Times.
Nation.
New York Times.
North American Review.
Oregonian (Morning Oregonian).
Oregon Journal.
Overland Monthly.
Pacific Northwest Commerce.
Putnam's Magazine.
Salt Lake Tribune.
San Diego Evening Tribune.
San Diego Sun.
San Diego Union.
San Francisco Chronicle.
Santa Fe Magazine.
Scribner's Magazine.
Seattle Daily Times.
Seattle Post-Intelligencer.
Social Hygiene.
Sunset Magazine.
Town Crier (Seattle).
Washington Post.
World's Work.

Primary Published Material

1915 All the Year, Panama-California Exposition. archive.org/details/C1002013084.

"Address delivered by Mr. James J. Hill at the Opening of the Alaska-Yukon-Pacific Exposition, Seattle, WA, June 1, 1909." www.mnhs.org/library/findaids/00698/pdf/00698 000034.pdf.

Alaska-Yukon-Pacific Exposition. "Report," Committee on Industrial Arts and Expositions; House of Representatives (60th Congress, 1st session: 1907–1908). archive.org/details/alaskayukonpacif01unit.

Alaska Yukon Pacific Exposition Seattle U.S.A., June 1st to October 15th, 1909. Seattle: Issued by Department of Publicity, 1907. Seattle Public Library AYPE Digital Collection.

The Alaska-Yukon-Pacific Exposition: Seattle, June 1–October 16, 1909. St. Paul, MN: Northern Pacific Railway, 1909. Alaska-Yukon-Pacific Exposition Digital Collection. Seattle Public Library.

The Alaska-Yukon-Pacific Exposition and Seattle the Beautiful Exposition City. Seattle: Robert A. Reid Publisher, 1909.

Alaska-Yukon-Pacific Exposition Souvenir Cookbook, 1909. Special Collections, University of Washington.

Back, Seid, Jr. *A Trip Through Chinatown: Chinese Souvenir of the Lewis and Clark Exposition.* Portland: R. W. Steele, 1905. Oregon Historical Society.

Bagley, Clarence B. *The History of Seattle from the Earliest Settlement to the Present*, vol. 2. Chicago: S. J. Clarke Publishing Co., 1916.

Barker, A. C. "Educational Opportunities of Oakland," *National Education Association and International Congress of Education, 1915, Complimentary Souvenir Program.*

Bernier, R. L. "To the Public." *California Magazine* 1.1 (July 1915).

Bishop, A. E., ed. "San Diego Exposition." *Journal of Education* 81.4 (January 28, 1915).

Blethen, Joseph. "What the Northwest Is: The Size and Qualities of the Country and the Characteristics of the People." *World's Work* 10.4 (1905).

Bradley, Lewis G. *Official Guide to the Lewis and Clark Exposition.* Portland, 1905. archive.org/details/officialguidetoloolewi.

Brown, Elton T. *The 1916 Exposition in Black and White: Being a series of pencil drawings of the Panama California International Exposition, 1916.* Coronado, CA: The Coronado Strand, 1916. archive.org/details/1916expositionin01brow.

Buchanan, John A. *Indian Legends and Other Poems: Souvenir Edition of the Lewis and Clark Fair.* San Francisco: Whitaker & Ray, 1905.

California and the Expositions—Union Pacific System. www.books-about-california.com/Pages/California_and_the_Expositions/California_and_Expos_text.html.

California for the Tourist: The Charm of the Land of Sunshine by Summit Sea and Shore. San Francisco: Southern Pacific, 1910. archive.org/details/californiafortou00sout.

The Carlisle Arrow: A Weekly Letter to Our People, vol. 11 (May 28, 1915); vol. 12 (October 22, 1915).

Chamberlain, Arthur Henry. "Our Western Wonderlands." *National Education Association and International Congress of Education, 1915, Complimentary Souvenir Program.* books.google.com.

Choate, Rufus. "San Diego to Control the Canal Commerce of the Southwest." *Exposition News* 1.1 (December 1911).

The Cities of Puget Sound, Your Hosts for 1909. Special Collections. University of Washington.

Committee on Industrial Arts and Exposition of the House of Representatives. Alaska-Yukon-Pacific Exposition, March 18, 1908. Washington, DC: Government Printing Office, 1908.

Connolly, Robert E. "California's Opportunity." *Sunset Magazine* 25.4 (December 1910).

Corbett, H. W. "The Exposition: Extract from the Annual Report of President Corbett to the Board of Commissioners." *The Centennial: Bulletin of Scope and Progress* 1.1 (1903).

Curtis, Henry S. *The Play Movement and Its Significance*. New York: Macmillan, 1917. archive.org/details/playmovementitssoocurt.

Daniels, Mark. "California as a Place of Homes." *California's Magazine* 1.1 (July 1915).

Dosch, Henry E. *Official Catalogue of the Alaska-Yukon-Pacific Exposition, Seattle, Washington*. Special Collections, University of Washington.

Egilbert, W. D. "California's Education Exhibit—The Panama-Pacific International Exposition," National Education Association and International Congress of Education, 1915, Complimentary Souvenir Program.

The Exposition Beautiful. Seattle: Seattle Publishing Company, ca. 1909. Alaska-Yukon Pacific Exposition Digital Collection. Seattle Public Library.

The Exposition: A Magazine Devoted to the Lewis and Clark Centennial, American Pacific Exposition and Oriental Fair 1:7 (June 1903). Wilson Room. Portland Public Library.

Falk, Lewis H. "Panama-California Exposition at San Diego." *Overland Monthly* 66.3 (November 1915).

Fore-Glance at Panama-California Exposition, San Diego, 1915: Unique International Year 'Round Jan. 1–Dec. 31. archive.org/details/Fore-glanceAtPanamaCalifornia ExpositionSanDiego1915Unique.

Forbes, Edgar Allen. "California Coming Into Its Own." *California Magazine* 1.1 (July 1915).

Foster, J. S. "The Alaska-Yukon-Pacific Exposition: How it Differs From Other World's Fairs and What it Means to the Great Northwest 57 Exposition Number." *The 57* 9.8. Pittsburgh: H. J. Heinz Company, 1909. Alaska-Yukon-Pacific Exposition Digital Collection, Seattle Public Library.

Gaston, Joseph. *Portland Oregon: Its History and Builders*, vol. 1. Chicago-Portland: S. J. Clarke Publishers, 1911.

General History Alaska-Yukon-Pacific Exposition: Meet Me in Seattle 1909. Seattle Public Library Digital Collection.

Gilbert, Menard. "California: Playground of the World." *California's Magazine* 1.1 (July 1915).

Gillett, Governor James N. "What California Offers." *Sunset Magazine* 25.6 (December 1910).

Glimpses of the Lewis and Clark Exposition and the Golden West. Chicago, 1905. archive .org/details/glimpsesoflewiscoolairrich.

Guide to San Francisco and the Panama Pacific Exposition, 1915. San Francisco: Baldwin

Piano Company, 1915. www.books-about california.com/Pages/Guide_to_SF_and_Expo/Guide_to_SF_and_Expo_main.html.

Guide to San Francisco and the Panama Pacific Exposition; Information for Visitors to the Panama-Pacific International Exhibition, San Francisco, 1915: An Analysis of the Plan and Scope of the Exposition. San Francisco: Kirchner & Mante, 1914. www.books-about-california.com/Pages/Info_for_Visitors_PPIE/Info_for_Visitor_PPIE_text.html.

Hall, Rinaldo M. *Oregon, Washington, Idaho and Their Resources.* Portland: Oregon Railroad and Navigation Company and Southern Pacific Company Lines in Oregon, 1903. OHS.

Harrison, George B. "Roads and Highways of California." *California's Magazine* 1.1 (July 1915).

Hearing before the Committee on Industrial Arts and Exposition of the House of Representatives. Alaska-Yukon-Pacific Exposition. January 27, 1908. Washington, DC: Government Printing Office, 1908.

Hearing before the Committee on Industrial Arts and Exposition of the House of Representatives. Proposed Panama Canal Exposition. January 10, 1911. Washington, DC: Government Printing Office, 1911.

Higgins, C.A. *To California over the Santa Fe Trail.* Chicago: Passenger Department, Santa Fe Railway Company, 1915. archive.org/details/tocaliforniaoveroohigg.

Hogaboom, Winfield. "Looking into the Future: The Purpose of the Panama-California Exposition, at San Diego, in 1915, 'To Show What Will Be By What Has Been.'" *Sunset Magazine* 32.2 (February 1913).

Hurlbut, Edward H. "Features of the Panama-Pacific Exposition." *Overland Monthly* 66.5 (November 1915).

Information for Visitors to the Panama-Pacific International Exposition. San Francisco: The Panama-Pacific International Exposition Company, 1915. www.books-about-california.com/Pages/Info_for_Visitors_PPIE/Info_for_Visitor_PPIE_text.html.

Johnson, Bascom. "Moral Conditions in San Francisco and at the Panama-California Exposition." *Social Hygiene* 1.4 (September 1915).

Johnson, Emory R. "What The Canal Will Accomplish." *Scribner's Magazine* 54.1 (July 1913).

Jones, R. S., Jr. "What the Visitor Sees at the Seattle Fair." *The American Review of Reviews* 40 (July 1909).

Kahn, Julius. "The Immigration Problem in California." *California's Magazine* 1.1 (July 1915).

Keliehor, Helen Chase. *Memories: The Alaska-Yukon-Pacific Exposition, Seattle Washington, June 1 to October 15, 1909.* Seattle, Washington, 1984. Special Collections, University of Washington.

Kelly, Arthur R. "Homes of California." *California's Magazine* 1.1 (July 1915).

King, Homer S. "California's Exposition Ambitions." *Sunset Magazine* 25.4 (December 1910).

"The Little Landers' Colony." *Exposition News* 1.1 (December 1911).

Los Angeles Standard Guide San Diego, Including the Panama-California Exposition at San Diego. Published by North American Press Association, 1915. archive.org/details/LosAngelesStandardGuideSanDiegoIncludingThePanamaCalifornia Exposition.

Love, Robertus. "The Lewis and Clark Fair." *The World's Work* 10.4 (1905).

Lynch, Robert Newton. "Looking East From the West." *California Magazine* 1.1 (July 1915).

———. "Welcoming the Immigrant." *Sunset Magazine* 32.3 (March 1913).

MacDonald, William. "The California Expositions." *The Nation* (October 21, 1915), reprinted in *Fifty Years of American Idealism: The New York Nation, 1865–1915* (Boston: Houghton Mifflin, 1915).

MacLafferty, James Henry. "San Francisco and the Panama-Pacific International Exposition." 1915. www.books-about california.com/Pages/San_Francisco_PPIE/San_Francisco_PPIE_text.html.

Macomber, Ben. *The Jewel City: Its Planning and Achievements; Its Architecture, Sculpture, Symbolism, and Music; Its Gardens, Palaces, and Exhibits*. San Francisco: John H. Williams Publisher, 1915.

McLeary, F. Burnham. "Following the Sunset to the Golden Gate." *World's Work* 29.6 (April 1915).

McNab, Gavin. "California's Promise to Posterity." *California Magazine* 1.1 (July 1915).

Meikle, James B. "American Mastery of the Pacific." *World's Work* 10.4 (1905).

Moore, Charles C. "San Francisco and the Exposition: The Relation of the City to the Nation as Regards the World's Fair." *Sunset Magazine* 28.4 (April 1912).

———. " 'San Francisco Knows How!' An Answer to the World's Questions: 'Can This Exposition Be Different?' " *Sunset Magazine* 28.1 (January 1912).

Murphy, Jerre C. "San Diego's Evolutionary Exposition." *Collier's: The National Weekly* (December 5, 1914).

Museum of History and Industry. "Hello Bill! Meet Me on the Pay Streak at the Alaska Yukon Pacific Exposition, Seattle USA, 1909." digitalcollections.lib.washington .edu/cdm/ref/collection/imlsmohai/id/3501.

"News Notes From San Diego." *Santa Fe Magazine* 9.6 (April 1914/15).

Nordhoff, Charles. *California: For Health, Pleasure, and Residence. A Book for Travellers and Settlers*. New York: Harper & Brothers Publishers, 1873.

Official Catalogue of the Lewis and Clark Centennial and American Pacific Exposition and Oriental Fair. Portland: A. Hess & Co., 1905. archive.org/details/officialcataloguoolewi.

Official Guidebook to the Lewis and Clark Exposition. Lewis and Clark Centennial and American Pacific Exposition and Oriental Fair, 1905.

Official Guide Book of the Panama-California Exposition. San Diego, 1915. archive.org/stream/TheOfficialGuideBookOfThePanama-CaliforniaExpositionSanDiego 1915/c100_2012_007#page/n0/mode/2up.

The Official Guide Book of the Panama California Exposition; *The Official Guide and Descriptive Book: Panama California International Exposition*. San Diego, 1916. archive.org/details/TheOfficialGuideAndDescriptiveBookPanama-california International.

Official Guide Panama-Pacific International Exposition San Francisco 1915. San Francisco: Wahlgreen, 1915.

Official Guide to the Alaska-Yukon-Pacific Exposition. Seattle: Alaska-Yukon-Pacific Exposition Publishing Company, 1909. Alaska-Yukon-Pacific Exposition Digital Collection, Seattle Public Library.

Oregon: Land of Opportunity. Portland: Portland Chamber of Commerce, 1911. babel.hathitrust.org/cgi/pt?id=mdp.39015027928319;view=1up;seq=5.

"Oregon as a Health Resort." *Lewis and Clark Journal* 2.1 (July 1904).

Page, Walter H. "The Larger Coast Cities." *World's Work* 10.4 (1905).

Painted Desert Exhibit—San Diego Exposition. 1915. archive.org/details/C100 2013086_201308.

Panama California Exposition Entire Year 1915. www.books-about california.com/Pages/San_Diego_Brochure/San_Diego_Brochure_text.html.

Panama-California International Exposition: Unique, Entrancing, Educational, San Diego, 1915. archive.org/details/PanamaCaliforniaInternationalExpositionUniqueEntrancingEducationalSan.

Panama Canal, Panama-Pacific International and Panama-California Expositions. Souvenir issued by International Harvester Companies (1915). https://archive.org/details/Panama-pacificPanama-californiaSouvenir1915.

Panama Pacific International Exposition: Popular Information. 1915. babel.hathitrust.org/cgi/pt?id=mdp.39015058345524.

Panama-Pacific International Exposition, San Francisco, 1915. [Hercules cover.] San Francisco: Panama-Pacific International Exposition Company, 1914. archive.org/details/cu31924101862732.

Panama-Pacific International Exposition, San Francisco, 1915. Virtual Museum of the City of San Francisco. www.sfmuseum.net/hist9/ppietxt1.html.

Participation in the Alaska-Yukon-Pacific Exposition: Message from the President of the United States, transmitting the report of the United States Government Board of Managers of the Government participation in the Alaska-Yukon-Pacific Exposition. Washington, DC: Government Printing Office, 1911. catalog.hathitrust.org/Record/011209847.

Perkins, E. T. "Redeeming the West: Present Status of Government Irrigation Projects Involving the Expenditure of $33,000,000, and Making Fertile Over 18,000,000 Acres of Land." *Sunset Magazine* 16.1 (November 1905).

Perry, George Hough. "How Country Editors Can Get National Advertising." *University of Kansas News-Bulletin* 15.4 (October 1914). babel.hathitrust.org/cgi/pt?id=osu.32435014436927;view=1up;seq=5.

"The Philippine Exhibit." *The Coast* 18.1 (July 1909).

The Philippine Islands: Their Industrial and Commercial Possibilities. 1914. archive.org/details/philippineislandoopanarich.

The Philippine Public Schools at the Panama-Pacific International Exposition. San Francisco: Marnell & Co., 1915. archive.org/details/philippinepublicoophil.

Piper, Edgar B. "Portland and the Lewis and Clark Centennial Exposition." *American Monthly Review of Reviews* 31 (April 1905).

"The Railways and the California Expositions." *Railway Age Gazette* 59.11 (September 10, 1915). babel.hathitrust.org.

Reardon, Timothy A. "Modern City Building." *California's Magazine* 1.1 (July 1915).

The Red Book of Views of the Panama-Pacific International Exposition. San Francisco: The Panama-Pacific International Exposition Company, 1915.

Reed, Henry E. "Material Development of the Oregon Country." *Lewis and Clark Journal* 1.1 (January 1904).

———. *Oregon: A Story of Progress and Development Together with an Account of the Lewis and Clark Centennial Exposition*. Portland, 1905. Oregon Historical Society.

———. "The Great West and the Two Easts." *North American Review* 178 (April 1904).

Reed, William G. "The Climate of California." *California Magazine* 1.1 (July 1915).

Report of the Alaska-Yukon-Exposition Commission of the State of Washington. Seattle: Pacific Press, Inc., 1910. Special Collections, University of Washington.

Report of the Country Life Commission: Special Message from the President of the United States Transmitting the Report of the Country Life Commission. Washington, DC: Government Printing Office, 1909.

Report of the Legislative Committee from the State of New York to the AYP Exposition (1910). Special Collections, University of Washington.

Roosevelt, Theodore. *The Strenuous Life: Essays and Addresses*. New York: Century, 1900. www.bartleby.com/58/10.html.

Rowell, Chester H. "Philippine Independence." *California Outlook* 18.2 (January 9, 1915).

San Diego: All the Year 1915, Panama-California Exposition. archive.org/details/SanDiegoAllTheYear1915PanamaCaliforniaExposition.

San Diego California: The Harbor City of the Southwest. Issued by San Diego Board of Supervisors, San Diego County, 1911. archive.org/details/C1002013095.

San Diego History Center Exposition Postcards. sandiegohistory.org/collection/photographs/list390.

"San Diego Is a City of Peace, Happiness and Plenty." *San Diego Exposition Bulletin* 1.5 (May 1912).

San Francisco and Vicinity—When the Golden State . . . Is Golden. San Francisco: Cardinell Vincent, 1915. www.books-about-california.com/Pages/SF_and_Vicinity/SF_and_Vicinity_main.html.

Seattle and the Pacific Northwest: Washington, Oregon, California, Alaska, British Columbia, Yukon. Seattle: Seattle Publishing Company, 1909. In Special Collections, University of Washington.

"Seattle Opens Doors of Country to Japanese Commissioners," *Pacific Northwest Commerce* 1.4 (October 1909).

Seattle: The Exposition City. Seattle, 1909. Seattle Public Library Alaska-Yukon-Pacific Exposition Digital Collection.

Seventh Annual Convention of the Associated Advertising Clubs of America, 1911. Boston: Pilgrim Publicity Association, 1912. books.google.com.

Sights and Scenes at the Lewis and Clark Centennial Exposition, Portland, Oregon. archive.org/details/sightsscenesatleoolewi.

"Smithsonian and National Museum Exhibit." *Coast* 18.1 (July 1909).

Smythe, William E. *The Conquest of Arid America.* New York: Harper & Brothers Publishers, 1900. archive.org/stream/ofaridconquestamoosmytrich#page/n5/mode/2up.

Southern California: Comprising the Counties of Imperial, Los Angeles, Orange, Riverside, San Bernardino, San Diego, Ventura. Southern California Panama Expositions Commission, 1914. books.google.com.

Souvenir Information Guide: Seattle and A. Y. P. Exposition Diary and Official Calendar. Seattle, 1909. Alaska-Yukon-Pacific Exposition Digital Collection, Seattle Public Library.

Souvenir View Book of the Lewis and Clark Centennial Exposition and Oriental Fair. Portland: Robert A. Reid, 1905. Oregon Historical Society.

"Speech of Charles W. Fulton of Oregon in the Senate of the United States, December 18, 1903." Washington, DC: 1904. Oregon Historical Society.

"Speech of Hon. Samuel H. Piles of Washington in the Senate of the United States." February 3, 1908. Washington, DC: Seattle Public Library Alaska-Yukon-Pacific Exposition Digital Collection.

Standard Guide to Los Angeles, San Diego, and the Panama-California Exposition. Los Angeles, 1916. archive.org/details/standardguidetolooooffi.

"Statement of Congressman W. E. Humphrey." *United States House Hearings, Industrial Art and Exposition Committee.* 1908. Special Collections. University of Washington.

"Statement of Hon. Harvey W. Scott of Portland, Oreg., President of the Lewis and Clark Centennial Exposition." House of Representatives, Committee on Industrial Arts and Expositions. January 14, 1904. archive.org/details/lewisclarkcentenoounit.

"Statement of John H. McGraw, Vice-President of the Exposition Company of Seattle, Wash., and President of the Seattle Chamber of Commerce." *United States House Hearings, Industrial Art and Exposition Committee.* 1908. Special Collections. University of Washington.

Steele, Rufus. "A Matter of Millions: How the Experts Are Hearing in Advance the Click of the Expositions Gates." *Sunset Magazine* 34.1 (January 1915).

———. "San Francisco the Exposition City." *Sunset Magazine* 25.4 (December 1910).

Street, Arthur I. "Another 'Go West' Period." *Sunset Magazine* 14.3 (January 1905).

Thirteenth Census of the United States: Manufactures, Vol. IX. Washington, DC: Government Printing Office, 1912.

Todd, Frank Morton. *The Story of the Exposition: Being the Official History of the International Celebration Held at San Francisco in 1915 to Commemorate the Discovery of the Pacific Ocean and the Construction of the Panama Canal.* Vols. 1–4. New York: G. P. Putnam's Sons, 1921.

United States House Hearings, Industrial Art and Exposition Committee (1908). Special Collections. University of Washington.

Warner, Charles Dudley. *Our Italy.* New York: Harper & Brothers, 1891.

Watson, Mark S. "The Panama-California Exposition." *California's Magazine* 1.1 (July 1915). Archive.org, https://archive.org/details/californiasmagazoosanf.

Wheeler, Benjamin Ide. "A Forecast for California and the True Significance of the Panama Canal." *California Magazine* 1.1 (July 1915).

———."The Meaning of the Canal." *American Review of Reviews* 51.2 (February 1915).

Wheeler, Olin D. *The Lewis and Clark Exposition: Portland, Oregon June 1 to October 15, 1905*. St. Paul, MN: Northern Pacific Railway Company, 1905.
"Where Rolls the Oregon." *Lewis and Clark Journal* 1.1 (January 1904).
Wickson, E. J. "The High Quality of California Rural Life." *California Magazine* 1.1 (July 1915).
Willey, Day Allen. "The Course of Empire: As Exemplified by the Lewis and Clark Exposition," n.d. Wilson Room, Portland Public Library.
Williams, Daniel R. "Watchful Waiting for the Philippines." *Sunset Magazine* 35 (December 1915).
Woehlke, Walter V. "Nueva España by the Silver Gate." *Sunset, the Pacific Monthly* 33.6 (December 1914).
———. "Real Wild-West Shows." *Sunset, the Pacific Monthly* 32.2 (February 1913).
———. "Staging the Big Show: An Inside Story of What Is Going on Behind the Scenes at the Panama-California Exposition at San Diego." *Sunset Magazine* 33.2 (August 1914).
———."The Land of Before-and-After: The Miracle-Story of Imperial Valley, California." *Sunset, The Pacific Monthly* 28.4 (April 1912).

Secondary Published Material

Abbott, Carl. *Boosters and Businessmen: Popular Economic Thought and Urban Growth in the Antebellum Middle West*. Westport, CT: Greenwood Press, 1981.
———. *The Great Extravaganza: Portland and the Lewis and Clark Exposition*. Portland: Oregon Historical Society, 1981.
———. *How Cities Won the West: Four Centuries of Urban Change in Western North America*. Albuquerque: University of New Mexico Press, 2008.
———. *Portland in Three Centuries: The Place and the People*. Corvallis: Oregon State University Press, 2011.
———. *Portland: Planning, Politics, and Growth in a Twentieth-Century City*. Lincoln: University of Nebraska Press, 1983.
Adams, David Wallace. *Education for Extinction: American Indians and the Boarding School Experience, 1875–1928*. Lawrence: University Press of Kansas, 1995.
Amero, Richard W. *Balboa Park History*. San Diego: History Press, 2013. balboapark history.net.
———. "The Making of the Panama-California Exposition, 1909–1915." *Journal of San Diego History* 36.1 (Winter 1990). www.sandiegohistory.org/journal/1990/january/expo.
———. *Panama-California Exposition San Diego, 1915–1916*. San Diego History Center. www.sandiegohistory.org/archives/amero/1915expo.
Aquila, Richard. ed. *Wanted Dead or Alive: The American West in Popular Culture*. Urbana: University of Illinois Press, 1996.
Armitage, Kevin. "Commercial Indians: Authenticity, Nature, and Industrial Capitalism in Advertising at the Turn of the Twentieth Century." *Michigan Historical Review* 29.2 (Fall 2003).

Ashworth, G. J., and H. Voogd. *Selling the City: Marketing Approaches in Public Sector Urban Planning.* London: Belhaven Press, 1990.

Athearn, Robert G. *The Mythic West in Twentieth-Century America.* Lawrence: University Press of Kansas, 1986.

Bauer, William J., Jr. "The Economy of Indian Education in California, 1902–1945." In *Indian Subjects: Hemispheric Perspectives on the History of Indigenous Education,* edited by Brenda J. Child and Brian Klopotek. Santa Fe, NM: School for Advanced Research Press, 2014.

Beck, David R. M. "The Myth of the Vanishing Race." https://davidrmbeck.files.wordpress.com/2017/09/myth-of-the-vanishing-race-web-grab.pdf.

Becker, Paula. "Miss Columbia Is Declared Queen of the Carnival at the Alaska-Yukon-Pacific Exposition in Seattle on August 19, 1909." *Historylink.org: The Free Online Encyclopedia of Washington State History.* www.historylink.org/index.cfm?DisplayPage=output.cfm&file_id=8881.

Benedict, Burton. *The Anthropology of World's Fairs: San Francisco's Panama Pacific International Exposition of 1915.* Berkeley: Scholar Press, 1983.

Berglund, Barbara. "'The Days of Old, the Days of Gold, the Days of '49': Identity, History, and Memory at the California Midwinter International Exposition, 1894." *Public Historian* 25.4 (Fall 2003).

Blee, Lisa. "Completing Lewis and Clark's Westward March: Exhibiting a History of Empire at the 1905 Portland World's Fair." *Oregon Historical Quarterly* 106.2 (Summer 2005).

———. "'I came voluntarily to work, sing and dance': Stories from the Eskimo Village at the 1909 Alaska-Yukon-Pacific Exposition." *Pacific Northwest Quarterly* 101.3/4 (Summer/Fall 2010).

Blethen, Joseph. "What the Northwest Is: The Size and Qualities of the Country and the Characteristics of the People." *World's Work* 10.4 (1905), 6474.

Bloodworth, William. "Writers of the Purple Sage: Novelists and the American West." In *Wanted Dead or Alive: The American West in Popular Culture,* edited by Richard Aquila. Urbana: University of Illinois Press, 1996.

Bokovoy, Matthew F. "Inventing Agriculture in Southern California." *Journal of San Diego History* 45.3 (Summer 1999).

———. *The San Diego World's Fairs and Southwestern Memory, 1880–1940.* Albuquerque: University of New Mexico Press, 2005.

Bowers, William L. "Country-Life Reform, 1900–1920: A Neglected Aspect of Progressive Era History." *Agricultural History* 45.3 (July 1971).

Chalana, Manish. "The Pay Streak Spectacle: Representations of Race and Gender in the Amusement Quarters of the Alaska-Yukon-Pacific Exposition." *Pacific Northwest Quarterly* 100.1, Part 1 (Winter 2008/2009).

Child, Brenda J., and Brian Klopotek. *Indian Subjects: Hemispheric Perspectives on the History of Indigenous Education.* Santa Fe, NM: School for Advanced Research Press, 2014.

Cocks, Catherine. *Doing the Town: The Rise of Urban Tourism in the United States, 1850–1915.* Berkeley: University of California Press, 2001.

Coleman, Michael C. *American Indians, the Irish, and Government Schooling.* Lincoln: University of Nebraska Press, 2007.

Corbey, Raymond. "Ethnographic Showcases, 1870–1930." *Cultural Anthropology* 8.3 (August 1993).

Cronon, William, George Miles, and Jay Gitlin, eds. *Under an Open Sky: Rethinking America's Western Past.* New York: W. W. Norton and Company, 1992.

Daniels, Roger. *Asian America: Chinese and Japanese in the United States since 1850.* Seattle: University of Washington Press, 1988.

DeLyser, Dydia. *Ramona Memories: Tourism and the Shaping of Southern California.* Minneapolis: University of Minnesota Press, 2005.

Deverell, William. *Railroad Crossing: Californians and the Railroad, 1850–1910.* Berkeley: University of California Press, 1994.

Deverell, William, and Tom Sitton, eds. *California Progressivism Revisited.* Berkeley: University of California Press, 1994.

Dilworth, Leah. *Imaging Indians in the Southwest: Persistent Visions of a Primitive Past.* Washington, DC: Smithsonian Institution Press, 1996.

Dougherty, Phil. "Alaska-Yukon-Pacific Exposition (1909): Chinese Village." History Link.org. www.historylink.org/index.cfm?DisplayPage=output.cfm&file_id=8964.

———. "Alaska-Yukon-Pacific Exposition in Seattle Celebrates China Day and Montesano Day on September 13, 1909." HistoryLink.org. www.historylink.org/index.cfm?DisplayPage=output.cfm&file_id=8962.

Dubofsky, Melvin. *We Shall Be All: A History of the Industrial Workers of the World.* Urbana: University of Illinois Press, 1988.

Dye, Victoria E. *All Aboard the Santa Fe: Railway Promotion of the Southwest, 1890s to 1930s.* Albuquerque: University of New Mexico Press, 2005.

Emmons, David M. "Constructed Province: History and the Making of the Last American West." *Western Historical Quarterly* 25.4 (Winter 1994).

Engstrand, Iris. *San Diego: California's Cornerstone.* San Diego: Sunbelt Publications, 2005.

Espiritu, Yen Le. *Filipino American Lives.* Philadelphia: Temple University Press, 1995.

Etulain, Richard W., ed. *Does the Frontier Experience Make America Exceptional?* Boston: Bedford/St. Martin's, 1999.

Ewald, Donna, and Peter Clute. *San Francisco Invites the World: The Panama-Pacific International Exposition of 1915.* San Francisco: Chronicle Books, 1991.

Fear-Segal, Jacqueline. "Nineteenth-Century Indian Education: Universalism versus Evolutionism." *Journal of American Studies* 33.2 (August 1999).

Ficken, Robert E. *The Forested Land: A History of Lumbering in Western Washington.* Seattle: University of Washington Press, 1987.

———. *Washington Territory.* Pullman: Washington State Press, 2002.

Fiege, Mark. *Irrigated Eden: The Making of an Agricultural Landscape in the American West.* Seattle: University of Washington Press, 2000.

Findlay, John M. "Fair City: Seattle as Host of the 1909 Alaska-Yukon-Pacific Exposition." *Pacific Northwest Quarterly* 100.1 (Winter 2008/2009).

———. "A Fishy Proposition: Regional Identity in the Pacific Northwest." In *Many Wests:*

Place, Culture, and Regional Identity, edited by David M. Wrobel and Michael C. Steiner. Lawrence: University Press of Kansas, 1997.

Gilbert, James. *Perfect Cities: Chicago's Utopias of 1893*. Chicago: University of Chicago Press, 1991.

Glass, Fred. *From Mission to Microchip: A History of the California Labor Movement*. Berkeley: University of California Press, 2016.

Haddad, John R. "The Wild West Turns East: Audience, Ritual, and Regeneration in Buffalo Bill's Boxer Uprising." *American Studies* 49.3/4 (Winter 2008).

Harris, Neil, Wim De Wit, James Gilbert, and Robert W. Rydell, *Grand Illusions: Chicago's World's Fair of 1893*. Chicago: Chicago Historical Society, 1993.

Hays, Samuel P. *Conservation and the Gospel of Efficiency: The Progressive Conservation Movement, 1890–1920*. Pittsburgh: University of Pittsburgh Press, 1999; originally published Harvard University Press, 1959.

Hinsley, Curtis, and David Wilcox, ed. *Coming of Age in Chicago: The 1893 World's Fair and the Coalescence of American Anthropology*. Lincoln: University of Nebraska Press, 2016.

Hoxie, Frederick E. *A Final Promise: The Campaign to Assimilate the Indians, 1880–1920*. Lincoln: University of Nebraska Press, 1984.

———. "Redefining Indian Education: Thomas J. Morgan's Program in Disarray." *Arizona and the West* 24.1 (Spring 1982).

Hyde, Anne Farrar. *An American Vision: Far Western Landscape and National Culture, 1820–1920*. New York: New York University Press, 1990.

Jacobson, Matthew Frye. *Barbarian Virtues: The United States Encounters Foreign Peoples at Home and Abroad, 1876–1917*. New York: Hill and Wang, 2000.

Kasson, Joy S. *Buffalo Bill's Wild West: Celebrity, Memory, and Popular History*. New York: Hill and Wang, 2000.

Kramer, Paul. "Making Concessions: Race and Empire Revisted at the Philippine Exposition, St. Louis, 1901–1905." *Radical History Review* 73 (Winter 1991).

Kropp, Phoebe S. *California Vieja: Culture and Memory in a Modern American Place*. Berkeley: University of California Press, 2006.

———. "'There is a little sermon in That': Constructing the Native Southwest at the San Diego Panama-California Exposition of 1915." In *The Great Southwest of the Fred Harvey Company and the Santa Fe Railway*, edited by Marta Weigle and Barbara A. Babcock. Phoenix, AZ: Heard Museum, 1996.

Laird, Pamela Walker. *Advertising Progress: American Business and the Rise of Consumer Marketing*. Baltimore: Johns Hopkins University Press, 1998.

Lane, L.W. "Bill" Jr. "*Sunset* Magazine: A Century of Western Living." sunset-magazine .stanford.edu/html/magazine.html.

Lears, Jackson. *Fable of Abundance: A Cultural History of Advertising in America*. New York: Basic Books, 1994.

———. *No Place of Grace: Antimodernism and the Transformation of American Culture, 1880–1920*. New York: Pantheon Books, 1981.

Lee, Lawrence B. "The Little Landers Colony of San Ysidro." *Journal of San Diego History* 21.1 (Winter 1975).

Lee, Shelley S. "The Contradictions of Cosmopolitanism: Consuming the Orient at the Alaska-Yukon-Pacific Exposition and the International Potlatch Festival, 1909–1934." *Western Historical Quarterly* 38.3 (Autumn 2007).

Limerick, Patricia N., Clyde A. Milner II, and Charles E. Rankin, eds. *Trails: Toward a New Western History.* Lawrence: University Press of Kansas, 1991.

Lipsky, William. *San Francisco's Panama-Pacific International Exposition.* Charleston, SC: Arcadia Publishing, 2005.

Lomawaima, K. Tsianina. "Domesticity in the Federal Indian Schools: The Power of Authority over Mind and Body." *American Ethnologist* 20.2 (May 1993).

———. "Estelle Reel, Superintendent of Indian Schools, 1898–1910: Politics, Curriculum, and Land." *Journal of American Indian Education* 35.3 (Spring 1996).

MacColl, E. Kimbark. *The Shaping of a City: Business and Politics in Portland, Oregon, 1885–1915.* Portland: Georgian Press, 1967.

MacPhall, Elizabeth. "San Diego's Chinese Mission." *Journal of San Diego History* 23.2 (Spring 1977).

Marchand, Roland. *Advertising the American Dream: Making Way for Modernity, 1920–1940.* Berkeley: University of California Press, 1985.

Markwyn, Abigail M. "Beyond *The End of the Trail*: Indians at San Francisco's 1915 World's Fair." *Ethnohistory* 63.2 (April 2016).

———. "Economic Partner and Exotic Other: China and Japan at San Francisco's Panama-Pacific International Exposition." *Western Historical Quarterly* 39.4 (Winter 2008).

———. *Empress San Francisco: The Pacific Rim, the Great West, and California at the Panama-Pacific International Exposition.* Lincoln: University of Nebraska Press, 2014.

McEnroe, Sean. "Painting the Philippines with an American Brush: Visions of Race and National Mission among the Oregon Volunteers in the Philippine Wars of 1898 and 1899." *Oregon Historical Quarterly* 104.1 (Spring 2003).

McGerr, Michael. *A Fierce Discontent: The Rise and Fall of the Progressive Movement in America, 1870–1920.* New York: Free Press, 2003.

McMahon, Michael. "An American Courtship: Psychologists and Advertising Theory in the Progressive Era." *American Studies* 13.2 (Fall 1972).

Miller, Bonnie M. "The Incoherencies of Empire: The 'Imperial' Image of the Indian at the Omaha World's Fairs of 1898–99." *American Studies* 49.3/4 (Fall/Winter 2008).

Miller, Grace L. "The I.W.W. Free Speech Fight: San Diego, 1912." *Southern California Quarterly* 54.3 (Fall 1972).

Milner, Clyde A., II, ed. *A New Significance: Re-envisioning the History of the American West.* New York: Oxford University Press, 1996.

Milner, Clyde A., II, Carol A. O'Connor, and Martha A. Sandweiss. *The Oxford History of the American West.* New York: Oxford University Press, 1994.

Moehring, Eugene P. *Urbanism and Empire in the Far West, 1840–1890.* Reno: University of Nevada Press, 2004.

Moore, Charles C. "San Francisco and the Exposition: The Relation of the City to the Nation as Regards the World's Fair." *Sunset Magazine* 28.4 (April 1912), 196–98.

Moore, Sarah J. *Empire on Display: San Francisco's Panama-Pacific International Exposition of 1915.* Norman: University of Oklahoma Press, 2013.

Morgan, Murray. *Skid Road: An Informal Portrait of Seattle.* New York: Viking Press, 1951.
Morgan, Neil. *Westward Tilt: The American West Today.* New York: Random House, 1963.
Moses, L. G. *Wild West Shows and the Images of American Indians, 1883–1933.* Albuquerque: University of New Mexico Press, 1996.
Nash, Gerald D., and Richard W. Etulain, eds. *The Twentieth-Century West: Historical Interpretations.* Albuquerque: University of New Mexico Press, 1989.
Neel, Susan Rhoades. "A Place of Extremes: Nature, History, and the American West." *Western Historical Quarterly* 25.4 (Winter 1994).
Nesbit, Robert C. *"He Built Seattle": A Biography of Judge Thomas Burke.* Seattle: University of Washington Press, 1961.
Norris, James D. *Advertising and the Transformation of American Society, 1865–1920.* New York: Greenwood Press, 1990.
Nugent, Walter. "The People of the West Since 1890." In Gerald D. Nash and Richard W. Etulain, eds. *The Twentieth-Century West: Historical Interpretations* (Albuquerque: University of New Mexico Press, 1989).
Olivera, Jon. "Colonial Ethnology and the Igorrote Village at the AYP." *Pacific Northwest Quarterly* 101.3/4 (Summer/Fall 2010).
Ott, Jennifer. "Siberian Yupik Arrive in Olympia en Route to the Alaska-Yukon-Pacific Exposition on September 27, 1908." *Historylink.org: The Free Online Encyclopedia of Washington State History.* www.historylink.org/index.cfm?DisplayPage=output.cfm&file_id=8913.
———. "Washington State Legislature on February 10, 1909, tables a proposed bill that would have required visitors from Japan to the A-Y-P Exposition to post bond ensuring their return to Japan." *Historylink.org: The Free Online Encyclopedia of Washington State History.* www.historylink.org/index.cfm?DisplayPage=output.cfm&file_id=9037.
Page, Walter H. "The Larger Coast Cities." *World's Work* 10.4 (1905), 6502.
Parezo, Nancy J., and Don D. Fowler. *Anthropology Goes to the Fair: The 1904 Louisiana Purchase Exposition.* Lincoln: University of Nebraska Press, 2007.
Peavy, Linda, and Ursula Smith. "World Champions: The 1904 Girls' Basketball Team from Fort Shaw Indian Boarding School." *Montana: The Magazine of Western History* 51.4 (Winter 2001).
Perlman, Selig, and Philip Taft. *History of Labor in the United States*, 4 vols. New York: Macmillan, 1921–35.
Peters, Scott J., and Paul A. Morgan. "The Country Life Commission: Reconsidering a Milestone in American Agricultural History." *Agricultural History* 78.3 (Summer 2004).
Pomeroy, Earl. *In Search of the Golden West: The Tourist in Western America*, 2nd ed. Lincoln: University of Nebraska Press, 1957.
———. *The Pacific Slope: A History of California, Oregon, Washington, Idaho, Utah, and Nevada.* Seattle: University of Washington Press, 1973, originally Knopf, 1965.
Pope, Daniel. *The Making of Modern Advertising.* New York: Basic Books Inc., 1983.
Ports, Uldis. "Geraniums vs. Smokestacks: San Diego's Mayoralty Campaign of 1917." *Journal of San Diego History* 21.3 (Summer 1975).

Putman, John C. *Class and Gender Politics in Progressive-Era Seattle.* Reno: University of Nevada Press, 2008.

———. "Racism and Temperance: The Politics of Class and Gender in Late 19th-Century Seattle." *Pacific Northwest Quarterly* 95.2 (Spring 2004).

Raibmon, Paige. *Authentic Indians: Episodes of Encounter from the Late-Nineteenth-Century Northwest Coast.* Durham, NC: Duke University Press, 2005.

Reid, Josh. "Professor Igloo Jimmie and Dr. Boombang Meet the Heathens: Indigenous Representations and the Geography of Empire at the Alaska-Yukon-Pacific Exposition." *Pacific Northwest Quarterly* 101.3/4 (Summer/Fall 2010).

Reisner, Marc. *Cadillac Desert: The American West and Its Disappearing Water.* New York: Viking Penguin, 1986.

Robbins, William G. *Colony and Empire: The Capitalist Transformation of the American West.* Lawrence: University Press of Kansas, 1994.

———. *Landscapes of Promise: The Oregon Story, 1800–1940.* Seattle: University of Washington Press, 2008.

———. "The 'Plundered Province' Thesis and the Recent Historiography of the American West." *Pacific Historical Review* 55.4 (November 1986).

Robbins, William G., Robert J. Frank, and Richard E. Ross, eds. *Regionalism and the Pacific Northwest.* Corvallis: Oregon State University Press, 1983.

Rothman, Hal. *Devil's Bargain: Tourism in the Twentieth-Century American West.* Lawrence: University Press of Kansas, 2000.

———. "Selling the Meaning of Place: Entrepreneurship, Tourism, and Community Transformation in the Twentieth-Century American West." *Pacific Historical Review* 65.4 (November 1996).

Runte, Alfred. "Promoting the Golden West: Advertising and the Railroad." *California History* 70.1 (Spring 1991).

Russell, Don. *The Wild West or, A History of the Wild West Shows, Being an Account of the Prestigious, Peregrinatory Pageants Pretentiously Presented before the Citizens of the Republic, the Crowned Heads of Europe, and Multitudes of Awe-Struck Men, Women, and Children around the Globe, Which Created a Wonderfully Imaginative and Unrealistic Image of the American West.* Fort Worth: Amon Carter Museum of Western Art, 1970.

Rydell, Robert W. *All the World's a Fair: Visions of Empire at American International Expositions, 1876–1916.* Chicago: University of Chicago Press, 1984.

———. "Visions of Empire: International Expositions in Portland and Seattle, 1905–09." *Pacific Historical Review* 52.1 (February 1983).

Rydell, Robert W., John E. Findling, and Kimberly D. Pelle. *Fair America: World's Fairs in the United States.* Washington, DC: Smithsonian Institution Press, 2000.

Sabin, Paul. "Home and Abroad: The Two 'Wests' of Twentieth-Century United States History." *Pacific Historical Review* 66.3 (August 1997).

Sandul, Paul J. P. *California Dreaming: Boosterism, Memory, and Rural Suburbs in the Golden State.* Morgantown: West Virginia University Press, 2014.

Schmid, Calvin. *Social Trends in Seattle.* Seattle: University of Washington Press, 1944.

Schorman, Rob. "Claude Hopkins, Earnest Calkins, Bissell Carpet Sweepers and the

Birth of Modern Advertising." *The Journal of the Gilded Age and Progressive Era* 7.2 (April 2008).

Schwantes, Carlos A. "The Concept of the Wageworkers' Frontier: A Framework for Future Research." *Western Historical Quarterly* 18.1 (January 1987).

———. "Landscapes of Opportunity: Phases of Railroad Promotion of the Pacific Northwest." *Montana: The Magazine of Western History* 43.2 (Spring 1993).

———. *Radical Heritage: Labor, Socialism, and Reform in Washington and British Columbia, 1885–1917*. Seattle: University of Washington Press, 1979.

Shaffer, Marguerite S. "'See America First': Re-Envisioning Nation and Region through Western Tourism." *Pacific Historical Review* 65.4 (November 1996).

———. *See America First: Tourism and National Identity, 1880–1940*. Washington, DC: Smithsonian Institution Scholarly Press, 2001.

Sherow, James E., ed. *A Sense of the American West: An Anthology of Environmental History*. Albuquerque: University of New Mexico Press, 1998.

Shoemaker, Nancy. *American Indian Population Recovery in the Twentieth Century*. Albuquerque: University of New Mexico Press, 1999.

Slotkin, Richard. *Gunfighter Nation: The Myth of the Frontier in Twentieth-Century America*. New York: Atheneum, 1992.

Smith, Erik. "Selling Seattle's First World's Fair." *Columbia: The Magazine of Northwest History* 23.3 (Fall 2009).

Smith, Sherry L. *Reimaging Indians: Native Americans through the Anglo Eyes, 1880–1940*. Oxford: Oxford University Press, 2000.

Starr, Kevin. *Inventing the Dream: California through the Progressive Era*. New York: Oxford University Press, 1985.

Stein, Alan, and Paula Becker. *Alaska-Yukon-Pacific Exposition: Washington's First World Fair, A Timeline History*. Seattle: History Ink/History Link and the University of Washington Press, 2009.

Stoll, Steven. *The Fruits of Natural Advantage: Making the Industrial Countryside in California*. Berkeley: University of California Press, 1998.

Strasser, Susan. "Customer to Consumer: The New Consumption in the Progressive Era." *OAH Magazine of History* 13.3 (Spring 1999).

Thrush, Coll. *Native Seattle: Histories from the Crossing-Over Place*. Seattle: University of Washington Press, 2007.

Tisdale, Shelby J. "Railroads, Tourism, and Native Americans in the Greater Southwest." *Journal of the Southwest* 38.4 (Winter 1996).

"Tourism and the American West." *Pacific Historical Review* 65.4 (November 1996).

Trachtenberg, Alan. *Shades of Hiawatha: Staging Indians, Making Americans, 1880–1930*. New York: Hill and Wang, 2004.

Trafford, Emily. "Hitting the Trail: Live Displays of Native American, Filipino, and Japanese People at the Portland World's Fair." *Oregon Historical Quarterly* 116.2 (Summer 2015).

Trennert, Robert A. "From Carlisle to Phoenix: The Rise and Fall of the Indian Outing System, 1878–1930." *Pacific Historical Review* 52.3 (August 1983).

———. *The Phoenix Indian School: Forced Assimilation in Arizona, 1891–1935*. Norman: University of Oklahoma Press, 1988.

Tygiel, Jules. "Where Unionism Holds Undisputed Sway: A Reappraisal of San Francisco's Union Labor Party." *California History* 62.3 (Fall 1983).

Van Nuys, Frank W. "A Progressive Confronts the Race Question: Chester Rowell, the California Alien Land Act of 1913, and the Contradictions of Early Twentieth-Century Racial Thought." *California History* 73.1 (Spring 1994).

Vaught, David. *Cultivating California: Growers, Specialty Crops, and Labor, 1875–1920*. Baltimore: Johns Hopkins, 2002.

Wallis, Michael. *The Real Wild West: The 101 Ranch and the Creation of the American West*. New York: St. Martin's Press, 1999.

Ward, Steven V., and John R. Gold, eds. *Place Promotion: The Use of Publicity and Marketing to Sell Towns and Regions*. Chichester, GB: John Wiley & Sons, 1994.

Watson, Kenneth Greg. "Chief Seattle." *Historylink.org: The Free Online Encyclopedia of Washington State History*. www.historylink.org/index.cfm?DisplayPage=output.cfm&file_id=5071.

Weigle, Marta, and Barbara A. Babcock. *The Great Southwest of the Fred Harvey Company and the Santa Fe Railway*. Phoenix, AZ: Heard Museum, 1996.

Welch, Christina. "Savagery on Show: The Popular Visual Representation of Native American Peoples and Their Lifeways at the World's Fairs (1851–1904) and in Buffalo Bill's Wild West (1884–1904)." *Early Popular Visual Culture* 9.4 (November 2011).

West, Elliott. "Selling the Myth: Western Images in Advertising." *Montana: The Magazine of Western History* 46.2 (Summer 1996).

White, Richard. *"It's Your Misfortune and None of My Own": A New History of the American West*. Norman: University of Oklahoma Press, 1991.

———. "Poor Men on Poor Lands: The Back-to-the-Land Movement of the Early Twentieth Century: A Case Study." *Pacific Historical Review* 49.1 (February 1980).

White, Richard, Patricia Nelson Limerick, and James R. Grossman. *The Frontier in American Culture*. Berkeley: University of California Press, 1994.

Wilson, John A. "Formidable Places: Building a Railroad in Carriso Gorge." *Journal of San Diego History* 40.4 (Fall 1994).

Wong, Marie Rose. *Sweet Cakes, Long Journey: The Chinatowns of Portland, Oregon*. Seattle: University of Washington Press, 2004.

Worster, Donald. *Rivers of Empire: Water, Aridity, and the Growth of the American West*. New York: Pantheon Books, 1985.

Wrobel, David M. "Beyond the Frontier-Region Dichotomy." *Pacific Historical Review* 65.3 (August 1996).

———. *The End of American Exceptionalism: Frontier Anxiety from the Old West to the New Deal*. Lawrence: University Press of Kansas, 1993.

———. *Promised Lands: Promotion, Memory, and the Creation of the American West*. Lawrence: University Press of Kansas, 2002.

Wrobel, David M., and Michael C. Steiner, eds. *Many Wests: Place, Culture, and Regional Identity*. Lawrence: University Press of Kansas, 1997.

Wrobel, David M., and Patrick T. Long, eds. *Seeing and Being Seen: Tourism in the American West.* Lawrence: University Press of Kansas, 2001.

Wunder, John. "What's Old about the New Western History? Race and Gender, Part 1." *Pacific Northwest Quarterly* 85.2 (April 1994).

———. "What's Old about the New Western History? Part II: Environment and Economy." *Pacific Northwest Quarterly* 88.2 (Spring 1998).

Zega, Michael E. "Advertising the Southwest." *Journal of the Southwest* 43.3 (Autumn 2001).

Dissertation and Thesis

Cleland, Kat. "Disruptions in the Dream City: Unsettled Ideologies at the 1905 World's Fair in Portland, Oregon." Master's thesis. Portland State University, 2013.

Kropp, Phoebe S. "'All Our Yesterdays': The Spanish Fantasy Past and the Politics of Public Memory in Southern California, 1884–1939." Ph.D. dissertation. University of California, San Diego, 1999.

MacDonald, Alexander Norbert. "Seattle's Economic Development, 1880–1910." Ph.D. dissertation. University of Washington, 1959.

Reiff, Janice L. "Urbanization and the Social Structure: Seattle, Washington, 1852–1910," Ph.D. dissertation. University of Washington, 1981.

INDEX

Numbers in italic refer to illustrations